21世纪英语专业系列教材

西方人文经典解读

Reading Through Occidental Philosophy

主编 谭 颖

副主编 张 进 赵 莉

图书在版编目(CIP)数据

西方人文经典解读/谭颖主编. —北京：北京大学出版社，2012.8
(21世纪英语专业系列教材)
ISBN 978-7-301-16209-5

Ⅰ. ①西… Ⅱ. ①谭… Ⅲ. ①英语－阅读教学－高等学校－教材②人文科学－西方国家 Ⅳ. ①H319.4:C

中国版本图书馆CIP数据核字(2012)第205567号

书　　　名：	西方人文经典解读
著作责任者：	谭　颖　主编
责　任　编　辑：	孙　莹
标　准　书　号：	ISBN 978-7-301-16209-5/H·3121
出　版　发　行：	北京大学出版社
地　　　址：	北京市海淀区成府路205号　100871
网　　　址：	http://www.pup.cn
电　　　话：	邮购部 62752015　发行部 62750672　编辑部 62754382　出版部 62754962
电　子　信　箱：	zbing@pup.pku.edu.cn
印　刷　者：	三河市北燕印装有限公司
经　销　者：	新华书店
	787毫米×1092毫米　16开本　13印张　200千字
	2012年8月第1版　2012年8月第1次印刷
定　　　价：	32.00元

未经许可，不得以任何方式复制或抄袭本书之部分或全部内容。
版权所有，侵权必究
举报电话：(010)62752024　电子信箱：fd@pup.pku.edu.cn

前　言

　　学习哲学对人生观的形成和发展有着深远的影响。"哲学"一词源自古希腊的"philo""sophia",意即"爱智慧",通常用来说明人对生活的看法和处事的基本原则。西方哲人苏格拉底说过:"未经审慎的生活是不值得过的人生。"通过阅读哲学经典文论帮助学生了解、反思并最终认同自身以及世界,并带着这种思辨的智慧去生活,去感受,学会用理智和心灵去选择属于自己的人生轨迹。

　　了解西方哲学的发展历程对英语专业的学生尤为重要。哲学是文化的重要组成部分。对于英语学习者来说,要掌握一门语言,了解承载她的文化,是十分必要的。而西方哲学无疑浓缩了西方历史、传统及思想的精华。马克思曾经说过,"任何真正的哲学都是自己时代精神的精华",列宁在《哲学笔记》中也曾指出:"哲学史,简略地说,就是整个认识的历史。"因此,要想更好地掌握英语这门语言,深刻地理解西方文化传统和历史,就必须阅读西方哲学经典。然而,西方文化有着两千多年的历史,经典文论浩如烟海,一个人就算穷其一生也不可能读完。所以,本书挑选了16位西方最具代表性的思想家进行介绍,并节选他们最经典的作品进行解读。

　　本教材综合西方哲学理论发展的特点,引导学生对西方人文经典进行深度阅读,通过各种独创环节,如片段鉴赏、头脑风暴等,帮助学生梳理西方思想史的发展脉络,激发学生的发散性思维。

前　言

目 录

Chapter 1　　Seeking the Ideal — Plato ················· (1)

Chapter 2　　Trusting the Senses — Aristotle ················· (13)

Chapter 3　　Establishing Anew Ancient Faith — Augustine ················· (23)

Chapter 4　　Knowledge Is Power — Bacon ················· (32)

Chapter 5　　I Am, I Exist — Descartes ················· (42)

Chapter 6　　To Be Is to Be Perceived — Berkeley ················· (53)

Chapter 7　　Custom as Our Guide — Hume ················· (62)

Chapter 8　　Society Corrupts — Rousseau ················· (75)

Chapter 9　　The Starry Heavens above and the Moral Law within — Kant ········· (85)

Chapter 10　　Greatest Good of the Greatest Number — Mill ················· (97)

Chapter 11　　Truth and Usefulness — James ················· (109)

Chapter 12　　Overturning Old Values — Nietzsche ················· (118)

Chapter 13　　Anatomy Is Destiny — Freud ················· (131)

Chapter 14　　Language Is a Game — Wittgenstein ················· (142)

Chapter 15　　Living Authentically — Heidegger ················· (151)

Chapter 16　　Man Makes Himself — Sartre ················· (161)

Sketch of the History of Western Philosophy ················· (177)

Directory ················· (182)

Glossary ················· (196)

References ················· (202)

Seeking the Ideal
—— Plato

Chapter 1

Plato is philosophy, and philosophy Plato.
—— *Waldo Emerson*

The safest characterization of the European philosophical tradition is that it consists of a series of footnotes to Plato.
—— *Alfred North Whitehead*

In this chapter
- Getting to know Plato
- Peering into Plato's major theory
- Appreciating Plato's hero —— Socrates

Plato

Born into an aristocratic family in the city state of Athens at a time of great ferment and change, Plato (c. 427—347 BC) is Socrates' pupil and Aristotle's teacher. As a young man he became an enthusiastic admirer of Socrates and later wrote the philosophical dialogues through which Socrates is known to us. Although probably destined for a life in politics, he was disillusioned with Athens and spent a lot of time travelling after his teacher Socrates was persecuted. Back in Athens, he founded a school known as the Academy (from which the word "academic" comes), remaining its head until his death.

Plato was widely regarded as occupying the high peak of Greek philosophy. His influence on philosophy and culture in general is rivaled only by Aristotle's. The thought of both is woven not only into Christian theology but into many of western ways of thinking and talking about the world.

Distinctive insights[①]

Plato is seen by many to be the ultimate fount of all western philosophy. By proposing that the use of reason, rather than observation, is the only way to acquire knowledge, Plato also laid the foundations of 17th century rationalism. His influence can still be felt today. The following is his major thinking.

1. The Forms (Ideas)

The most fundamental distinction in Plato's philosophy is between the many observable objects that appear beautiful (good, just, unified, equal, big) and the one object that is what beauty (goodness, justice, unity) really is, from which those many beautiful (good, just, unified, equal, big) things receive their names and their corresponding characteristics. He believes that the world that appears to our senses is in some way defective and filled with error, but there is a more real and perfect realm, populated by entities (called "Forms" or "Ideas") that are eternal, changeless, and in some sense paradigmatic for the structure and character of our world. That is to say, the material world we can sense is not the real world, but only an image or copy of the real world. The forms, according to Plato, are roughly archetypes or abstract representations of the many types of things, and properties we feel and see around us can only be perceived by reason. Take horse for example, the "form" or "idea" of horse is intelligible, abstract and can be applied to all horses. It is something that never changes no matter how horse is different from another, or even all horses on the earth vanish.

To illustrate his theory, Plato presents what has become known as "Allegory of the Cave" in his work, *The Republic*. In the allegory, a group of prisoners were chained in a fixed position in a cave, and they were only able to look at the wall in front of them. Behind them is an elevation that rises abruptly from the level where the prisoners are seated. On this elevation there are other persons walking back and forth carrying artificial objects, including the figures of animals and human beings made out of wood and stone and various other materials. Behind these walking persons is a fire, and further back still is the entrance to the cave. The chained prisoners can look only forward against the wall at the end of the cave and see neither each other nor the moving persons nor the fire behind them. All that the prisoners can ever see are the shadows on the wall in front of them, which are projected as people walk in front of the fire. They never see the objects or the people carrying them, nor are they aware that the shadows are shadows of other things. The prisoners are "like ourselves", says Plato. The world of our experience, which we take to be real, is only a shadow world. The real world is the world of ideas, which we

---

① 柏拉图建立了欧洲哲学史上第一个庞大的客观唯心主义体系,其中心为理念论。柏拉图认为世界由"理念世界"和"现象世界"所组成。理念的世界是真实的存在,永恒不变,而人类感官所接触到的这个现实的世界,只不过是理念世界的微弱的影子,它由现象所组成,而每种现象是因时空等因素而表现出暂时变动等特征。

can reach only by intuitive contemplation, not by sense-knowledge.

2. The Divided Line[①]

In his metaphor of the Divided Line, Plato provides more details about the levels of knowledge that we can obtain. Through Socrates, Plato imagines that there exists a line between the actual world, dividing it into two parts. The lower part of the line consists of the visible world and the upper part of the line makes up the intelligible world. And each half of the line relates to a certain type of knowledge: in the visible world, we can only have opinion; in the intelligible world we achieve knowledge. Each of these divisions can be subdivided into two. The visible or changing world can be divided into a lower region, "illusion", which is made up of shadows, reflections, paintings, poetry, etc., and an upper region, "belief", which refers to any kind of knowledge of things that change, such as individual horses. "Belief" may be true some or most of the time but sometimes it is wrong because things in the visible world change. Belief is practical and may serve as a relatively reliable guide to life. The upper region can be divided into "reason" and "intelligence". "Reason" is the knowledge like mathematics and requires that some postulates be accepted without question. "Intelligence" is the knowledge of the highest and most abstract categories of things, an understanding of the ultimate good. We approach this highest level of knowledge to the extent that we are able to move beyond the restrictions of hypotheses toward the unity of all Forms.

3. The Recollection[②]

Plato argues that we have the ability to recognize the imperfect instances of the Form in the world we inhabit. He believes that our conception of Ideal Forms must be innate, even if we are not aware of this. Human beings are divided into two parts: the body and the soul. Our bodies possess the senses, through which we are able to perceive the material world, while the soul possesses the reason with which we can perceive the realm of Ideas or Forms. Plato concludes that our soul, which is immortal and eternal, must have inhabited the world of Ideas before our birth, and still yearns to return to that realm after our death. So when we see variations of the Ideas in the world with our senses, we recognize them as a sort of recollection. Recalling the innate memories of these Ideas requires reason — an attribute of the soul.

4. The Philosopher-king

According to Plato, as in the case of a ship, where the pilot's authority rests upon knowledge of navigation, so as the ship of state should be piloted by someone who has adequate knowledge. Plato develops this theme in his *Republic*. He believes that competence should be the qualification for authority. The people who, brave or strong but are not intelligent, are suited for various productive professions, such as farming, building etc.. The people who are somewhat bright, strong and especially courageous are suited to defensive and policing

---

① 柏拉图认为这个世界可分为可知世界和可见世界。可见世界由影子、反射物、绘画、诗歌等幻想和信念组成,是变化无常的,相对的,不真实的。而由像数学这样的理性知识构成的可知世界中的理念却是永恒不变的,绝对的,是唯一的真实存在。它只能为思维所认识。

② 柏拉图的回忆说认为真正的知识是对理念的认识,是人出世以前灵魂早就具有,但在灵魂投生到人体后,由于肉体的玷污,而被暂时忘却。人们要得到知识,只需唤起自己的灵魂对理念的回忆。认为人只有摆脱肉体的干扰,才能重新获得对理念的认识。

professions. The ruler, said Plato, should be the one who has been fully educated and has come to understand the difference between the visible world and the intelligible world — between the realm of opinion and the realm of knowledge, between appearance and reality. In short, the philosopher-king is one whose education has led him up step by step through the ascending degrees of knowledge of the Divided Line until at last he has knowledge of the Good, the synoptic vision of the interrelation of all truths to each other.

5. Platonic Love

Plato goes beyond accepting homoerotic relationships as part of his social world. He takes the romantic view of them, and takes it further, in two ways. He stresses the mentoring aspect of the lover-beloved relation, elevating it to an idealized relation between teacher and pupil which is above physical attraction. It consists in concern for the other's soul — that is, their psychological and mental well-being. This is what is often labeled "Platonic love" — love with the form of a romantic relation, but transformed by concern with the soul rather than the body. By using the language of homoerotic romantic love, Plato presents the urge to philosophical enquiry and understanding as itself being a transformation of sexual desire. In a passage on the "ascent of love" in the *Symposium*, Plato, through Socrates, describes how erotic urge can become sublimated and transfigured, leading the person to move beyond particular gratifications, finding satisfaction only in the transformation from individual possession to contemplation and understanding universal rules.

The reason why Plato did everything as unlikely as tracing the drive for philosophical understanding to the energy of love probably lies in the fact that he is often attracted by an explanation which has the promise of harmonizing two very different demands on what is to be explained. The drive to do philosophy has to come from within you, and be genuine. Plato is struck by its likeness to the lover's desire: it comes from within you in a way that cannot be deliberately produced, and, like love, it drives you to focus all your efforts to achieve an aim which you feel you cannot live without, however impossible the attainment may seem to be. But philosophy is also like a joint activity; and few philosophers have stressed as much as Plato the importance of mutual discussion and argument: philosophical achievement is produced from the conversations of two or more, not just the intense thoughts of one. Plato stresses at times the way that love can produce a couple with joint concerns which transcend what each gets separately out of the relationship; philosophy similarly requires the stimulus and co-operation of joint discussion and argument. Philosophy and love thus share puzzling features.

6. Women's Potential and the Family

Plato's *Republic* is also famous for the idea that in an ideally governed society the nuclear family should be either abolished or severely limited. Plato is stuck by the way that families not only serve as schools for selfishness and a competitive and hostile attitude to outsiders, but also close the spread of attachment to wider groups. Cities will have citizens with real attachment to their city and its ideals, he thinks, only if the kind of influences provided within the nuclear family are reined in.

Among the benefits of this idea he sees a release of the potential in women, who will exchange a narrow life of caring for husband and children at home for one in which their physical and mental capacities can be developed in wider contexts, just as those of men are.

Introductory remarks

(The) *Apology* is Plato's version of speech given by Socrates as he defends himself against the charges of being a man "who corrupted the young of the Athens, refused to worship the gods recognized by the state and invented new deities". Socrates' speech, however, is by no means an "apology" in our modern understanding of the word. It here has its earlier meaning (now usually expressed by the word "*apologia*") of speaking in defense of a cause or of one's beliefs or actions. Thus, in *The Apology*, Socrates attempts to defend himself and his conduct — certainly not to apologize for it.

(The) *Apology* can be divided into three parts. The first part is Socrates' own defense of himself including the famous recounting of the Oracle at Delphi① with occasional comments from Miletus his accuser. The second part is Socrates' Proposal for his Sentence. And the third part, which is our present selection, is Socrates' comments on his own sentence.

Text

The Apology②(excerpt)

Not much time will be gained, O Athenians, in return for the evil name which you will get from the detractors of the city, who will say that you killed Socrates, a wise man; for they will call me wise, even although I am not wise, when they want to reproach you. If you had waited a little while, your desire would have been fulfilled in the course of nature③. For I am far advanced in years, as you may perceive, and not far from death. I am speaking now not to all of you, but only to those who have condemned me to death. And I have another thing to say to them: you think that I was convicted because I had no words of the sort which would have procured my acquittal — I mean, if I had thought fit to leave nothing undone or unsaid④. Not so; the deficiency which led to my conviction was not of words — certainly not. But I had not the boldness or impudence or inclination to address you as you would have liked me to do, weeping and wailing and lamenting, and saying and doing many things which you have been accustomed to hear from others, and which, as I maintain, are unworthy of me⑤. I thought at

---

① 德尔菲神喻。古希腊的德尔菲被称为神谕之地,是古代神谕者聚居的地方。
② 公元前 399 年,雅典法庭以"亵渎神灵,腐蚀青年"的罪名判处苏格拉底死刑。柏拉图的《申辩篇》叙述了宣判后苏格拉底在法庭上为自己所作的最后的辩护。
③ ...your desire...the course of nature:如果稍作等待,自然的进程就会帮助你们完成这个愿望。(即,至苏格拉底于死地)。
④ you think that...undone or unsaid:你们以为我之所以被判刑是由于我的辩护不充分,我的意思是,如果我尽可能用言词和行为打动陪审团,以求获得赦免,也许不至于被判死刑。procured my acquittal:判无罪。
⑤ But I had not...unworthy of me. 我不愿哭泣哀嚎,不想厚颜无耻地进行表演,说些和做些我认为毫无价值,而你们却惯于用别人那里听到和看到的事情来取悦你们。wail:恸哭;嚎啕。lament:悲痛;伤心。

the time that I ought not to do anything common or mean when in danger; nor do I now repent of the style of my defense; I would rather die having spoken after my manner, than speak in your manner and live. For neither in war nor yet at law ought I or any man to use every way of escaping death①. Often in battle there can be no doubt that if a man will throw away his arms, and fall on his knees before his pursuers, he may escape death; and in other dangers there are other ways of escaping death, if a man is willing to say and do anything. The difficulty, my friends, is not to avoid death, but to avoid unrighteousness; for that runs faster than death②. I am old and move slowly, and the slower runner has overtaken me, and my accusers are keen and quick, and the faster runner, who is unrighteousness, has overtaken them③. And now I depart hence condemned by you to suffer the penalty of death, — they too go their ways condemned by the truth to suffer the penalty of villainy and wrong④; and I must abide by⑤ my award — let them abide by theirs. I suppose that these things may be regarded as fated, — and I think that they are well.

And now, O men who have condemned me, I would fain⑥ prophesy to you; for I am about to die, and in the hour of death men are gifted with prophetic power⑦. And I prophesy to you who are my murderers, that immediately after my departure punishment far heavier than you have inflicted on me will surely await you. Me you have killed because you wanted to escape the accuser, and not to give an account of your lives. But that will not be as you suppose: far otherwise. For I say that there will be more accusers of you than there are now; accusers whom hitherto I have restrained: and as they are younger they will be more inconsiderate with you, and you will be more offended at them. If you think that by killing men you can prevent some one from censuring⑧ your evil lives, you are mistaken; that is not a way of escape which is either possible or honorable; the easiest and the noblest way is not to be disabling others, but to be improving yourselves. This is the prophecy which I utter before my departure to the judges who have condemned me.

Friends, who would have acquitted⑨ me, I would like also to talk with you about the thing which has come to pass, while the magistrates are busy, and before I go to the place at which I must die. Stay then a little, for we may as well talk with one another while there is time. You are my friends, and I should like to show you the meaning of this event which has happened to me. O my judges — for you I may truly call judges — I should like to tell you of a wonderful circumstance. Hitherto the divine faculty of which

---

① For neither in war...escaping death: 法庭如同战场,无论我和他人都不应费尽心机去逃避死亡。
② The difficulty...faster than death: 真正困难的不是逃避死亡,而是规避不义;不义之事比死亡更难逃避。(这里,苏格拉底指出为善去死比活得于世更有价值。)
③ I am old...overtaken them: 我老了,迟钝了,逃避不了死亡;但聪明而敏捷的原告却不能逃避不义。
④ they too go...villainy and wrong: 他们也会因为邪恶和道德败坏而被真理宣判死刑。villainy and wrong: 邪恶和道德败坏。
⑤ abide by: 承担;承受。
⑥ would fain: fain 用在 would 后[古][诗]: 欣然;乐意。
⑦ in the hour...prophetic power: 临死之时是最能作出预言之时。
⑧ censure: 指责;谴责。
⑨ acquit(sb. of): 宣判……无罪。

the internal oracle is the source has constantly been in the habit of opposing me even about trifles, if I was going to make a slip or error in any matter①; and now as you see there has come upon me that which may be thought, and is generally believed to be, the last and worst evil. But the oracle made no sign of opposition②, either when I was leaving my house in the morning, or when I was on my way to the court, or while I was speaking, at anything which I was going to say; and yet I have often been stopped in the middle of a speech, but now in nothing I either said or did touching the matter in hand has the oracle opposed me. What do I take to be the explanation of this silence③? I will tell you. It is an intimation that what has happened to me is a good, and that those of us who think that death is an evil are in error. For the customary sign would surely have opposed me had I been going to evil and not to good.

　　Let us reflect in another way, and we shall see that there is great reason to hope that death is a good; for one of two things — either death is a state of nothingness and utter unconsciousness, or, as men say, there is a change and migration of the soul from this world to another④. Now if you suppose that there is no consciousness, but a sleep like the sleep of him who is undisturbed even by dreams, death will be an unspeakable gain. For if a person were to select the night in which his sleep was undisturbed even by dreams, and were to compare with this the other days and nights of his life, and then were to tell us how many days and nights he had passed in the course of his life better and more pleasantly than this one, I think that any man, I will not say a private man, but even the great king will not find many such days or nights, when compared with the others⑤. Now if death be of such a nature, I say that to die is gain; for eternity is then only a single night. But if death is the journey to another place, and there, as men say, all the dead abide, what good, O my friends and judges, can be greater than this? If indeed when the pilgrim arrives in the world below, he is delivered from the professors of justice in this world⑥, and finds the true judges who are said to give judgment there, Minos and Rhadamanthus and Aeacus⑦ and Triptolemus, and other sons of God who were righteous in their own life, that pilgrimage will be worth making. What would not a man give if he might converse with Orpheus⑧ and Musaeus and Hesiod

---

　　① Hitherto...in any matter：一种预言的声音一直伴随着我，如果我要去做我不该做的事，哪怕是无足轻重的小事，它都要阻止我。
　　② But the oracle...opposition：神却没降一点征兆阻止我。
　　③ What do I...this silence：我怎么解释神的这种沉默呢？
　　④ For one of two thing...to another：死是两种境界之一：或是灵魂和肉体虚无，死者已毫无知觉；或者如世俗所说，死亡就是灵魂从一处移居到另一处。
　　⑤ For if a person...with the others：如果让任何人把他沉睡无梦的夜晚与他一身中度过的其他日日夜夜相比较，在充分思考后指出，他的一生中有多少日日夜夜比他沉睡无梦的夜晚更美好、更幸福，我想即使是波斯王都会发现这样的日子屈指可数，更不要说一般人了。a private man：一般平民。great king：指当时的波斯王。
　　⑥ If indeed...in this world：如果到了另一个世界，他则摆脱了这个世界所谓的法官的纠缠。the world below：另一个世界，指死亡。
　　⑦ 米诺斯，克里特国王，死后成为冥府判官之一，以严密的法治闻名；拉达曼提斯，米诺斯的兄弟，死后亦是冥府判官之一；埃阿科斯，蚁民王，作为对他生前的正义和虔诚的报偿，宙斯也让他在阴间当了法官。
　　⑧ Orpheus：俄耳甫斯。太阳神兼音乐之神阿波罗和司管文艺的缪斯(Muse)女神卡利俄帕(Calliope)之子。

and Homer①? Nay, if this be true, let me die again and again. I myself, too, shall have a wonderful interest in their meeting and conversing with Palamedes②, and Ajax the son of Telamon③, and any other ancient hero who has suffered death through an unjust judgment; and there will be no small pleasure, as I think, in comparing my own sufferings with theirs. Above all, I shall then be able to continue my search into true and false knowledge; as in this world, so also in the next; and I shall find out who is wise, and who pretends to be wise, and is not. What would not a man give, O judges, to be able to examine the leader of the great Trojan expedition④; or Odysseus or Sisyphus⑤, or numberless others, men and women too! What infinite delight would there be in conversing with them and asking them questions! In another world they do not put a man to death for asking questions: assuredly not. For besides being happier than we are, they will be immortal, if what is said is true.

Wherefore, O judges, be of good cheer about death, and know of a certainty, that no evil can happen to a good man, either in life or after death. He and his are not neglected by the gods; nor has my own approaching end happened by mere chance. But I see clearly that the time had arrived when it was better for me to die and be released from trouble; wherefore the oracle gave no sign. For which reason, also, I am not angry with my condemners, or with my accusers; they have done me no harm, although they did not mean to do me any good; and for this I may gently blame them.

Still I have a favor to ask of them. When my sons are grown up, I would ask you, O my friends, to punish them; and I would have you trouble them, as I have troubled you, if they seem to care about riches, or anything, more than about virtue; or if they pretend to be something when they are really nothing, — then reprove them, as I have reproved you, for not caring about that for which they ought to care, and thinking that they are something when they are really nothing. And if you do this, both I and my sons will have received justice at your hands.

The hour of departure has arrived, and we go our ways — I to die, and you to live. Which is better God only know.

Brainstorming

1. Was Socrates trying to get himself acquitted? If he was not, what effect was he trying to exert on the jury?

2. Why does Socrates assume that his condemnation is actually something good?

3. What is the supernatural sign or divine oracle that Socrates alludes to? Might we

---

① 穆萨欧斯,传说是诗歌的创始人;赫西奥德(c700 BC)古希腊诗人;荷马(c700 BC)古希腊诗人。
② Palamedes:帕拉墨德斯,特洛伊战争中的希腊英雄。
③ Ajax the son of Telamon:特拉蒙的阿雅克斯,古希腊神话中的英雄。
④ Trojan expedition:特洛伊之战,以争夺漂亮的女人海伦(Helen)为起因。是一场以阿伽门农(Agamemnon)及阿喀琉斯(Achilles)为首的希腊军进攻以帕里斯(Paris)及赫克托尔(Hector)为首的特洛伊城的十年攻城战。
⑤ Odysseus or Sisyphus:奥德修斯或西绪福斯,皆为希腊神话传说中的英雄人物。

count this as some kind of specialized knowledge, the kind which Socrates vehemently denies having? Or is this kind of intuition or inspiration of the kind Socrates identifies with the poets?

4. What is Socrates' view of death? Why does Socrates especially want to talk to Palamedes and Ajax (son of Telamon) in the afterlife?

5. What moral values does Socrates uphold?

6. Is Socrates a theist? If he is, what does his "god" symbolize?

7. How does the text illuminate Socrates' maxim "An unexamined life is not worth living"? How, do you think, does Socrates examine his own life?

Supplementary reading

The famous *Allegory of the Cave*, also known as Plato's Cave is taken from his *Republic* Book VII (514a—520a). Written as a fictional dialogue between Socrates and Plato's brother Glaucon, it depicts Plato's Theory of Forms, according to which, the "Form" or "Idea", and not the material world of change known to us through sensation, possess the highest and most fundamental kind of reality. And it is philosophers' task to enlighten the "prisoners".

As Plato's most widely read work, The Allegory has exercised a profound influence upon Western thought.

The Allegory of the Cave[①] (excerpt)

Next, said I, here is a parable to illustrate the degrees in which our nature may be enlightened or unenlightened. Imagine the condition of men living in a sort of cavernous chamber underground, with an entrance open to the light and a long passage all down the cave. Here they have been from childhood, chained by the leg and also by the neck, so that they cannot move and can see only what is in front of them, because the chains will not let them turn their head. At some distance higher up is the light of a fire burning behind them; and between the prisoners and the fire is a track with a parapet built along it, like the screen at a puppet show, which hides the performers while they show their puppets over the top.

I see, said he.

Now behind this parapet imagine persons carrying along various artificial objects, including figures of men and animals in wood or stone or other materials, which project above the parapet. Naturally, some of these persons will be talking, others silent.

It is a strange picture, he said, and a strange sort of prisoners.

Like ourselves, I replied; for in the first place prisoners so confined would have seen nothing of themselves or of one another, except the shadows thrown by the fire-light in

---

① 洞穴寓言,暗喻那些无知并不愿听取他人意见的人,或不愿面对真相的人。

the wall of the Cave facing them, would they?

Not if all their lives they had been prevented from moving their heads.

And they would have seen as little of the objects carried past.

Of course.

Now, if they could talk to one another, would they not suppose that their words referred only to those passing shadows which they saw?

Necessarily.

And suppose their prison had an echo from the wall facing them? When one of the people crossing behind them spoke, they could only suppose that the sound came from the shadow passing before their eyes.

No doubt.

In every way, then, such prisoners would recognize as reality nothing but the shadows of those artificial objects.

Inevitably.

Now consider what would happen if their release from the chains and the healing of their unwisdom should come about in this way. Suppose one of them was set free and forced suddenly to stand up, turn his head, and walk with eyes lifted to the light; all these movements would be painful, and he would be too dazzled to make out the objects whose shadows he had been used to see. What do you think he would say, if someone told him that he had formerly seen was meaningless illusion, but now, being somewhat nearer to reality and turned towards more real objects, he was getting a true view? Suppose further that he were shown the various objects being carried by and were made to say, in reply to questions, what each of them was. Would he not be perplexed and believe the objects now shown him to be not so real as what he formerly saw?

Yes, not nearly so real.

And if he were forced to look at the fire-light itself, would not his eyes ache, so that he would try to escape and turn back to the things which he could see distinctly, convinced that they really were clearer than these other objects now being shown to him?

Yes.

And suppose someone were to drag him away forcibly up the steep and rugged ascent and not let him go until he had hauled him out into the sunlight, would he not suffer pain and vexation at such treatment, and, when he had come out into the light, find his eyes so full of its radiance that he could not see a single one of the things that he was now told were real?

Certainly he would not see them all at once.

He would need, then, to grow accustomed before he could see things in that upper world. At first it would be easiest to make out shadows, and then the images of men and things reflected in water, and later on the things themselves. After that, it would be easier to watch the heavenly bodies and the sky itself by night, looking at the light of the moon and stars rather than the Sun and the Sun's light in the daytime.

Yes, surely.

Last of all, he would be able to look at the Sun and contemplate its nature, not as it appears when reflected in water or any alien medium, but as it is in itself in its own domain.

No doubt.

And now he would begin to draw the conclusion that it is the Sun that produces the seasons and the course of the year and controls everything in the visible world, and moreover is in a way the cause of all that he and his companions used to see.

Clearly he would come at last to that conclusion.

Then if he called to mind his fellow prisoners and what passed for wisdom in his former dwelling-place, he would surely think himself happy in the change and be sorry for them. They may have had a practice of honoring and commending one another, with prizes for the man who had the keenest eye for the passing shadows and the best memory for the order in which they followed or accompanied one another so that he could make a good guess as to which was going to come next. Would our released prisoner be likely to covet those prizes or to envy the men exalted to honor and power in the Cave? Would he not feel like Homer's Achilles, that he would far sooner "be on earth as a hired servant in the house of a landless man" or endure anything rather than go back to his old beliefs and live in the old way?

Yes, he would prefer any fate to such a life.

Now imagine what would happen if he went down again to take his former seat in the Cave. Coming suddenly out of the sunlight, his eyes would be filled with darkness. He might be required once more to deliver his opinion on those shadows, in competition with the prisoners who had never been released, while his eyesight was still dim and unsteady, and it might take some time to become used to the darkness. They would laugh at him and say that he had gone up only to come back with his sight ruined; it was worth no one's while even to attempt the ascent. If they could lay hands on the man who was trying to set them free and lead them up, they would kill him.

Yes, they would.

Every feature in this parable, my dear Glaucon, is meant to fit our earlier analysis. The prison dwelling corresponds to the region revealed to us through the sense of sight, and the fire-light within it to the power of the Sun. The ascent to see the things in the upper world you may take as standing for the upward journey of the soul into the region of the intelligible; then you will be in possession of what I surmise, since that is what you wish to be told. Heaven knows whether it is true; but this, at any rate, is how it appears to me. In the world of knowledge, the last thing to be perceived and only with great difficulty is the essential Form of Goodness. Once it is perceived, the conclusion must follow that, for all things, this is the cause of whatever is right and good; in the visible world it gives birth to light and to the lord of light, while it is itself sovereign in the intelligible world and the parent of intelligence and truth. Without having had a vision of this form no one can act with wisdom, either in his own life or in matters of state.

Famous quotations

Man is a prisoner who has no right to open the door of his prison and run away ... A man should wait, and not take his own life until God summons him①.

—— *Phaedo*, 62

False words are not only evil in themselves, but they infect the soul with evil②.

—— 91

Friends have all things in common③.

—— *Phaedrus*, 279

He who is of a calm and happy nature will hardly feel the pressure of age, but to him who is of an opposite disposition youth and age are equally a burden④.

—— *The Republic*, bk. i, 329d

Mankind ensures injustice fearing that they may be the victims of it, and not because they shrink from committing it⑤.

—— 344c

Bodily exercise, when compulsory, does no harm to the body; but knowledge which is acquired under compulsion obtains no hold on the mind⑥.

—— vii, 536e

Wealth is the parent of luxury and indolence, and poverty of meanness and viciousness, and both of discontent⑦.

—— iv, 422a

The direction in which education starts a man will determine his future life⑧.

—— 425b

Socrates was put to death in 399 BC, ultimately for questioning the basis of Athenian morality. Here he accepts the bowl of hemlock that will kill him, and gestures defiantly at the heavens.

---

① 人是一个无权打开牢门逃跑的囚犯……一个人应该等待神的召唤,而不要自寻短见。——《斐多篇》,第62节
② 虚假的言辞不仅本身是邪恶的,而且以邪恶侵害人们的灵魂。——第91节
③ 朋友之间有相通之处。——《斐德罗篇》
④ 生性恬淡且又达观的人不会感到年岁的沉重压力;可是对于性格迥异的人,年轻与年老同样都是负担。——《国家篇》,第1卷第329d节
⑤ 人类谴责不仁不义,唯恐自己沦为它的受害者,而并非要约束自己,免犯此类过失。——第344c节
⑥ 体格锻炼即便是强制性的,也不会损害身体;知识如果是强迫灌输的,就不会在头脑中生根。——第7卷第536e节
⑦ 富有是奢侈与懒怠之父,贫穷是卑劣与邪恶之父;富有和贫穷又都是怨愤之父。——第4卷第422a节
⑧ 一个人接受启蒙教育的方向将会确定他今后的一生。——第425b节

Trusting the Senses
—— Aristotle

Linnaeus and Cuvier have been my two Gods, though in every different ways, but they were mere schoolboys to old Aristotle.
—— Charles Darwin

In this chapter
- Getting to know Aristotle
- Appreciating Aristotle's political doctrines
- Looking at his proposed ethics

Aristotle

Born in Stagira, in the northeast region of modern Greece, Aristotle (384—322 BC) was educated as a member of the aristocracy. He was sent to study in Plato's Academy at the age of 17, where he spent almost 20 years both as a student and as a teacher. After Plato died, he left Athens and was invited to return to Macedonia as tutor to the young Alexander the Great, who later encouraged him to set up his own school the Lyceum in Athens. But when Alexander died in 323 BC anti-Macedonian feeling flared up, and Aristotle had to flee to Chalcis, where he died the following year.

Aristotle is widely known as "The Philosopher" well into the 18th century. The scope of his work is immense, ranging from the charting of planets to the classification of fishes; from study of the winds, the seas and the weather to the analysis of dramatic tragedy; from morals and politics to geometry and number. Although he lived and worked nearly two and a half thousand years ago, his thought, like Plato's, is still vital and indeed constitutive part of Western culture.

Distinctive insights①

Being a universal preeminent philosopher, Aristotle's concern covers a wide range.

1. The Syllogism②

The first distinction of Aristotle is that almost without predecessors, almost entirely by his own hard thinking, he created a new science — Logic. He founded a system of logic which was the basis of logical studies until the nineteenth century. He regarded logic as a kind of general tool for the study and acquisition of knowledge of all kinds and his writings on the subject are known as the *Organon* meaning instrument or tool. The central feature of his logic is the syllogism, defined by him as a "discourse in which, certain things being stated, something other than what is stated follows of necessity from their being so". The most usual form of syllogism consists of three propositions, two of which are the premises and one the conclusion of an argument. A typical syllogism runs as follows:

All men are mortal.
Socrates is a man.
Therefore Socrates is mortal.

If the premises in a syllogism are true and if its form, or pattern, is valid, then the conclusion of the syllogism is and must be true. The valid syllogism that has true premises therefore constitutes a proof of what its conclusion states.

2. The Four Causes③

Aristotle is a problem-centered philosopher, beginning from puzzles which arise in everyday thinking about nature. His *Physics* analyzes the most general features of natural phenomena: cause, change, time, place, infinity, and continuity. The doctrine of the *four causes* is especially important in his work. A cause (*aitia*) is something like an explanatory factor. One is the *material* or *matter cause*, the physical make-up of the thing, which puts considerable restrictions on what it can be and do. The material cause of a house, for instance, is the matter from which it is built. The second is the *moving* or *efficient cause*, the item initiating a change, the moving cause in the case of the house is the builder. *The formal cause* is the plan or form of the house. *The final cause* is the purpose or end of the house: for provision of shelter. The complete explanation of the coming to be of a house will factor in all of these causes. In natural phenomena efficient, formal, and

---

① 哲学上提出了关于第一哲学、实体、四因、潜能与现实、第一推动力、灵魂等于蜡块等学说。社会政治观上,认为人是政治动物,国家高于个人,主张由"中等阶级"来治理国家。伦理学上,提倡中道,认为道德包括行德和知德。美学上,曾给悲剧下过定义,提出净化说,并指出艺术作品在"摹仿"个别事物时,目的在于使事物的一般特征得以表现出来。在教育上,认为理性的发展是教育的最终目的。在历史学、修辞学、心理学、生物学、生理学、医学等方面也有贡献。

② 三段论,是由一个共同概念联系着的两个性质判断作前提,推出另一个性质判断作结论的演绎推理。由大前提、小前提、结论三部分组成。其特点在于通过中项的媒介绍,把大项和小项联系起来,因而能从两个前提必然地推出结论。

③ 四因说。亚里士多德认为事物的生灭变化有四种原因,即:(1)质料因,指事物是有什么东西构成的;(2)形式因,指事物的本质结构;(3)动力因,指促使一定的质料取得一定的形式结构的力量;(4)目的因,指事物所要达到的目的。

final causes often coincide. The form transmitted by the father is both the efficient cause and the form of the child, and the latter is glossed in terms of the child's end or complete development. A natural process counts essentially as the development of, say, an oak or a man because its very identity depends on the complete form realized at its end. As with all things natural, the end is an internal governing principle of the process rather than an external goal.

3. The Unmoved Mover[①]

Aristotle's concept of God was importantly influential in the later development of rational Christian philosophy and theology. In his *Physics*, Aristotle argues that everything is in motion and that it is impossible to conceive of either a beginning or end of motion; there must therefore be an eternal mover producing the eternal motion and this mover must itself be unmoved since, if it were not, a mover would have to be sought for it. God is therefore the Unmoved Mover. He is eternal, non-material, unchanging and perfect; he must be actuality without potentiality[②], for potentiality involves change and is less than perfect. The Unmoved Mover is also a Person, but his thought is of thought itself and he is supremely happy in his perfect knowledge of all things.

4. The Golden Mean[③]

Aristotle thinks that the chief condition of happiness, barring certain physical prerequisites, is the life of reason — the specific glory and power of man. Virtue, or rather excellence, will depend on clear judgment, self-control, symmetry of desire, artistry of means; it is not the possession of the simple man, nor the gift of innocent intent, but the achievement of experience in the fully developed man. Yet there is a road to it, a guide to excellence, which may save many detours and delays: it is the middle way, the golden mean. But what is the golden mean? For Aristotle, it is a mean between the excess of rashness and the deficiency of cowardice with respect to acting in the face of danger; a mean between the excess of intemperance and the deficiency of insensibility with respect to the enjoyment of pleasures; and a mean between the excess of being ingratiating and the deficiency of being surly with respect to relations with strangers...

However, the golden mean is not like the mathematical mean, an exact average of two precisely calculable extremes; it fluctuates with the collateral circumstances of each situation, and discovers itself only to mature and flexible reason. Excellence is an art won by training and habituation: we do not act rightly because we have virtue or excellence, but we rather have these because we have acted rightly.

5. Achieving Happiness

Aristotle argues that since every activity has a final cause, there must be a highest good at which all human activity ultimately aims. This end of human life could be called happiness (or living well). But what is it really? Neither the ordinary notions of

---

① 第一推动力,亦称"第一推动者",指一切事物的目的与运动的终极原因。中世纪第一推动力转为神的别称。
② 潜能与实现。亚里士多德认为,任何东西一旦存在,它必然包含潜能,随时准备发挥出来,变化就是由潜能走向实现的过程,而"第一动因"却只有实现没有潜能。
③ 中道学说。亚里士多德认为,德行是两个偏颇极端的中间道,两个极端都是罪恶。

pleasure, wealth, and honor nor fame, social status provide an adequate account of this ultimate goal, for even individuals who acquire the material goods or achieve intellectual knowledge may not be happy. He concludes that genuine happiness should lie in action that leads to virtue, since this alone provides true value and not just amusement. Thus, Aristotle holds that contemplation is the highest form of moral activity because it is continuous, pleasant, self-sufficient, and complete. In intellectual activity, human beings most nearly approach divine blessedness, while realizing all of the genuine human virtues as well.

Introductory remarks

Aristotle holds the idea that the best regime corresponds to the best way of life for a human being. Since the best way of life is living nobly and according to virtue, the best regime is the one, which promotes this life. So he thinks that the best government looks to the common advantage which provides an active and "happy" life for its people while a deviant government looks to the advantage of the rule which involves mastery rather than political rule. In the *Politics* he speculates about the origins of the state, describes and assesses the relative merits of various types of government and lists the obligations of the individual citizens.

The following is an excerpt taken from his *Politics*, Part IX, Book 3, in which he considers six forms of government: Monarchy, Aristocracy, and Polity on one side as "good" forms of government, and Tyranny, Oligarchy, and Democracy as "bad" forms. Considering each in turn, Aristotle rejects Monarchy as infantilizing of citizens, Oligarchy as too profit-motivated, Tyranny as against the will of the people, Democracy as serving only to the poor, and Aristocracy (known today as Meritocracy) as ideal but ultimately impossible. Aristotle finally concludes that a polity — a combination between democracy and oligarchy, where most can vote but must choose among the rich and virtuous for governors — is the best compromise between idealism and realism.

Text

On Politics① (excerpt)

Let us begin by considering the common definitions of oligarchy and democracy, and what is justice, oligarchical and democratical. For all men cling to justice of some kind, but their conceptions are imperfect and they do not express the whole idea. For example, justice is thought by them to be, and is, equality. Not however, for whoever, but only for equals. And inequality is thought to be, and is, justice; neither is this for all, but only for unequals②. When the persons are omitted, then men judge erroneously. The

---

① 《政治学》,西方第一部系统的政治学著作,其目的在于维护当时的城邦奴隶制。

② And inequality is thought... but only for unequals: 不平等被认为是,而且事实上也是公正的,不过也不是对所有人而是对彼此不平等的人而言。

reason is that they are passing judgment on themselves, and most people are bad judges in their own case. And whereas justice implies a relation to persons as well as to things, and a just distribution, as I have already said in the *Ethics*, implies the same ratio between the persons and between the things, they agree about the equality of the things, but dispute about the equality of the persons①, chiefly for the reason which I have just given—because they are bad judges in their own affairs; and secondly, because both the parties to the argument are speaking of a limited and partial justice, but imagine themselves to be speaking of absolute justice. For the one party, if they are unequal in one respect, for example wealth, consider themselves to be unequal in all; and the other party, if they are equal in one respect, for example free birth, consider themselves to be equal in all. But they leave out the capital point. For if men met and associated out of regard to wealth only, their share in the state would be proportioned to their property and the oligarchical doctrine would then seem to carry the day②. It would not be just that he who paid one mina should have the same share of a hundred minae③, whether of the principal or of the profits, as he who paid the remaining ninety-nine. But a state exists for the sake of a good life, and not for the sake of life only: if life only were the object, slaves and brute animals might form a state, but they cannot, for they have no share in happiness or in a life of free choice. Nor does a state exist for the sake of alliance and security from injustice, nor yet for the sake of exchange and mutual intercourse; for then the Tyrrhenians and the Carthaginians, and all who have commercial treaties with one another, would be the citizens of one state④. True, they have agreements about imports, and engagements that they will do no wrong to one another, and written articles of alliance. But there are no magistrates common to the contracting parties who will enforce their engagements; different states have each their own magistracies⑤. Nor does one state take care that the citizens of the other are such as they ought to be, nor see that those who come under the terms of the treaty do no wrong or wickedness at an, but only that they do no injustice to one another. Whereas, those who care for good government take into consideration virtue and vice in states. Whence it may be further inferred that virtue must be the care of a state which is truly so called, and not merely enjoys the name: for without this end the community becomes a mere alliance which differs only in place from alliances of which the members live apart; and law is only a convention, a surety to one another of

---

① And whereas justice implies... about the equality of the person: 一旦关系到人和事,正如我在《伦理学》中提到过,公正的区别以相同的方式在事物和人之间体现,人们主张事物的平等,但涉及到人就会发生分歧;

② For if men met and... to carry the day: 如果财产是人们结合成共同体时所为的目的,那么人们理应按财产的状况在城邦中享有其他地位。因此,寡头政体的拥护者的主张似乎更有说服力。carry the day: 得胜。

③ minae: 米那(金钱单位)。

④ Nor does a state exist... the citizens of one state: 城邦之所以存在也不是为了联合抵御一切不公正的行为,也不是为了交易和彼此间的贸易往来,否则,第勒塞尼亚人和迦太基人,以及所有彼此间订有商贸条约的城邦公民,都将同属一个城邦了。intercourse: 相互往来; Tyrrhenians: 第勒塞尼亚人; Carthaginians: 迦太基人。

⑤ magistracy: 地方行政官,执法官。

justice, as the sophist Lycophron says, and has no real power to make the citizens①.

　　This is obvious; for suppose distinct places, such as Corinth and Megara, to be brought together so that their walls touched, still they would not be one city, not even if the citizens had the right to intermarry②, which is one of the rights peculiarly characteristic of states. Again, if men dwelt at a distance from one another, but not so far off as to have no intercourse, and there were laws among them that they should not wrong each other in their exchanges, neither would this be a state. Let us suppose that one man is a carpenter, another a husbandman③, another a shoemaker, and so on, and that their number is ten thousand; nevertheless, if they have nothing in common but exchange, alliance, and the like, that would not constitute a state. Why is this? Surely not because they are at a distance from one another: for even supposing that such a community were to meet in one place, but that each man had a house of his own, which was in a manner his state, and that they made alliance with one another, but only against evil-doers; still an accurate thinker would not deem this to be a state, if their intercourse with one another was of the same character after as before their union. It is clear then that a state is not a mere society, having a common place, established for the prevention of mutual crime and for the sake of exchange. These are conditions without which a state cannot exist; but all of them together do not constitute a state, which is a community of families and aggregations of families in well-being, for the sake of a perfect and self-sufficing life. Such a community can only be established among those who live in the same place and intermarry. Hence arise in cities family connections, brotherhoods, common sacrifices, amusements which draw men together. But these are created by friendship, for the will to live together is friendship. The end of the state is the good life, and these are the means towards it. And the state is the union of families and villages in a perfect and self-sufficing life, by which we mean a happy and honorable life④.

　　Our conclusion, then, is that political society exists for the sake of noble actions, and not of mere companionship. Hence they who contribute most to such a society have a greater share in it than those who have the same or a greater freedom or nobility of birth but are inferior to them in political virtue; or than those who exceed them in wealth but are surpassed by them in virtue⑤.

　　From what has been said it will be clearly seen that all the partisans of different forms

---

　　① and law is only a convention... make the citizens: 而法律也只是一纸条约，用智者吕科富隆的话来说，法律是"人们互相确保正义的契约"，却对公民没有实际效力。吕科富隆（285—247 BC），古希腊悲剧诗人，文法家。

　　② for suppose distinct places... the right to intermarry: 假如有人把麦加拉城和科林斯城用一道城墙围起来，也不会造出一个统一的城邦，即使是城邦之间有权通婚，也无济于事。Corinth: 科林斯，古希腊南部海港城市；Megara: 麦加拉，古希腊重要城市。

　　③ husbandman: (古义)农夫，庄稼汉。

　　④ And the state is the union... and honorable life: 城邦是若干家族和村落的共同体，追求完美的、自给自足的生活。我们说，这就是幸福而高尚的生活。

　　⑤ Hence they who contribute most... by them in virtue: 因此，凡是对城邦共同体有卓著贡献的人，与那些在出身方面同样是自由人或更加尊贵但是在政治德性方面却不及的人相比，或者与在财产方面超出他人而在德性方面却被人超出的人相比，理应在城邦中享有更加显赫的地位。

of government speak of a part of justice only.

Brainstorming

1. What does Aristotle mean when he says "all men cling to justice of some kind, but their conceptions are imperfect"?
2. Do you agree with Aristotle that quality is relative? Why or why not?
3. What does Aristotle consider as the essential features of a true political community?
4. How do you understand Aristotle's statement "a state exists for the sake of a good life, and not for the sake of life only"? In your opinion, what is this "good life" and "life only"?
5. Assess Aristotle's claim that political society exists for the sake of noble actions, and not of mere companionship.
6. List Aristotle's essential conditions for a state to exist.
7. Do you agree with Aristotle that a state would be well-governed in which the middle class is large and strong? Why?
8. Is a good citizen the same thing as a good man? Why or why not?

Supplementary reading

The following excerpt is taken from *Nicomachean Ethics*[①], Book 1, VII, a treatise in practical philosophy. Its aim is effective action in matters of conduct. In this book Aristotle reminds us, "not in order to know what virtue is, but in order to become good." One becomes good by becoming a good chooser and doer. This is not simply a matter of choosing and doing right actions but of choosing or doing them in the right way.

Good for Something Else (excerpt)

Let us again return to the good we are seeking, and ask what it can be. It seems different in different actions and arts; it is different in medicine, in strategy, and in the other arts likewise. What then is the good of each? Surely that for whose sake everything else is done. In medicine this is health, in strategy victory, in architecture a house, in any other sphere something else, and in every action and pursuit the end; for it is for the sake of this that all men do whatever else they do. Therefore, if there is an end for all that we do, this will be the good achievable by action, and if there are more than one, these will be the goods achievable by action.

So the argument has by a different course reached the same point; but we must try to state this even more clearly. Since there are evidently more than one end, and we choose

---

① 《尼各马科伦理学》,系统论证了德行在于合乎理性的活动,至善就是幸福等观点,成为西方伦理思想发展的主要渊源之一。

some of these (e.g. wealth, flutes, and in general instruments) for the sake of something else, clearly not all ends are final ends; but the chief good is evidently something final. Therefore, if there is only one final end, this will be what we are seeking, and if there are more than one, the most final of these will be what we are seeking. Now we call that which is in itself worthy of pursuit more final than that which is worthy of pursuit for the sake of something else, and that which is never desirable for the sake of something else more final than the things that are desirable both in themselves and for the sake of that other thing, and therefore we call final without qualification that which is always desirable in itself and never for the sake of something else.

Now such a thing happiness, above all else, is held to be; for this we choose always for self and never for the sake of something else, but honor, pleasure, reason, and every virtue we choose indeed for themselves (for if nothing resulted from them we should still choose each of them), but we choose them also for the sake of happiness, judging that by means of them we shall be happy. Happiness, on the other hand, no one chooses for the sake of these, nor, in general, for anything other than itself.

From the point of view of self-sufficiency the same result seems to follow; for the final good is thought to be self-sufficient. Now by self-sufficient we do not mean that which is sufficient for a man by himself, for one who lives a solitary life, but also for parents, children, wife, and in general for his friends and fellow citizens, since man is born for citizenship. But some limit must be set to this; for if we extend our requirement to ancestors and descendants and friends' friends we are in for an infinite series. Let us examine this question, however, on another occasion; the self-sufficient we now define as that which when isolated makes life desirable and lacking in nothing; and such we think happiness to be; and further we think it most desirable of all things, without being counted as one good thing among others — if it were so counted it would clearly be made more desirable by the addition of even the least of goods; for that which is added becomes an excess of goods, and of goods the greater is always more desirable. Happiness, then, is something final and self-sufficient, and is the end of action.

Presumably, however, to say that happiness is the chief good seems a platitude, and a clearer account of what it is still desired. This might perhaps be given, if we could first ascertain the function of man. For just as for a flute-player, a sculptor, or an artist, and, in general, for all things that have a function or activity, the good and the "well" is thought to reside in the function, so would it seem to be for man, if he has a function. Have the carpenter, then, and the tanner certain functions or activities, and has man none? Is he born without a function? Or as eye, hand, foot, and in general each of the parts evidently has a function, may one lay it down that man similarly has a function apart from all these? What then can this be? Life seems to be common even to plants, but we are seeking what is peculiar to man. Let us exclude, therefore, the life of nutrition and growth. Next there would be a life of perception, but it also seems to be common even to the horse, the ox, and every animal. There remains, then, an active life of the element that has a rational principle; of this, one part has such a principle in the sense of being obedient to one, the other in the sense of possessing one and exercising thought. And, as "life of the rational element" also has two meanings, we must state that life in the sense of activity is what we mean; for this seems to be the more proper sense of the term. Now if the function of man is an activity of soul which follows or implies a rational principle, and if we say "so-and-so" and "a good so-and-so" have a function which is the same in kind, e. g. a lyre, and a good lyre-player, and so without qualification in all cases, eminence in respect of goodness being added to the name of the function (for the function of a lyre-player is to play the lyre, and that of a good lyre-player is to do so well): if this is the case, and we state the function of man to be a certain kind of life, and this to be an activity or actions of the soul implying a rational principle, and the function of a good man to be the good and noble performance of these, and if any action is well performed when it is performed in accordance with the appropriate excellence: if this is the case, human good turns out to be activity of soul in accordance with virtue, and if there are more than one virtue, in accordance with the best and most complete.

But we must add "in a complete life". For one swallow does not make a summer, nor does one day; and so too one day, or a short time, does not make a man blessed and happy.

Let this serve as an outline of the good; for we must presumably first sketch it roughly, and then later fill in the details. But it would seem that any one is capable of carrying on and articulating what has once been well outlined, and that time is a good discoverer or partner in such a work; to which facts the advances of the arts are due; for any one can add what is lacking. And we must also remember what has been said before, and not look for precision in all things alike, but in each class of things such precision as accords with the subject-matter, and so much as is appropriate to the inquiry. For a carpenter and a geometer investigate the right angle in different ways; the former does so in so far as the right angle is useful for his work, while the latter inquires what it is or what sort of thing it is; for he is a spectator of the truth. We must act in the same way, then, in all other matters as well, that our main task may not be subordinated to minor questions. Nor must we demand the cause in all matters alike; it is enough in some cases that the fact be well established, as in the case of the first principles; the fact is the primary thing or first principle. Now of first principles we see some by induction, some by perception, some by a certain habituation, and others too in other ways. But each set of principles we must try to investigate in the natural way, and we must take pains to state them definitely, since they have a great influence on what follows. For the beginning is thought to be more than half of the whole, and many of the questions we ask are cleared up by it.

Famous quotations

Man is by nature a political animal.[①]

—— *Politics*, i. 2. 1253a

---

① 人生来是一种政治动物。——《政治学》第 1 卷第 2 章第 1253 节。

Even when laws have been written down, they ought not always to remain unaltered.①

—— ii, 8

Where some people are very wealthy and others have nothing, the result will be either extreme democracy or absolute oligarchy, or despotism will come from either of those excesses.②

—— 4. 1296a

The basis of a democratic state is liberty.③

—— vi, 2

All men by nature desire knowledge.④

—— *Metaphysics*, bk. I, ch. 1

So the good has been well explained as that at which all things aim.⑤

—— *Nicomachean Ethics*, I. 1, 1094a

One swallow does not make a summer.⑥

—— ch. 7

Misfortune shows those who are not really friends⑦.

—— *Eudemian Ethics*, bk, vii, ch. 2

What is a friend? A single soul dwelling in two bodies.⑧

—— 20.

Plato and Aristotle differ in their opinions of the nature of universal truth. For Plato, it resides in the higher realm of the Forms, but for Aristotle it resides here on Earth, and can be acquired through observation and experience.

---

① 即使在法律成文以后,它们也不应该始终保持一成不变。——第2卷第8章
② 有些人非常富裕,另一些人则一贫如洗,这时就会产生极端的民主政体或专制的寡头政体。这两个极端中的任何一个都会导致暴政。——第4章1296a节。
③ 民主国家的基础是自由。——第6卷第2章。
④ 求知是所有人的本性。——《形而上学》,第1卷第1章。
⑤ 所以善被合理地认为是万物所追求的目标。——《尼各马可伦理学》第1卷第1章1094a节。
⑥ 一只燕子成不了夏。——第7章。(亚氏用形象的比喻说明,最崇高的善是完美的终极的善。在短暂的时间里行善,并不能使人得到终身幸福。)
⑦ 不幸能表明哪些人不是真正的朋友。——《乐生伦理学》,第7卷第2章。
⑧ 朋友是什么?一个灵魂居住在两个肉体中。——第20节

Establishing Anew Ancient Faith
—— Augustine

Chapter 3

> *Understanding is the reward of faith.*
> *Seek therefore not to understand in order*
> *that you may believe, but believe in order*
> *that you may understand.*
>
> —— Augustine

In this chapter
- Getting to know St. Augustine
- Glimpsing an unusual insight about Augustine's religious belief

Augustine

St. Augustine of Hippo (354—430) was born in the city of Thagaste in North Africa at a time when the Roman Empire was being destroyed by the barbarian invasions. Educated to be a rhetorician when he was young, he went on to teach rhetoric in his home town, and at Carthage, Rome, and Milan, where he occupied a prestigious position. Augustine suffered a spiritual crisis before he converted to Christianity. In 386 he abandoned his career and devoted himself entirely to writing Christian works. He was ordained the Bishop of Hippo in 395. Thereafter he lived with his clergy and preached, wrote and traveled in pursuit of his duties until his death.

Generally considered the "Apostle to the English" and a founder of the English church, Augustine is well known for his works the *Confessions* and the *City of God*. In the *Confessions* he writes of his early life, his repentance and conversion, and discusses questions about time and the presence of evil in the world. In the *City of God* his main themes are the human will, the relationship between theology and reason, and the division of history into two "cities", one formed by self-love, the other by the love of God. These philosophical reflections have exerted an enduring philosophical influence on later philosophers.

Distinctive insights①

Augustine's works deal with many topics in philosophical psychology and anthropology. It teaches such cosmological doctrines as the "seed-reasons" by which creatures are given intelligible form. It elaborates in subtle detail the distinguishable "traces" of Father, Son, and Spirit in the created world and particularly in the human soul's triad of memory, intellect, and will. The following doctrines are typically attributed to Augustine:

1. The Theory of Illumination②

One of Augustine's doctrines concerns divine "illumination" of the human intellect, i.e., some active intervention by God in ordinary processes of human understanding. Like Plato, he thinks of the soul as inhabiting and deploying the body. He says, "Man is, as far as we can see, a rational soul making use of a mortal and material body." At the same time, because of his Christian conviction that God creates each soul when a human being comes into existence, he does not endorse Plato's view of the soul as being in exile from its real home during its habitation of a human body. Though he holds that all knowledge is the product of the rational soul, he believes that it may be of two kinds of objects: objects of sense and objects known independently of sense experience, the latter being perceived by the mind "through itself". In the case of sensory knowledge he regards the mind as using the bodily senses as instruments for obtaining knowledge and thus of perception as fundamentally an activity of mind; for the mind at its highest intellectual level is able, he says, to judge and interpret the information it is made aware of through the senses. For Augustine, the highest intellectual activity results in an illumination of certain ultimate and eternal truths which are latent in all human minds. These truths, he maintains, furnish us with standards against which we make our judgments of how things should be, and in apprehending them.

2. Faith and Reason

Augustine is not interested in mere theoretical speculations about the existence of God, but rather, he expounds Christian philosophical reflections that sought to combine faith and reason. By claiming "Understanding is the reward of faith", he means that faith is primary because it provides the prerequisite for a Christian philosophy. But faith alone, he holds, is simply a kind of blind assent. It must be consolidated and made intelligible by means of reason. This reconciling of his long pursuit of philosophy with his serious faith

---

① 奥古斯丁用新柏拉图主义论证基督教教义，把神学和哲学结合起来。宣扬"恩宠论"，认为人只有依赖上帝的恩宠才能得救。提出"预定论"，认为人的灵魂去处为上帝所预定。强调教权，声称人们虽应服从世俗政权，但世俗政权只是"世人之城"，最后终将覆灭，而由"上帝之城"取代，教会则是"上帝之城"在地上的体现。这一说法为中世纪西欧基督教的教权至上论提供了理论根据。

② 奥古斯丁认为，上帝除了创造及监管万物之外，还需以"光启"使人了解永恒而必然的真理。而永恒真理的存在又证明了上帝的存在。

in the Catholic church guides his work for the rest of his life.

3. Free Will as the Cause of Evil

Augustine assumes that the will is free and seeks to determine how we choose good or evil. This continues to be "debated" in our age and has great implications on one's perspective on life. How one answers the question of free will often helps determine whether one believes life has any ultimate "meaning" at all. Augustine's approach to the "free choice of the will" assumes that "there can be no denying that we have a will." "Good will" as he defines, is "a will by which we seek to live a good and upright life and to attain unto perfect wisdom". Free will, or sin, according to him, is a product of the will. It is not, as Plato said, ignorance, nor as the Medichaeans① said, the work of the principle permeating the body. In spite of the fact of original sin, we still possess freedom of the will, which is not, however, the same as spiritual freedom, for true spiritual liberty is no longer possible in its fullness in this life. We now use free will to choose wrongly. But even when we choose rightly, we do not possess the spiritual power to do the good we have chosen. We must have the help of God's grace. Whereas evil is caused by an act of free will, virtue on the other hand, is the product not of our will but of God's grace. The moral law tells us what we must do, but in the end it really shows us what we can't do on our own. Hence, Augustine concludes that "the law was … given that grace might be sought; grace was given that the law might be fulfilled."

4. The Nature of Time

Augustine's philosophical reflections on the nature of time are of enduring interest. In a famous passage in the *Confessions* he says: "What then is time? If no one asks me, I know what it is. If I wish to explain it to him who asks me, I do not know." When he does try to explain what time is, he finds he produces paradox. He argues, for example, that we measure time in many ways yet, if we think carefully about the nature of time, it does not seem to be anything that can be measured since past time does not exist once it is past, future time does not exist since it has not yet come and present time becomes past time as soon as it comes into existence. Time is a kind of extendedness, but he cannot say what it is that is extended. We measure the motion of a body — how long it takes, or how long it is in motion from one place to another. He says he could not measure the time unless he knows what it is. He seems to conclude that we use time to measure time and this, of course, brings him no nearer to being able to say what time is, and that time is nothing in reality but exists only in the human mind's apprehension of reality.

Introductory remarks

(The) *Confessions* consists of 13 books. It is a diverse blend of autobiography, philosophy, theology and critical exegesis of the Christian Bible. The first nine books (or chapters) trace the story of Augustine's life, from his birth up to the events that took

---

① 摩尼教，又称明教，源自古代波斯宗教袄教，是将基督教与伊朗马兹达（见袄教）教义混合而成的哲学体系。

place just after his conversion to Catholicism, while the remaining part addresses more strictly philosophical and theological issues.

The following excerpt is taken from Book Eight of *Confession* out of the events of the first half of his life. It tells the story of his conversion expevience in Milan, which begins with an agonizing state of spiritual paralysis and ends with an ecstatic decision to wholly embrace celibacy and the catholic faith.

Text

The Confession① (excerpt)

CHAPTER XI

Thus I was sick and tormented, reproaching myself more bitterly than ever, rolling and writhing in my chain till it should be utterly broken. By now I was held but slightly, but still was held. And thou, O Lord, didst press upon me in my inmost heart with a severe mercy, redoubling the lashes of fear and shame; lest I should again give way and that same slender remaining tie not be broken off, but recover strength and enchain me yet more securely②. I kept saying to myself, "See, let it be done now; let it be done now." And as I said this I all but came to a firm decision. I all but did it — yet I did not quite. Still I did not fall back to my old condition, but stood aside for a moment and drew breath. And I tried again, and lacked only a very little of reaching the resolve — and then somewhat less, and then all but touched and grasped it. Yet I still did not quite reach or touch or grasp the goal, because I hesitated to die to death and to live to life. And the worse way, to which I was habituated③, was stronger in me than the better, which I had not tried. And up to the very moment in which I was to become another man, the nearer the moment approached, the greater horror did it strike in me. But it did not strike me back, nor turn me aside, but held me in suspense.

It was, in fact, my old mistresses, trifles of trifles and vanities of vanities, who still enthralled④ me. They tugged at my fleshly garments and softly whispered: "Are you going to part with us? And from that moment will we never be with you any more? And from that moment will not this and that be forbidden you forever?" What were they suggesting to me in those words "this or that"? What is it they suggested, O my God? Let thy mercy guard the soul of thy servant from the vileness and the shame they did suggest⑤! And now

---

① 《忏悔录》以祷告自传手法写成,主要描写早期奥古斯丁皈依基督教时的内心挣扎及转变经历。

② O Lord, didst press upon...chain me yet more securely: 主啊,你在我心坎中催迫我,你严肃的慈爱用恐惧悔恨的鞭子在加倍地鞭策我,使我不放弃,不去挣断剩下的细脆的链子,而让它恢复力量,把我更加牢牢束缚。didst=did, 是古体诗歌用语,用在 thou 后。

③ habituate:使习惯。

④ enthrall:迷住,吸引住,使感到非常愉快。

⑤ Let thy mercy guard... and the shame they did suggest:求您的慈爱把这一切肮脏与可耻从您仆人的灵魂中全部清除。vile:卑鄙的,可耻的,邪恶的。

I scarcely heard them, for they were not openly showing themselves and opposing me face to face; but muttering, as it were, behind my back; and furtively① plucking at me as I was leaving, trying to make me look back at them. Still they delayed me, so that I hesitated to break loose and shake myself free of them and leap over to the place to which I was being called — for unruly habit kept saying to me, "Do you think you can live without them?"

But now it said this very faintly; for in the direction I had set my face, and yet toward which I still trembled to go, the chaste dignity of continence appeared to me — cheerful but not wanton, modestly alluring me to come and doubt nothing, extending her holy hands, full of a multitude of good examples — to receive and embrace me②. There were there so many young men and maidens, a multitude of youth and every age, grave widows and ancient virgins; and continence herself in their midst: not barren, but a fruitful mother of children — her joys — by thee, O Lord, her husband. And she smiled on me with a challenging smile as if to say: "Can you not do what these young men and maidens can? Or can any of them do it of themselves, and not rather in the Lord their God? The Lord their God gave me to them. Why do you stand in your own strength, and so stand not? Cast yourself on him; fear not. He will not flinch③ and you will not fall. Cast yourself on him without fear, for he will receive and heal you." And I blushed violently, for I still heard the muttering of those "trifles" and hung suspended. Again she seemed to speak: "Stop your ears against those unclean members of yours, that they may be mortified④. They tell you of delights, but not according to the law of the Lord thy God." This struggle raging in my heart was nothing but the contest of self against self. And Alypius kept close beside me, and awaited in silence the outcome of my extraordinary agitation⑤.

CHAPTER XII

Now when deep reflection had drawn up out of the secret depths of my soul all my misery and had heaped it up before the sight of my heart, there arose a mighty storm, accompanied by a mighty rain of tears. That I might give way fully to my tears and lamentations, I stole away from Alypius, for it seemed to me that solitude was more appropriate for the business of weeping. I went far enough away that I could feel that even his presence was no restraint upon me. This was the way I felt at the time, and he realized it. I suppose I had said something before I started up and he noticed that the sound of my voice was choked with weeping. And so he stayed alone, where we had been sitting together, greatly astonished. I flung myself down under a fig tree — how I know not — and gave free course to my tears. The streams of my eyes gushed out an acceptable sacrifice to thee. And, not indeed in these words, but to this effect, I cried to thee: "And thou, O Lord, how long? How long, O Lord? Wilt thou be angry forever?

---

① futively：偷偷摸摸地，鬼鬼祟祟地，秘密地。

② cheerful but not wanton... of a multitude of good examples — to receive and embrace me：……明朗而肃穆地微笑着，庄重地邀请我上前，向我伸出充满着圣善的双手，准备接纳我，拥抱我。

③ flinch：缩；退缩；畏缩。

④ mortified：失面子的，受辱的；羞愧的；窘迫的。

⑤ This struggle raging in... of my extraordinary agitation：这种争斗在我心中搅扰，正是我与我的决斗。阿利比乌斯静静地傍我而坐，等待着我这次异乎寻常的内心斗争的结果。（阿利比乌斯是奥古斯丁的同乡及好友。）

Oh, remember not against us our former iniquities."① For I felt that I was still enthralled by them. I sent up these sorrowful cries: "How long, how long? Tomorrow and tomorrow? Why not now? Why not this very hour make an end to my uncleanness?"②

I was saying these things and weeping in the most bitter contrition of my heart, when suddenly I heard the voice of a boy or a girl I know not which — coming from the neighboring house, chanting over and over again, "Pick it up, read it; pick it up, read it." Immediately I ceased weeping and began most earnestly to think whether it was usual for children in some kind of game to sing such a song, but I could not remember ever having heard the like. So, damming the torrent of my tears, I got to my feet, for I could not but think that this was a divine command to open the Bible and read the first passage I should light upon. For I had heard how Anthony, accidentally coming into church while the gospel was being read, received the admonition as if what was read had been addressed to him: "Go and sell what you have and give it to the poor, and you shall have treasure in heaven; and come and follow me."③ By such an oracle he was forthwith converted to thee.

So I quickly returned to the bench where Alypius was sitting, for there I had put down the apostle's book when I had left there. I snatched it up, opened it, and in silence read the paragraph on which my eyes first fell: "Not in rioting and drunkenness, not in chambering and wantonness, not in strife and envying, but put on the Lord Jesus Christ, and make no provision for the flesh to fulfill the lusts thereof."④ I wanted to read no further, nor did I need to. For instantly, as the sentence ended, there was infused in my heart something like the light of full certainty and all the gloom of doubt vanished away.

Closing the book, then, and putting my finger or something else for a mark I began — now with a tranquil countenance — to tell it all to Alypius. And he in turn disclosed to me what had been going on in himself, of which I knew nothing. He asked to see what I had read. I showed him, and he looked on even further than I had read. I had not known what followed. But indeed it was this, "Him that is weak in the faith, receive."⑤ This he applied to himself, and told me so. By these words of warning he was strengthened, and by exercising his good resolution and purpose — all very much in keeping with his character, in which, in these respects, he was always far different from and better than I — he joined me in full commitment without any restless hesitation.

Then we went in to my mother, and told her what happened, to her great joy. We explained to her how it had occurred — and she leaped for joy triumphant; and she blessed

---

① And thou, O Lord, how long?... against us our former iniquities: 主啊,你的发怒到何时为止? 请你不要记着我过去的罪恶。(出自《诗篇》78首5、8节)。iniquities: 邪恶,不公正,罪行。

② How long... end to my uncleanness: 还要多久? 还要多久? 明天吗? 又是明天! 为何不是现在? 为何不在此时此刻结束我的恶?

③ Go and sell... and come and follow me: 去变卖你所有的,分给穷人;你积财于天,然后来跟随我。(出自《马太福音》第19章21节)。

④ Not in rioting... the lusts thereof: 不可耽于酒食,不可溺于淫荡,不可趋于竞争嫉妒,应被服主耶稣基督,勿使纵恣于肉体的嗜欲。(出自《罗马书》第13章13节)。

⑤ Him that is weak in the faith, receive: 信心软弱的人,你们要接纳他。出自《罗马书》第14章1节。

thee, who art "able to do exceedingly abundantly above all that we ask or think."① For she saw that thou hadst granted her far more than she had ever asked for in all her pitiful and doleful lamentations. For thou didst so convert me to thee that I sought neither a wife nor any other of this world's hopes, but set my feet on that rule of faith which so many years before thou hadst showed her in her dream about me. And so thou didst turn her grief into gladness more plentiful than she had ventured to desire, and dearer and purer than the desire she used to cherish of having grandchildren of my flesh.

Brainstorming

1. How does Augustine describe his state of mind just prior to his conversion experience?
2. What practical changes does Augustine make following his decision to convert to Catholicism?
3. Can the existence of God be proved or disproved? Is religious faith reasonable or unreasonable?
4. According to Augustine, God is not the parent of evil, as God endowed human with free will. What is the implication of man having free will?
5. "Since the innocent often suffer and the guilty go unpunished in this life, there must be another life in which these wrongs are righted and each person is judged by an impartial God according to his or her deserts." Evaluate this argument.
6. Describe the kind of universe (if any) that would make each of the following hypotheses probable.
   a. There are two Gods (one good, one evil) fighting for control of the world.
   b. There are many gods, each with his own sphere of influence.
   c. Everything in the universe tends toward good.
   d. Everything in the universe tends toward evil.
   e. Everything that appears to be bad in the world will in the end turn out for the best.
   f. Everything that appears to be good in the world will in the end turn out for the worst.
   g. There is one God, both omnipotent and benevolent.
   h. There is one God, omnipotent but not benevolent.
   i. There is one God, benevolent but not omnipotent

Supplementary reading

The following excerpt is taken from Augustine's *Confession* Book X, a narrative also fashioned out of the events of the first half of his life. The story is an unexcelled introduction to his views of philosophy and his final conversion to Christianity.

Chapter 1. In God Alone is the Hope and Joy of Man (excerpt)

Let me know You, O Thou who know me; let me know You, as I am known. O

---

① able to do exceedingly abundantly above all that we ask or think: 你所能成全于我们的,超越我们的意想。(出自《以弗所书》第 3 章 20 节)。

Thou strength of my soul, enter into it, and prepare it for Yourself, that You may have and hold it without spot or wrinkle. This is my hope, therefore have I spoken; and in this hope do I rejoice, when I rejoice soberly. Other things of this life ought the less to be sorrowed for, the more they are sorrowed for; and ought the more to be sorrowed for, the less men do sorrow for them. For behold, You desire truth, seeing that he who does it comes to the light. This wish I to do in confession in my heart before You, and in my writing before many witnesses.

Chapter 2. That All Things are Manifest to God. That Confession Unto Him is Not Made by the Words of the Flesh, But of the Soul, and the Cry of Reflection.

And from You, O Lord, unto whose eyes the depths of man's conscience are naked, what in me could be hidden though I were unwilling to confess to You? For so should I hide You from myself, not myself from You. But now, because my groaning witnesses that I am dissatisfied with myself, Thou shinest forth, and satisfiest, and art beloved and desired; that I may blush for myself, and renounce myself, and choose You, and may neither please You nor myself, except in You. To You, then, O Lord, am I manifest, whatever I am, and with what fruit I may confess unto You I have spoken. Nor do I it with words and sounds of the flesh, but with the words of the soul, and that cry of reflection which Your ear knows. For when I am wicked, to confess to You is naught but to be dissatisfied with myself; but when I am truly devout, it is naught but not to attribute it to myself, because Thou, O Lord, dost bless the righteous; but first Thou justifiest him ungodly. My confession, therefore, O my God, in Your sight, is made unto You silently, and yet not silently. For in noise it is silent, in affection it cries aloud. For neither do I give utterance to anything that is right unto men which You have not heard from me before, nor do You hear anything of the kind from me which Yourself said not first unto me.

Chapter 3. He Who Confesses Rightly Unto God Best Knows Himself.

What then have I to do with men, that they should hear my confessions, as if they were going to cure all my diseases? A people curious to know the lives of others, but slow to correct their own. Why do they desire to hear from me what I am, who are unwilling to hear from You what they are? And how can they tell, when they hear from me of myself, whether I speak the truth, seeing that no man knows what is in man, save the spirit of man which is in him? But if they hear from You anything concerning themselves, they will not be able to say, The Lord lies. For what is it to hear from You of themselves, but to know themselves? And who is he that knows himself and says, It is false, unless he himself lies? But because charity believes all things (among those at all events whom by union with itself it makes one), I too, O Lord, also so confess unto You that men may hear, to whom I cannot prove whether I confess the truth, yet do they believe me whose ears charity opens unto me.

But yet do Thou, my most secret Physician, make clear to me what fruit I may reap by doing it. For the confessions of my past sins — which You have forgiven and covered, that You might make me happy in You, changing my soul by faith and Your sacrament, — when they are read and heard, stir up the heart, that it sleep not in despair and say, I cannot; but that it may awake in the love of Your mercy and the sweetness of Your grace, by which he that is weak is strong, if by it he is made conscious of his own weakness. As for the good, they take delight in hearing of the past errors of such as are now freed from them; and they delight, not because they are errors, but because they have been and are so no longer. For what fruit, then, O Lord my God, to whom my conscience makes her daily confession, more confident in the hope of Your mercy than in her own innocency, — for what fruit, I beseech You, do I confess even to men in Your presence by this book what I am at this time, not what I have been? For that fruit I have both seen and spoken of, but what I am at this time, at the very moment of making my confessions, various people desire to know, both who knew me and who knew me not — who have heard of or from me — but their ear is not at my heart, where I am whatsoever I am. They are desirous, then, of hearing me confess what I am within, where they can neither stretch eye, nor ear, nor mind; they desire it as those willing to believe — but will they understand? For charity, by which they are good, says unto them that I do not lie in my confessions, and she in them believes me.

Famous quotations

I love not yet, yet I loved to love ··· I sought what I might love, in love with loving①.

—— *Confessions*, bk, iii, ch. 1

Hear the other side②.

—— *De Duabus Animabus*, XIV, ii

We make ourselves a ladder out of our vices if we trample the vices themselves underfoot③.

—— *Sermons*, iii

Anger is a weed; hate is the tree④.

—— lviii

The dove loves when it quarrels; the wolf hates when it flatters⑤.

—— lxiv

Grant me chastity and continence, but not yet.⑥

—— *Confessions*, bk, viii, ch. 7

God is not the Parent of evils. A world without evil, Augustine says, would be a world without us — rational being able to choose their actions. Just as for Cain, who has killed his brother Abel, our moral choice allow for the possibility of evil.

---

① 我还不曾爱过，但我愿意去爱我在寻找我所爱慕的事物，怀着深沉的爱——《忏悔录》，第3卷第1章。
② 要听取另一方的言辞。（兼听则明，偏听则暗）——《论生活的两面》，第14章第2节。
③ 倘若我们把罪恶踩在脚下，就能架起一座摆脱罪恶的云梯。——《布道文》第3篇
④ 愤怒是株草，仇恨是棵树。——第58篇
⑤ 鸽群在争吵，那是出于爱；豺狼献殷勤，那是出于恨。——第64篇
⑥ 给我高洁和自持能力——但时机未到。——《忏悔录》第八卷第7章（奥古斯丁的人生理想是：淡泊名利，自我约束，洁身自好，超然物外；但目前尚未达到这种精神境界。）

Knowledge Is Power
—— Bacon

Chapter 4

Bacon, Locke and Newton, I consider them as the three greatest men that have ever lived, without any exception, and as having laid the foundation of those superstructures which have been raised in the Physical Moral sciences.

—— Thomas Jefferson

In this chapter
- Glimpsing the life of Francis Bacon
- Looking at Bacon's Four Idols
- Introducing his proposed scientific method

Francis Bacon

Born in London, Bacon (1561—1626) was educated privately before being sent to Trinity College, Cambridge, at the age of 12. After graduation he started first as a lawyer, but soon gave up his studies to take up a diplomatic post in France at 16, fully expecting to become, in due course, a statesman in high office. But his father's sudden death left him penniless, forcing him to return to the legal profession. It wasn't until 1618 that he was appointed to the Lord Chancellorship, but was dismissed 2 years later, when convicted of taking bribes. Bacon continued to study and write before he died of a feverish bronchitis resulting from the chill he suffered when he filled a chicken's body with snow to see if the flesh could be preserved by the cold.

A philosopher, essayist, statesman, lawyer, jurist, and scientific methodologist, Bacon has been reputed as the "Father of Experimental Science". He is also considered to be the philosophical influence before the dawning of the industrial age, since his ideas created a profound impression during his lifetime and his strikingly modern empiricist methodology has ever since widely influenced many nineteenth-century figures.

Distinctive insights①

Bacon champions the new empiricism resulting from the achievements of early modern science. He does not propose an actual philosophy, but rather a method of developing philosophy. He opposes alleged knowledge based on appeals to authority, and on the barrenness of scholasticism. He believes that what is needed is a new attitude and methodology based strictly on scientific practices. The goal of acquiring knowledge is the good of mankind: Knowledge is power.

1. Baconian Inductive Methodology②

Bacon argues that the advancement of science depends on formulating laws of ever-increasing generality. He proposes a scientific method that includes a variation of this approach. His concept of experiment and method of observation rest on the notion of induction, that is deriving "laws" from the simple observation of particulars and their series and order. The alternative view, which he strongly criticized, was Aristotle's deductive method, the classic example of which is: (1) All men are mortal; (2) Socrates is a man; (3) Therefore, Socrates is mortal. The problem with this approach, according to Bacon, is that the conclusions we draw only perpetuate the errors that are already contained in the premises. Therefore, we should come up with an argumentative strategy that will provide us with new information upon which we can draw new conclusions. Induction does just this. Bacon's induction proceeds as follows. First, we look for those cases where, given certain changes, certain others invariably follow. In his example, if certain changes in the form (motion of particles) take place, heat always follows. We seek to find all of the "positive instances" of the form that give rise to the effect of that form. Next, we investigate the "negative instances," cases where in the absence of the form, the qualitative change does not take place. In the operation of these methods it is important to try to produce experimentally "prerogative instances," particularly striking or typical examples of the phenomenon under investigation. Finally, in cases where the object under study is present to some greater or lesser degree, we must be able to take into consideration why these changes occur. In the example, quantitative changes in degrees of heat will be correlated to quantitative changes in the speed of the motion of the particles. This method implies that in many cases we can invent instruments to measure changes in degree. Such inventions are of course the hoped-for outcome of scientific inquiry, because their

---

① 培根认为自然界是物质的,物质与运动不可分离,一切来源于感觉。主张采用归纳、分析、比较、观察和实验的理性方法整理感觉材料,对归纳法作了比较系统的论述,因而他被认为是归纳逻辑的创始人。在美学上,他强调想象虚构、理想化、动态美与艺术家的灵心妙运,开浪漫主义的先河。在教育上,强调学校应传授百科全书式的知识。

② 培根的归纳法分三个步骤。第一步,广泛收集相关事实材料作为归纳的基础;第二步,整理有关事实材料;第三步,通过比较再进行归纳。

possession improves the lot of human beings.

2. Idols of Mind[①]

According to Bacon, although philosophy at the time used the deductive syllogism to interpret nature, the philosopher should proceed through inductive reasoning from fact to axiom to law. But before beginning this induction, the inquirer is to free his/her mind from certain false notions or tendencies which distort the truth.

There are well-known hindrances to acquisition of knowledge of causal laws. Such hindrances (false opinions, prejudices), which "anticipate" nature rather than explain it, Bacon calls them the four idols (*idola*). Idols of the tribe are natural mental tendencies, among which are the idle search for purposes in nature, and the impulse to read our own desires and needs into nature. Idols of the cave are predispositions of particular individuals, who tend to form opinions based on idiosyncrasies of education, social intercourse, reading, and favored authorities. Idols of the marketplace are the most potentially dangerous of all dispositions as regarded by Bacon, because they arise from common uses of language that often result in verbal disputes. Many words though thought to be meaningful, stand for nonexistent things; others, although they name actual things, are poorly defined or used in confused ways. Idols of the theatre depend upon the influence of accepted theories or established authorities. Bacon maintains that the aim of acquiring genuine knowledge does not depend on superior skill in the use of words but rather on the discovery of natural laws. Once these idols are eliminated, the mind is free to seek knowledge of natural laws based on experimentation, which of course, would lead to the hoped-for outcome of scientific inquiry, because it in turn, may bring about benefits to all human beings.

Introductory remarks

Novum Organum — a reference to Aristotle's work *Organon* is Bacon's philosophical treatise on logic and syllogism, which details a new system of logic he believes to be superior to the old ways of syllogism. In this work, we see the development of the Baconian method consisting of procedures for isolating the form nature, or cause, of a phenomenon, including the method of agreement, method of difference, and method of concomitant variation.

Novum Organum is actually the second part of Bacon's larger work, the *Great Instauration*, which aims to offer a new method of investigating nature, called the Interpretation of Nature. It consists of two books of aphorisms. Our present selection is taken from Book One, in which he launches his scathing attack on current philosophy and on the scientific method. The main object of his assault consists largely in the syllogism, a

---

① idol 具有假想、偶像之意。培根借用该词指阻碍人们正确反映客观世界,阻碍人们获得真理性认识的主体心理障碍。依据这些障碍的不同性质,他将假象分为四种:即,源于"人的天性之中"的"种族假象";源于个人"所特有的天性中"的"洞穴假象";源于"人们彼此交往而形成"的词语上误解的"市场假象";以及源于"各种哲学教条"造成错误知识体系的"剧场假象"。他主张打破"假象",铲除各种幻想和偏见。

method that he believes to be completely inadequate in comparison to what Bacon calls "true Induction."

Text

Novum Organum① (excerpt)

XXXIX

There are four kinds of illusions which block men's minds. For instruction's sake, we have given them the following names: the first kind is called idols of the tribe, the second idols of the cave; the third idols of the marketplace; the fourth idols of the theatre.

XL

Formation of notions and axioms by means of true induction is certainly an appropriate way to banish idols and get rid of them; but it is also very useful to identify the idols. Instruction about idols has the same relation to the interpretation of nature as teaching the sophistic refutations has to ordinary logic.②

XLI

The idols of the tribe are founded in human nature itself and in the very tribe or race of mankind. The assertion that the human senses are the measure of things is false; to the contrary, all perceptions, both of sense and mind, are relative to man, not to the universe. The human understanding is like an uneven mirror receiving rays from things and merging its own nature with the nature of things, which thus distorts and corrupts it.③

XLII

The idols of the cave are the illusions of the individual man. For (apart from the aberrations of human nature in general④) each man has a kind of individual cave or cavern which fragments and distorts the light of nature. This may happen either because of the unique and particular nature of each man; or because of his upbringing and the company he keeps; or because of his reading of books and the authority of those whom he respects and admires; or because of the different impressions things make on different minds, preoccupied and prejudiced perhaps, or calm and detached, and so on. The evident

---

① 《新工具论》(1620),是培根未完成的巨著《伟大的复兴》六个部分中的第二部分。培根认为亚里士多德在《工具论》中提出的三段论演绎法一直为中世纪经院哲学所滥用,但对于科学原理的发现和技术发明,该演绎法是无用的,应予以抛弃,代之以归纳法。他把对这种新方法的论述称为"新工具",以示有别于亚里士多德以演绎逻辑为主的《工具论》。

② Instruction about idols...has to ordinary logic:论述"假象"的学说之对于"解释自然"和驳斥"诡辩"的学说之对于"普通逻辑"是一样的。sophistic refutations:诡辩的驳斥。

③ The human understanding...which thus distorts and corrupts it:人类理解力则正如一面凹凸镜,由于它接受的光线既不规则,反映事物时就掺入了它自己的性质而使得事物的性质变形和褪色。

④ apart from the aberrations of human nature in general:除普遍人性所共有的错误外。aberrations:脱离常轨,偏离。

consequence is that the human spirit (in its different dispositions in different men) is a variable thing, quite irregular, almost haphazard①. Heraclitus well said that men seek knowledge in lesser, private worlds, not in the great or common world.②

XLIII

There are also illusions which seem to arise by agreement and from men's association with each other, which we call idols of the marketplace; we take the name from human exchange and community. Men associate through talk; and words are chosen to suit the understanding of the common people. And thus a poor and unskillful code of words incredibly obstructs the understanding. The definitions and explanations with which learned men have been accustomed to protect and in some way liberate themselves, do not restore the situation at all. Plainly words do violence to the understanding, and confuse everything; and betray men into countless empty disputes and fictions.③

XLIV

Finally there are the illusions which have made their homes in men's minds from the various dogmas of different philosophies, and even from mistaken rules of demonstration. These I call idols of the theatre, for all the philosophies that men have learned or devised are, in our opinion, so many plays produced and performed which have created false and fictitious worlds. We are not speaking only of the philosophies and sects now in vogue④ or even of the ancient ones; many other such plays could be composed and concocted, seeing that the causes of their very different errors have a great deal in common. And we do not mean this only of the universal philosophies, but also of many principles and axioms of the sciences which have grown strong from tradition, belief and inertia. But we must speak at greater length and separately of each different kind of idol, to give warning to the human understanding...

XLVII

The human understanding is most affected by things which have the ability to strike and enter the mind all at once and suddenly⑤, and to fill and expand the imagination. It pretends and supposes that in some admittedly imperceptible way, everything else is just like the few things that took the mind by storm. The understanding is very slow and ill adapted to make the long journey to those remote and heterogeneous instances which test

---

① the human spirit...quite irregular, almost haphazard：人的元精（照各个不同的人所秉受而得的样子）实际上是一种易变多扰的东西，又似为机运所统治。human spirit：元精，意即一切有生的和无生的物体之中都包有元精，渗透于可触分子，它触摸不到，亦没有任何重量，只借动作或作用来显示它自己。haphazard：随意的，偶然任意的。

② Heraclitus well said...not in the great or common world. 赫拉克利特曾经说得好，人们之追求科学总是求诸他们自己的小天地，而不是求诸公共的大天地。赫拉克利特（约530—470 BC）古希腊前苏格拉底哲学家。

③ Plainly words do violence to...empty disputes and fictions：文字仍公然强制和统辖着理解力，弄得一切混乱，并把人们岔引到无数空洞的争论和无谓的幻想上去。

④ in vogue：正在流行。

⑤ The human understanding...all at once and suddenly：人类理解力最易被同时而陡然打入心中从而足以充填想像力的一些事物所引动。

axioms as in a fire, unless it is made to do so by harsh rules and the force of authority.①

XLVIII

The human understanding is ceaselessly active, and cannot stop or rest, and seeks to go further; but in vain. Therefore it is unthinkable that there is some boundary or farthest point of the world; it always appears, almost by necessity, that there is something beyond. Again it cannot be conceived how eternity has come down to this day; since the distinction which is commonly accepted that there is an infinity of the past and an infinity of the future can no way stand, because it would follow that there is one infinity which is greater than another infinity, and that infinity is being consumed and tends towards the finite. There is a similar subtlety about ever divisible lines, from thought's lack of restraint②. This indiscipline of the mind works with greater damage on the discovery of causes: for though the most universal things in nature must be brute facts, which are just as they are found, and are not themselves truly causable, the human understanding, not knowing how to rest, still seeks things better known. And then as it strives to go further, it falls back on things that are more familiar, namely final causes,③ which are plainly derived from the nature of man rather than of the universe, and from this origin have wonderfully corrupted philosophy. It is as much a mark of an inept and superficial thinker to look for a cause in the most universal cases as not to feel the need of a cause in subordinate and derivative④ cases.

XLIX

The human understanding is not composed of dry light, but is subject to influence from the will and the emotions⑤, a fact that creates fanciful knowledge; man prefers to believe what he wants to be true. He rejects what is difficult because he is too impatient to make the investigation; he rejects sensible ideas, because they limit his hopes; he rejects the deeper truths of nature because of superstition; he rejects the light of experience, because he is arrogant and fastidious, believing that the mind should not be seen to be spending its time on mean, unstable things; and he rejects anything unorthodox⑥ because of common opinion. In short, emotion marks and stains the understanding in countless ways which are sometimes impossible to perceive.

---

① The understanding is...and the force of authority: 至于说到要往复从事于许多远隔而相异的事例,促使原理经受如火一般的考验,那么人的智力就完全迟钝而不适宜,除非有严格的法则和强有力的权威来强制它。heterogeneous: 各种各样的;多种多样的。

② There is a similar subtlety...from thought's lack of restraint: 关于一条线的无限可分割性,同样由于思想欲罢不能之故,也有着相同的微妙情形。这是指亚里士多德的话;他的著作中有几处都说,在理论上,一尺一寸都可无限分割下去。

③ as it strives to go further, it falls back on things that are more familiar, namely final causes: 它在努力追求较远的东西中却回头落到近在手边的东西上,也就是说,落到目的因上。

④ derivative: 被引申出的,被推论出的。

⑤ The human understanding...from the will and the emotions: 人类理解力不是干燥的光,而是受到意志和各种情绪的灌浸的。"人类理解力不是干燥的光"借自赫拉克利特的名言"最聪明的心乃是一种干燥的光"。

⑥ unorthodox: 非正统的,非传统的。

Brainstorming

1. In what ways does each of Bacon's four idols hamper human understanding?

2. Are there any links or causal relationships between the four idols? Give your own examples.

3. How do you interpret Bacon's analogy between the hindrances to acquisition of knowledge and the four idols of mind?

4. What are the two ways of exploring truth according to Bacon? Which way does he advocate? Why?

5. According to Bacon, what would result from the adoption of his new method of scientific inquiry?

6. Discuss how to overcome the limitation of human understanding, drawing from your own knowledge and experience.

Supplementary reading

In *The Advancement of Learning*, from which the following excerpt is taken, Bacon argues that the only knowledge of importance is that which can be discovered by observation — "empirical" knowledge rooted in the natural world. He forcefully champions the idea of state funding for experimental science and the creation of an encyclopedia.

The Advancement of Learning① (excerpt)

The parts of human learning have reference to the three parts of man's understanding: history to his memory, poesy to his imagination, and philosophy to his reason. Divine learning receiveth the same distribution; theology consisteth of the history of the church; parables, which is divine poesy; and holy doctrine is but Divine History.

I am not ignorant that in divers sciences, as of the jurisconsults, the mathematicians, the rhetoricians, the philosophers, there are set down some memorials of the schools, authors, and books. But a just story of learning, containing the antiquities and originals of knowledges and their sects, their inventions, their traditions, their flourishings, decays, with the causes and occasions of them, throughout the ages of the world, I may truly affirm to be wanting.

As to those histories of marvels, those superstitious narrations of sorceries, witchcrafts, dreams, divinations, and the like, where there is an assurance and clear evidence of the fact, I am not of the opinion that they be altogether excluded. For it is not yet known in what cases the effects attributed to superstition do participate of natural causes: as your majesty hath showed in your own example; who with the two clear eyes of

---

① 《学术的进展》，以知识为其研究对象，抨击了中世纪的蒙昧主义，论证了知识的巨大作用，提示了知识不能令人满意的现状及补救办法。

religion and natural philosophy have looked deeply and wisely into these shadows, and yet proved yourself to be of the nature of the sun, which passeth through pollutions and itself remains as pure as before. But this I hold fit, that these narrations, which have mixture with superstition, be sorted by themselves, and not be mingled with the narrations which are merely and sincerely natural.

For history of nature wrought or mechanical, I find some collections made of agriculture, and likewise of manual arts; but it is esteemed a kind of dishonour unto learning to descend to inquiry upon matters mechanical. But the truth is, it be not the highest instances that give the securest information. He that enquireth into the nature of a great Commonwealth, must find it first in a family, and the simple conjugations of man and wife, which are in every cottage. So we see how that secret of nature, of the turning of iron touched with the loadstone towards the north, was found out in needles of iron, not in bars of iron.

If my judgment be of any weight, the use of history mechanical is of all others the most radical and fundamental towards natural philosophy and to the endowment and benefit of man's life.

As for civil history, it is of three kinds; not unfitly to be compared with the three kinds of pictures or images: for of pictures or images, we see some are unfinished, some are perfect, and some are defaced. So of histories we may find three kinds, memorials, perfect histories, and antiquities; for memorials are history unfinished, or the first or rough draughts of history; and antiquities are history defaced, or some remnants of history which have casually escaped the shipwreck of time.

History, which may be called just and perfect history, is of three kinds, according to the object which it propoundeth or pretendeth to represent: for it either representeth a time, or a person, or an action. The first we call chronicles, the second lives, and the third narrations or relations. But for modern histories, whereof there are some few very worthy, but the greater part beneath mediocrity.

There is another portion of history which Cornelius Tacitus maketh, which is not to be forgotten, especially with that application which he accoupleth it withal, annals and journals. I cannot likewise be ignorant of a form of writing which some wise and grave men have used, containing a scattered history of those actions which they have thought worthy of memory, with politic discourse and observation thereupon: not incorporate into the history, but separately, and as the more principal in their intention; which kind of ruminated history I think more fit to place amongst books of policy.

History ecclesiastical receiveth the same divisions with history civil: but further, in the propriety thereof, may be divided into the history of the church, by a general name; history of prophecy; and history of providence. Thus much therefore concerning history; which is that part of learning which answereth to one of the cells, domiciles, or offices of the mind of man: which is that of memory.

Poesy is a part of learning in measure of words extremely licensed, and doth truly refer to the imagination. It is taken in two senses in respect of words or matter; in the first sense it is but a character of style, and belongeth to arts of speech, and is not pertinent for the present: in the latter it is, as hath been said, one of the principal portions of learning, and is nothing else but feigned history, which may be styled as well in prose as in verse.

The use of this feigned history hath been to give some shadow of satisfaction to the mind of man in those points wherein the nature of things doth deny it. Therefore, because the acts or events of true history have not that magnitude which satisfieth the mind of man, poesy feigneth acts and events greater and more heroical.

In this third part of learning, which is poesy, I can report no deficience. For being as a plant that cometh of the lust of the earth, without a formal seed, it hath sprung up and spread abroad more than any other kind. But it is not good to stay too long in the theatre. Let us now pass on to the judicial place or palace of the mind, which we are to approach and view with more reverence and attention.

In Philosophy, the contemplations of man do either penetrate unto God, or are reflected or reverted upon himself. Out of which several inquiries there do arise three knowledges, divine philosophy, natural philosophy, and human philosophy or humanity. But because the distributions and partitions of knowledge are not like several lines that meet in one angle, and so touch but in a point; but are like branches of a tree, that meet in a stem: therefore it is good, before we enter into the former distribution, to erect and constitute one universal science, by the name of PHILOSOPHIA PRIMA, primitive or summary philosophy, as the main and common way: That it be a receptacle for all such profitable observations and axioms as fall not within the compass of any of the special parts of philosophy or sciences, but are more common and of a higher stage.

This science, as I understand it, I may justly report as deficient; for I see sometimes the profounder sort of wits in handling some particular argument will now and then draw a bucket of water out of this well for their present use; but the spring-head thereof seemeth to me not to have been visited; being of so excellent use, both for the disclosing of nature, and the abridgment of art.

Famous quotations

Hope is a good breakfast, but it is a bad supper[①].

—— *Apophthegms*（16240），36

Riches are a good handmaid, but the worst mistress[②].

—— *De Dignitate et Augmentis Scientiarum*, I. Vi, 3. Antitheta

Fame is like a river, that beareth up things light and swollen, and drowns things weighty and sold[③].

—— *53. Of Praise*

---

① 希望是一顿美好的早餐，但又是一顿糟糕的晚餐。——《箴言集》，第36则。
② 财富是出色的侍女，却是最猥劣的情妇。——《学术的进步》，第1卷第6章第3节《论对偶》。
③ 名誉有如江河，所承载的是轻盈疏松之物，而淹没沉重坚实之物。——第53篇《论称誉》。

Studies serve for delight, for ornament, and for ability①.

—— 50. *Of Studies*

Some books are to be tasted, others to be swallowed, and some few to be chewed and digested; that is, some books are to be read only in parts; others to be read but not curiously; and some few to be read wholly, and with diligence and attention. Some books also may be read by deputy, and extracts made of them by others②.

—— 50. *Of Studies*

Reading maketh a full man; conference a ready man; and writing an exact man③.

—— 50. *Of Studies*

Histories make men wise; poets, witty; the mathematics, subtile; natural philosophy deep; moral, grave; logic and rhetoric, able to contend④.

—— 50. *Of Studies*

It is science, not religion that was regarded increasingly as the key to knowledge from the 16th century onward.

---

① 读书足以怡情,足以博采,足以长才。——第 50 篇《论读书》。
② 有些书供浅尝,有些书供吞食,少数则需咀嚼消化。换言之,有些书只需读上半部分,有些只需大体浏览,少数则需全读,读时需全神贯注,孜孜不倦。书也可以请人读,事后取其读书摘要。——同上。
③ 读书使人充实,讨论使人机智,笔记使人准确。——同上。
④ 读史使人明智,读诗使人灵秀,数学使人周密,科学使人深刻,伦理学使人庄重,逻辑修辞学使人善辩。——同上。

I Am, I Exist
——Descartes

Chapter 5

With the interpretation of man as subiectum, Descartes creates the metaphysical presupposition for future anthropology of every kind and tendency.

—— Heidegger

In this chapter
- Glimpsing Descartes' life
- Appreciating Descartes' method of doubt
- Assessing Descartes' dualism

René Descartes

Born near Tours, France, Descartes (1596—1650) was educated at the Jesuit College Royale, in La Flèche. Due to his poor health he always stayed indoors and thus formed the habit of meditating. From the age of 16 he started to concentrate on studying mathematics, which later helped him find his philosophical calling. In 1649, in his fifties, he was invited to Sweden by Queen Christina to discuss philosophy: he was expected to get up very early, much against his normal practice. In consequence he fell prey to the cold northern winter and died of pneumonia one year later.

A major figure in 17th-century continental rationalism, Descartes is generally credited as the "Father of Modern Philosopher". During his lifetime, he was just as famous as an original physicist, physiologist and mathematician. But it is as a highly original philosopher that he is most frequently read today.

Distinctive insights[①]

1. The Cartesian System[②]

In a celebrated simile, Descartes describes the whole of philosophy as like a tree: the roots are metaphysics, the trunk the physics, and the branches are the various particular sciences, including mechanics, medicine, and morals. The analogy captures at least three important features of the Cartesian system. The first is its insistence on the essential unity of knowledge, which contrasts strongly with the Aristotelian conception of the sciences as a series of separate disciplines, each with its own methods and standards of precision. The sciences, as Descartes puts it in an early notebook, are all "linked together" in a sequence that is in principle as simple and straightforward as the series of numbers. The second point conveyed by the tree simile is the utility of philosophy for ordinary living: the tree is valued for its fruits, and these are gathered, Descartes points out, "not from the roots or the trunk but from the ends of the branches" — the practical sciences. Descartes frequently stresses that his principal motivation is not abstract theorizing for its own sake: in place of the "speculative philosophy taught in the schools," we can and should achieve knowledge that is "useful in life" and that will one day make us "masters and possessors of nature." Third, the likening of metaphysics or "first philosophy" to the roots of the tree nicely captures the Cartesian belief in what has come to be known as foundationalism — the view that knowledge must be constructed from the bottom up, and that nothing can be taken as established until we have gone back to first principles.

2. Method of Doubt

Descartes applies his systematic doubt to the very existence of the world. It is possible, he suggests, imaging that one's entire waking life is an illusion. But even so, it is not possible to doubt one's own existence. The difficult thing, however, is to discover the nature of the self. Is the self an amalgam of perceptions, memories and feelings, or are these too, like the physical body, inessential to its real nature? Thus, Descartes' ambition was to begin philosophy anew, establishing it on grounds certain enough to support an edifice of indoubitable knowledge. In *The Meditations*, he begins his construction project by observing that many of the preconceived opinions he has accepted since childhood have turned out to be unreliable; so it is necessary, "once in a lifetime" to "demolish everything and start again, right from the foundations." He puts all beliefs, ideas, thoughts, and matter in doubt. He proceeds, in other words, by applying what is sometimes called his method of doubt, which is explained in the earlier *Discourse on the Method*: "Since I now wished to devote myself solely to the search of truth, I thought it

---

① 笛卡尔试图建立无所不包的哲学体系,它由形而上学、物理学等各门具体科学组成。在形而上学方面,他提出"普遍怀疑"的理论以及"精神实体"与"物质实体"同时存在、互不相关的二元论世界观,并提出"我思故我在"的原则。在认识论上,主张唯理论,把几何学的推理方法或演绎法应用到哲学上,认为清晰明白的概念就是真理,从而提出"天赋观点"的唯心主义学说,是近代唯理论的创始人。

② 笛卡儿提出物质世界是否为精神的存在留有一席之地?精神的存在是怎样的?能否采用研究有形世界的方法来认识和研究它等等。笛卡儿自成体系,熔唯物主义与唯心主义于一炉,在哲学史上产生了深远的影响。

necessary to... reject as if absolutely false everything in which one could imagine the least doubt, in order to see if I was left believing anything that was entirely indubitable." He shows that his grounds, or reasoning, for any knowledge could just as well be false. Sensory experience, the primary mode of knowledge, is often erroneous and therefore must be doubted. Even such seemingly straightforward judgments as "I am sitting here by the fire" may be false, since there is no guarantee that my present experience is not a dream. The *dream argument* (as it has come to be called) leaves intact the truths of mathematics, since "whether I am awake or asleep two and three make five"; but Descartes now proceeds to introduce an even more radical argument for doubt based on the following dilemma. If there is an omnipotent God, he could presumably cause me to go wrong every time I count two and three; if, on the other hand, there is no God, then I owe my origins not to a powerful and intelligent creator, but to some random series of **imperfect causes**, and in this case there is even less reason to suppose that my basic intuitions about mathematics are reliable. From here Descartes dramatizes a morass of wholesale doubt by introducing an imaginary demon "of the utmost power and cunning" who is systematically deceiving him in every possible way. Everything I believe in — "the sky, the earth and all external things" — might be illusions that the demon has devised in order to trick me. Yet this very extreme doubt, when pushed as far as it will go, yields the first indubitable truth in the Cartesian quest for knowledge — the existence of the thinking subject.

3. The First Certainty

The axiom — "I think, therefore I am" — forms Descartes' First Certainty. It is at this point that Descartes realizes that there is one belief that he surely cannot doubt: his belief in his own existence. Each of us can think or say: "I am, I exist", and while we are thinking or saying it we cannot be wrong about it. When Descartes tries to apply the evil test to this belief, he realizes that the demon could only make him believe that he exists if he does in fact exist; how can he doubt his existence unless he exists in order to do the doubting. So "Let the demon deceive me as much as he may, he can never bring it about that I am nothing, so long as I think I am something... I am, I exist, is certain, as often as it is put forward by me or conceived in the mind." His conclusion is that "I exist" is impossible to doubt and is, therefore, absolutely certain. Descartes expresses this *cogito* argument in the famous phrase "Cogito ergo sum" ("I am thinking, therefore I exist")

4. Cartesian Dualism①

Descartes raises the central questions of modern philosophy. Is there a place in the world of matter for a spiritual being? What sort of thing could it be? Can it be known and investigated with the same methods as the physical world?

He is well known for discussing the dualist problem of mind and matter generated from his conclusion that mind is a non-corporeal substance distinct from material of bodily

---

① 笛卡尔的二元论,认为世界有两种各自独立、性质不同的实体:一种是物质的(身),另一种精神的(心)。这两个实体交互作用,心理通过感官获取有关物质世界的信息;身体的需要在意识中被感受,并指导身体活动。

substance. By "substance" he means "anything which has independent existence; which does not depend on anything else for existence". He further maintains that "every substance has a principal property that constitutes its essential nature"; that is, every substance has a property it must have in order to be what it is. Consciousness is the essential property of mind substance; extension in length, breadth and depth is the essential property of bodily or material substance. Descartes' realization that he cannot doubt the fact that he exists as a thinking substance (even though he can still doubt that he has a body), convinces him that mind can exist independently of matter. He argues that "my soul is not in my body as a pilot in a ship; I am most tightly bound to it..."; that is, the mind does not influence the body, as it were, operating levers and switches which set the body into the required motions but there is, he insists, a much closer union in which the mind directly moves the body and directly experiences, rather than observes, the pains and pleasures generated by means of the body. Although Descartes' dualist account goes no way towards showing how a material substance actually can affect a non-material substance, the Cartesian version of the mind-body problem has remained probably the most popular and most worked-over philosophical problem of the last three centuries.

Introductory remarks

The Discourse on the Method is a philosophical and autobiographical treatise published in 1637. The book is divided into six parts, described in the author's preface as: 1. Various considerations touching the Sciences; 2. The principal rules of the method discovered; 3. Certain rules of Morals deduced from this method; 4. The reasonings by which the author establishes the existence of God and of the Human Soul; 5. The order of the physical questions investigated, and, in particular, the explication of the motion of the heart and of some other difficulties pertaining to medicine, as also the difference between the soul of man and that of the brutes; 6. What the author believes to be required in order to greater advancement in the investigation of Nature than has yet been made, with the reasons that have induced him to write.

The following selection is an excerpt from Part IV, in which Descartes attempts to arrive at a fundamental set of principles that one can know as true without any doubt. To achieve this, Descartes employs a method called general doubt, also sometimes referred to as methodological skepticism: he rejects any ideas that can be doubted, and then reestablishes them in order to acquire a firm foundation for genuine knowledge. He finally arrives at his famous conclusion: I think, therefore I am. For if he didn't exist, he wouldn't be thinking. From this point, Descartes can begin to prove other truths, such as the existence of God. What is so important about his axiom of "I am, I exist" is that it privileges the individual over tradition and privileges the individual's perception of the truth over some objective truth or some commonly shared truth. In other words, the individual subjective experience is the foundation of truth. This notion would radically transform thinking in Europe and the West up through the present day.

Discourse On the Method① (excerpt)

I am in doubt as to the propriety of making my first meditations in the place above mentioned matter of discourse; for these are so metaphysical, and so uncommon, as not, perhaps, to be acceptable to every one. And yet, that it may be determined whether the foundations that I have laid are sufficiently secure, I find myself in a measure constrained to advert to them②. I had long before remarked that, in relation to practice, it is sometimes necessary to adopt, as if above doubt, opinions which we discern to be highly uncertain, as has been already said; but as I then desired to give my attention solely to the search after truth, I thought that a procedure exactly the opposite was called for, and that I ought to reject as absolutely false all opinions in regard to which I could suppose the least ground for doubt, in order to ascertain whether after that there remained aught in my belief that was wholly indubitable③. Accordingly, seeing that our senses sometimes deceive us, I was willing to suppose that there existed nothing really such as they presented to us; and because some men err in reasoning, and fall into paralogisms④, even on the simplest matters of geometry, I, convinced that I was as open to error as any other, rejected as false all the reasonings I had hitherto⑤ taken for demonstrations; and finally, when I considered that the very same thoughts (presentations) which we experience when awake may also be experienced when we are asleep, while there is at that time not one of them true, I supposed that all the objects (presentations) that had ever entered into my mind when awake, had in them no more truth than the illusions of my dreams⑥. But immediately upon this I observed that, whilst I thus wished to think that all was false, it was absolutely necessary that I, who thus thought, should be somewhat; and as I observed that this truth, I think, therefore I am (*cogito ergo sum*), was so certain and of such evidence that no ground of doubt, however extravagant, could be alleged by the skeptics

---

① 《方法论》,提出在传统演绎法的基础上创立一种以数学为基础的演绎法;以唯理论为根据,从自明的直观公理出发,运用数学的逻辑演绎,推出结论。
② And yet, that it may be... to advert to them:然而要使人判定我所建立的根基是否牢固,我不得不多少提及到它们。in a measure:部分地;advert to:提出看法。
③ to reject as absolutely false... there remained aught in my belief that was wholly indubitable:拒绝凡是我认为有丝毫疑问的一切看法,视它们为绝对谬切,以便查此此后在我的信念中是否只留下全部不可怀疑的事物。ascertain:查明,弄清,确定;in regard to:在……方面;aught:一切,全部;indubitable:不容置疑的。
④ paralogisms:不合逻辑的推论,谬误推理;谬论。
⑤ hitherto:到目前为止,迄今。
⑥ the very same thoughts... no more truth than the illusions of my dreams:我们在清醒时所有的思想也可以同样地在睡梦中发生,而睡梦中的一切都不是真实的,所以我假定凡在清醒时进入我脑海的一切物品和表象,亦必和我在睡梦中的幻想一样都没有真实的根据。

capable of shaking it①, I concluded that I might, without scruple②, accept it as the first principle of the philosophy of which I was in search.

In the next place, I attentively examined what I was and as I observed that I could suppose that I had no body, and that there was no world nor any place in which I might be; but that I could not therefore suppose that I was not; and that, on the contrary, from the very circumstance that I thought to doubt of the truth of other things, it most clearly and certainly followed that I was; while, on the other hand, if I had only ceased to think, although all the other objects which I had ever imagined had been in reality existent, I would have had no reason to believe that I existed③; I hence concluded that I was a substance whose whole essence or nature consists only in thinking, and which, that it may exist, has need of no place, nor is dependent on any material thing; so that "I", that is to say, the mind by which I am what I am, is wholly distinct from the body, and is even more easily known than the latter, and is such, that although the latter were not, it would still continue to be all that it is④.

After this I inquired in general into what is essential I to the truth and certainty of a proposition; for since I had discovered one which I knew to be true, I thought that I must likewise be able to discover the ground of this certitude⑤. And as I observed that in the words I think, therefore I am, there is nothing at all which gives me assurance of their truth beyond this, that I see very clearly that in order to think it is necessary to exist, I concluded that I might take, as a general rule, the principle, that all the things which we very clearly and distinctly conceive are true⑥, only observing, however, that there is some difficulty in rightly determining the objects which we distinctly conceive.

In the next place, from reflecting on the circumstance that I doubted, and that consequently my being was not wholly perfect (for I clearly saw that it was a greater perfection to know than to doubt), I was led to inquire whence I had learned to think of something more perfect than myself; and I clearly recognized that I must hold this notion from some nature which in reality was more perfect. As for the thoughts of many other objects external to me, as of the sky, the earth, light, heat, and a thousand more, I was less at a loss to know whence these came; for since I remarked in them nothing which seemed to render them superior to myself, I could believe that, if these were true, they were dependencies on my own nature, in so far as it possessed a certain perfection, and, if

---

① I observed that this truth... the skeptics capable of shaking it：我认定"我思，故我在"这一真理千真万确，不言而喻，即便怀疑论者用最激烈的怀疑理由也不能动摇它。*cogito ergo sum*：(拉丁语)"我思故我在"；extravagant：过度的，过分的；skeptics：怀疑论者。

② scruple：顾虑，顾忌，良心上的不安。

③ if I had only ceased to... to believe that I existed：如果我一旦停止了思想，虽然我所想象过的一切事物都存在着，我却没有理由相信我自己是存在的。

④ the mind... continue to be all that it is：所以"我"，就是那使我之所以成为我的心灵，它与身体完全不同，但比身体更容易被认识；身体虽可不存，心灵却能继续长留。

⑤ certitude：确信，自信。

⑥ I concluded that... distinctly conceive are true：于是我得出结论，我不妨拿这一原理作为一个普通的法则，即：大凡我们所能十分清晰而明确地认识的事物必都是真实的。

they were false, that I held them from nothing, that is to say, that they were in me because of a certain imperfection of my nature. But this could not be the case with the idea of a nature more perfect than myself; for to receive it from nothing was a thing manifestly impossible; and, because it is not less repugnant① that the more perfect should be an effect of, and dependence on the less perfect, than that something should proceed from nothing, it was equally impossible that I could hold it from myself: accordingly, it but remained that it had been placed in me by a nature which was in reality more perfect than mine, and which even possessed within itself all the perfections of which I could form any idea; that is to say, in a single word, which was God. And to this I added that, since I knew some perfections which I did not possess, I was not the only being in existence (I will here, with your permission, freely use the terms of the schools); but, on the contrary, that there was of necessity some other more perfect Being upon whom I was dependent, and from whom I had received all that I possessed; for if I had existed alone, and independently of every other being, so as to have had from myself all the perfection, however little, which I actually possessed, I should have been able, for the same reason, to have had from myself the whole remainder of perfection, of the want of which I was conscious, and thus could of myself have become infinite, eternal, immutable, omniscient, all-powerful, and, in fine, have possessed all the perfections which I could recognize in God②. For in order to know the nature of God (whose existence has been established by the preceding reasonings), as far as my own nature permitted, I had only to consider in reference to all the properties of which I found in my mind some idea, whether their possession was a mark of perfection; and I was assured that no one which indicated any imperfection was in him, and that none of the rest was awanting③. Thus I perceived that doubt, inconstancy④, sadness, and such like, could not be found in God, since I myself would have been happy to be free from them. Besides, I had ideas of many sensible and corporeal⑤ things; for although I might suppose that I was dreaming, and that all which I saw or imagined was false, I could not, nevertheless, deny that the ideas were in reality in my thoughts. But, because I had already very clearly recognized in myself that the intelligent nature is distinct from the corporeal, and as I observed that all composition is an evidence of dependency, and that a state of dependency is manifestly a state of imperfection, I therefore determined that it could not be a perfection in God to be compounded of these two natures and that consequently he was not so compounded; but that if there were any bodies in the world, or even any intelligences, or other natures that

---

① repugnant: 矛盾的,抵触的;不一致的。
② I should have been...I could recognize in God: 那么根据同样理由,我也应当能从我自身获取那些我感觉欠缺的所有其它一切的完善,从而成为无限、永生、不变、全知、全能。简言之,我可拥有凡我认为属于上帝的一切完善。immutable: 永恒不变的;omniscient: 无所不知的;in fine: 总而言之。
③ I was assured that...that none of the rest was awanting: 我深信凡是不够十全十美的特性,都不属于上帝,而其它完全无缺的,没有一样不在他里面。awanting: 缺乏的。
④ inconstancy: 易变,不定性。
⑤ corporeal: 有形的,物质的,肉体的。

were not wholly perfect, their existence depended on his power in such a way that they could not subsist without him for a single moment...①

Brainstorming

1. What is the first principle of the philosophy according to Descartes?
2. What eventually became Descartes sole object of investigation?
3. What method of rational inquiry did Descartes finally choose? Why?
4. Explain the sentence: I think; therefore I am.
5. What are the differences between Descartes and Bacon in the methods they advocated?
6. Evaluate these knowledge claims:
  a. "You can say what you like. You weren't there. I know what I saw, and what I saw was a spaceship manned by extra-terrestrials."
  b. A skeptic says he doesn't know he has a hand in front of him. But does he know, in spite of what he says?
7. Is it possible that I might be, not an illusion produced by a Cartesian evil demon, but a brain in a vat? Is it possible that I might look out of any window and see nothing — no shapes, no colors, no black or white, just nothing?
8. Would the following help in determining which is dream and which is waking life? Why? Why not?
  a. As Freud has shown, a person's dream experiences are a good basis for inferring what his waking-life experiences (especially conflicts) are; but his waking-life experiences provide no basis for inferences about his dreams. So we can tell which is which by discovering from which group inference is the more successful.
  b. All the people in a given locality have very similar waking-life experiences (seeing the same building, etc.), but the dreams of each person will be wildly discrepant with those of every other person. I can distinguish the waking-life experiences from the dream-experiences by checking with other people to see if they had experiences similar to mine.

Supplementary reading

In this selection from the "*On First Meditations*②", Descartes applies his systematic doubt to the very existence of the world. It is possible, he suggests, imaging that one's entire waking life is an illusion. But even so, it is not possible to doubt one's own existence. The difficult thing, however, is to discover the nature of the self. Is the self an amalgam of perceptions and memories and feelings, or are these too, like the physical

---

① if there were...for a single moment...如果世界上存在着任何不十分完善的质体,无论属智性的,或属其它本性,它们必然依靠上帝的能力而得以存在,没有上帝,它们将瞬间熄灭。
② 《第一哲学沉思录》(1641),通过普遍怀疑的方法,力图使心灵摆脱感官,通过纯粹理智来获得确定的知识。从"我思故我在"这一命题出发,推出上帝的存在和外界物体的存在,重新建立起心灵、上帝和物体的观念的可靠性。

body, inessential to its real nature?

Of the Nature of the Human Mind (excerpt)

  I suppose, then, that all the things that I see are false; I persuade myself that nothing has ever existed of all that I possess no senses; I imagine that body, figure, extension, movement and place are but the fictions of my mind...

  Can I affirm that I possess the least of all those things which I have just said pertain to the nature of body? I pause to consider, I revolve all these things in my mind, and I find none of which I can say that it pertains to me. It would be tedious to stop to enumerate them. Let us pass to the attributes of soul and see if there is any one which is in me. What of nutrition or walking the first mentioned? But if it is so that I have no body it is also true that I can neither walk nor take nourishment. Another attribute is sensation. But one cannot feel without body, and besides I have thought I perceived many things during sleep that I recognized in my walking moments as not having been experienced at all. What of thinking? I find here that thought is an attribute that belongs to me: it alone cannot be separated from me. I am, I exist, that is certain. But how often? Just when I think; for it might possibly be the case if I ceased entirely to think, that I should likewise cease altogether to exist. I do not now admit anything which is not necessarily true: to speak accurately I am not more than a thing which thinks, that is to say a mind or a soul, or an understanding, or a reason, which are terms whose significance was formerly unknown to me. I am, however, a real thing and really exist; but what thing? I have answered: a thing which thinks.

  And what more? I shall exercise my imagination in order to see if I am not something more. I am not a collection of members which we call the human body; I am not a subtle air distributed through these members. I am not a wind, a fire, a vapor, a breath, nor anything at all which I can imagine or conceive; because I have assumed that all there were nothing. Without changing that supposition I find that I only leave myself certain of the fact that I am somewhat. But perhaps it is true that these same things which I supposed were non-existent because they are unknown to me, are really not different from the self which I know. I am not sure about this. I shall not dispute about it now; I can only give judgment on things that are known to me; consequently it does not depend on those which I can feign in imagination...

  But what then am I? A thing which thinks. What is a thing which thinks? It is a thing which doubts, understands, conceives, affirms, denies, wills, refuses, which also imagines and feels.

  Certainly it is no small matter if all these things pertain to my nature. But why should they not so pertain? Am I not that being who now doubts nearly everything, who nevertheless understands certain things, who affirms that one only is true, who denies all the others, who desires to know more, is averse to be deceived, who imagines many things, sometimes indeed despite his will, and who perceives many likewise, as by the intervention of the bodily organs? Is there nothing in all this which is as true as it is certain that I exist, even though I should always sleep and though he who has given me being employed all his ingenuity in deceiving me? Is there likewise any one of these attributes which can be distinguished from my thought, or which might be said to be separated from myself?

For it is so evident of itself that it is I who doubts, who understands, and who desires, that likewise; for although it may happen (as I formerly supposed) that none of the things which I imagine are true, nevertheless this power of imagining does not cease to be really in use, and it forms part of my thought. Finally, I am the same who feels, that is to say, who perceives certain things, as by the organs of sense, since in truth I see light, I hear noise, I feel heat. But it will be said that these phenomena are false and that I am dreaming. Let it be so; still it is at least quite certain that it seems to me that I see light, that I hear noise and that I feel heat. That cannot be false; properly speaking it what is in me called feeling, and used in this precise sense that is no other thing than thinking...

But finally what shall I say of this mind, that is, of myself, for up to this point I do not admit in myself anything but mind? What then, I who seem to perceive this piece of wax so distinctly, do I not know myself not only with much more truth and certainty, but also with much more distinctness and clearness? For I judge that the wax is or exists from the fact that I am or that I do not possess eyes with which to see anything; but it cannot be that when I see, or (for I no longer take account of the distinction) when I think I see, I myself who think I am not. So if I judge that the wax exists from the fact that I touch it, the same thing will follow, to wit, that I am; and if I judge that my imagination, or some other cause, whatever it is, persuades me that the wax exists, I shall still conclude the same. And what I have here marked of wax may be applied to all other things which are external to me and which are met with outsider of me. And further, if the notion or perception of wax has seemed to me clearer and more distinct, not only after the sight or the touch, but also after many other causes have rendered it quite manifest to me, which how much more evidence and distinctness must it be said that I now know myself, since all the reasons which contribute to the knowledge of wax, or any other body whatever, are yet better proofs of the nature of my mind! And there are so many other things in the mind itself which may contribute to the elucidation of its nature, that those which depend on body such as these just mentioned, hardly merit being taken into account.

But finally here I am, having insensibly reverted to the point I desired for, since it is now manifest to me that even bodies are not properly speaking known by the senses or by the faculty of imagination, but by the understanding only, and since they are unknown from the fact that they are understood, I see clearly that there is nothing which is easier for me to know than my mind. But because it is difficult to rid oneself so promptly of an opinion to which one was accustomed for so long, it will be well that I should halt a little at this point, so that by the length of my meditation I may more deeply imprint on my memory this new knowledge.

Famous quotations

Common sense is the best distributed commodity in the world, for every man is convinced that he is well supplied with it①.

—— *Discourse on the Method*, pt. I

I think; therefore I am②.

—— pt. IV.

It is not enough to have a good mind; the main thing is to use it well. ③

—— pt. I

Doubt is the origin of wisdom④.

—— *Meditations on the First Principle*

Each problem that I have solved became a rule, which served afterwards to solve other problems. ⑤

—— *Discourse on the Method*, pt. I

The reading of all good books is like a conversation with the finest minds of past centuries. ⑥

—— *Discourse on the Method*

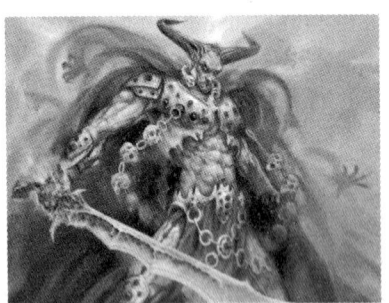

Sometimes I do not know whether I was then a man dreaming I was a butterfly, or whether I am now a butterfly dreaming I am a man. However, even there is an evil demon deceiving me about everything, he cannot make me doubt my existence; for if he tries, I am only more confirmed when forced to question my own existence.

---

① 常识是世上分配最多的商品,因为人人都相信自己是充分具备的。——《方法论》,第一部分。
② 我思故我在。——第四部分。
③ 仅仅具备出色的智力是不够的,主要的问题是如何出色地使用它。——第一部分。
④ 怀疑是智慧之源。——《第一哲学沉思录》。
⑤ 我解决的每一个问题变成了一个规则,为我以后解决其他问题服务。——《方法论》,第二章。
⑥ 阅读所有的优秀名著就像与过去时代那些最高尚的人物进行交谈。(读好书,如同与先哲们交谈)。——《方法论》。

To Be Is to Be Perceived
—— Berkeley

Chapter 6

Berkeley was, therefore, the first to treat the subjective starting-point really seriously and to demonstrate irrefutably its absolute necessity. He is the father of idealism...

—— Arthur Schopenhauer

In this chapter
- Getting to know Berkeley
- Sketching out the view of Berkeley's subjective idealism

George Berkeley

Born and brought up in the English noble family of Berkeley, Ireland, George Berkeley (1685—1753) attended first Kilkenny and then Trinity College, Dublin, where he became interested in philosophy through the influence of Newton, Boyle, and Locke. His publication of *A Treatise Concerning the Principles of Human Knowledge* in 1710 brought him great success and a lasting reputation, in which he propounded his system of philosophy, the leading principle of which is that the world, as represented by our senses, depends for its existence on being perceived. However his main concern had been founding a college in Bermuda, in pursuit of which he gave up his deanery of Derry. In 1731, when it became clear that funds were not available, he returned to London, then to Dublin, where he became Bishop and lived there for the rest of his life.

Berkeley's name is often linked to the notion *esse est percipi*, "to be is to be perceived". This startling proposal embodies what Berkeley regarded as a plainly apparent fact — a theory he called "immaterialism" (later referred to as "subjective idealism" by others). Though it sounds somewhat counter-intuitive, the idea contains a valuable insight that has been passed on to successive generations of thinkers, that is, the independent existence of things apart from our perception of them cannot simply be assumed, no matter how obvious it may seem.

Distinctive insights①

The main thrust of Berkeley's philosophy is the claim that there is no such thing as matter. While holding that all the objects we perceive and ordinarily take to exist in the world outside ourselves are simply collections of ideas existing only in minds, he maintains that everything that exists is either a mind or depends for its existence upon a mind.

1. *esse est percipi*②

According to Berkeley there are only two kinds of things: spirits and ideas. Spirits are simple, active being which produce and perceive ideas; ideas are passive beings which are produced and perceived. Such a proposal implies that ordinary physical objects exist if and only if they are perceived; for all sensible objects, i.e., objects capable of being perceived, their being is to be perceived. He gives essentially two arguments for his proposal. First, he holds that every physical object is just a collection of sensible qualities, and that every sensible quality is an idea. So, physical objects are just collections of sensible ideas. No ideas can exist unperceived, something everyone in the period would have granted. Hence, no physical object can exist unperceived. The second argument is the so-called master argument of *Principles* 22-24, in which Berkeley argues that one cannot conceive a sensible object existing unperceived, because if one attempts to do this one must thereby conceive that very object. He concludes from this that no such object can exist "without the mind," that is, wholly unperceived.

2. Immaterialism③

Berkeley regards it as a major error that some people had assumed that there are existing things which neither perceive nor are perceived. His own view is that only two kinds of things exist: spirits and ideas. Spirits perceive and ideas are perceived. Ideas are passive but spirits are active and able to cause ideas. God causes the ideas of what we ordinarily think of as our immediate perceptions of the external world. Subsequent reflections on what we perceived, as when, for example, I think about the wood pigeons I saw and heard this morning, are caused by ourselves. Berkeley believes not only that this thesis of immaterialism disposes of, or rather, prevents the generation of the tricky problems concerning substance, perception and knowledge that had afflicted earlier

---

① 贝克莱的非物质论是他"主观唯心主义"的核心。主观唯心主义把个人的某种主观精神如感觉、经验、心灵、意识、观念、意志等看作是世界上一切事物产生和存在的根源与基础,而世界上的一切事物则是由这些主观精神所派生的,是这些主观精神的显现。因此,主观的精神是本原的、第一性的,而客观世界的事物则是派生的、第二性的。贝克莱的"存在即被感知"、"物是观念的集合"等观点是主观唯心主义的典型代表。

② 存在即被感知。(以感知来确定存在与否,上帝存在论就能够站住脚了,因为,感觉上认为有上帝,进而可推论上帝就存在。)

③ 非物质论,认为绝对的、独立的物质的存在是难以理解的。实在的东西是感觉印象和观念。

philosophies, but that it is a natural consequence of plain, common-sense thinking.

3. The will of God

A central tenet of Berkeley's exposition is the will of God. Berkeley argues that we have indirect knowledge of spirits: "I perceive several motions, changes, and combinations of ideas, that inform me there are certain particular agents, like myself, which accompany them and concur in their production." And just as we do not directly perceive our fellow spirits, he says, so do we not directly perceive God. In Berkeley's system everything is dependent at all times on the will of God. It is God who "maintains that intercourse between spirits whereby they are able to perceive the existence of each other". Nature is not distinct from God, but is simply "the visible series of effects or sensations imprinted on our minds, according to certain fixed and general laws". We therefore must rely on God to supply us with our ideas of things around, and depend for our knowledge of the world and of the existence of other minds upon our faith in the God's will which would never deceive us.

Introductory remarks

Berkeley's *A Treatise Concerning the Principles of Human Knowledge* is regarded as a landmark of Western philosophy with a revolutionary concept "immaterialism". It seeks to refute the claims made by his contemporary John Locke about the nature of human perception. Whilst, like all the empiricist philosophers, both Locke and Berkeley agree that there is an outside world, and it is this world which causes the ideas one has within one's mind. Berkeley seeks to prove that the outside world is also composed solely of ideas. Berkeley does this by suggesting that "Ideas can only resemble Ideas" — the mental ideas that we possess can only resemble other ideas (not physical objects) and thus the external world consists not of physical form, but rather of ideas. This world was given logic and regularity by some other force, which Berkeley concludes was God.

The following text is selected from *The Treatise* in which Berkeley focuses on his claim that existence is the state of being perceived by a perceiver while human minds know only ideas, not objects.

Text

A Treatise Concerning the Principles of Human Knowledge①(excerpt)

It is evident to any one who takes a survey of the objects of human knowledge, that they are either ideas actually imprinted on the senses; or else such as are perceived by attending to the passions and operations of the mind; or lastly, ideas formed by help of memory and imagination

---

① 《人类知识原理》。书中否认物质的存在,认为所谓的"实体"(物体)都只是"被感官所感知的观念"。

— either compounding, dividing, or barely representing those originally perceived in the aforesaid ways①. — By sight I have the ideas of light and colors, with their several degrees and variations. By touch I perceive hard and soft, heat and cold, motion and resistance, and of all these more and less either as to quantity or degree. Smelling furnishes me with odors; the palate with tastes; and hearing conveys sounds to the mind in all their variety of tone and composition. — And as several of these are observed to accompany each other, they come to be marked by one name, and so to be reputed as one thing. Thus, for example, a certain color, taste, smell, figure and consistence having been observed to go together, are accounted one distinct thing, signified by the name *apple*; other collections of ideas constitute a stone, a tree, a book, and the like sensible things — which as they are pleasing or disagreeable excite the passions of love, hatred, joy, grief, and so forth.

But, besides all that endless variety of ideas or objects of knowledge, there is likewise something which knows or perceives them; and exercises divers operations, as willing, imagining, remembering, about them. This perceiving, active being is what I call MIND, SPIRIT, SOUL, or MYSELF②. By which words I do not denote any one of my ideas, but a thing entirely distinct from them, wherein they exist, or, which is the same thing, whereby they are perceived — for the existence of an idea consists in being perceived③.

That neither our thoughts, nor passions, nor ideas formed by the imagination, exist without the mind, is what everybody will allow — And to me it is no less evident that the various sensations, or ideas imprinted on the sense, however blended or combined together (that is, whatever objects they compose), cannot exist otherwise than in a mind perceiving them — I think an intuitive knowledge may be obtained of this by any one that shall attend to what is meant by the term exist when applied to sensible things. The table I write on I say exists, that is, I see and feel it; and if I were out of my study I should say it existed — meaning thereby that if I was in my study I might perceive it, or that some other spirit actually does perceive it. There was an odor, that is, it was smelt; there was a sound, that is, it was heard; a color or figure, and it was perceived by sight or touch. This is all that I can understand by these and the like expressions. — For as to what is said of the absolute existence of unthinking things without any relation to their being perceived, that is to me perfectly unintelligible Their *esse is percipi*, nor is it possible they should have any existence out of the minds or thinking things which perceive them④.

It is indeed an opinion strangely prevailing amongst men, that houses, mountains, rivers, and in a word all sensible objects, have an existence, natural or real, distinct from

---

① It is evident...in the aforesaid way：在任何一个观察过人类知识对象的人看来，显然这些对象或是实际刻印于感官之上的观念，或是由于关注心灵各种情感及作用而被感知的观念，或是借助于记忆和想象而形成的观念。这些记忆和想象要么混合，要么分开，或以上述方式仅代表那些原本感知的观念。

② This perceiving...MYSELF：这样一个能感知的主动实体，就是我所谓的心灵、精神、灵魂或自我。

③ By which words...perceived：观念只存在于这个东西之中，或者说，被这个东西所感知；因为一个观念的存在，就在于被感知。

④ Their *esse is percip*...which perceive them：它们的存在(*esse*)就是被感知(*percipi*)，它们不可能在心灵或感知它们的能思维的东西以外有任何存在。

their being perceived by the understanding. But, with how great an assurance and acquiescence so ever this principle may be entertained in the world, yet whoever shall find in his heart to call it in question may, if I mistake not, perceive it to involve a manifest contradiction. For, what are the fore-mentioned objects but the things we perceive by sense? And what do we perceive besides our own ideas or sensations? And is it not plainly repugnant① that any one of these, or any combination of them, should exist unperceived?

If we thoroughly examine this tenet it will, perhaps, be found at bottom to depend on the doctrine of abstract ideas. For can there be a nicer strain of abstraction than to distinguish the existence of sensible objects from their being perceived, so as to conceive them existing unperceived②? Light and colors, heat and cold, extension and figures — in a word the things we see and feel — what are they but so many sensations, notions, ideas, or impressions on the sense③? And is it possible to separate, even in thought, any of these from perception? For my part, I might as easily divide a thing from itself. I may, indeed, divide in my thoughts, or conceive apart from each other, those things which, perhaps, I never perceived by sense so divided. Thus, I imagine the trunk of a human body without the limbs, or conceive the smell of a rose without thinking on the rose itself. So far, I will not deny, I can abstract — if that may properly be called abstraction which extends only to the conceiving separately such objects as it is possible may really exist or be actually perceived asunder. But my conceiving or imagining power does not extend beyond the possibility of real existence or perception. Hence, as it is impossible for me to see or feel anything without an actual sensation of that thing, so is it impossible for me to conceive in my thoughts any sensible thing or object distinct from the sensation or perception of it.

Some truths there are so near and obvious to the mind that a man need only open his eyes to see them. Such I take this important one to be, viz. that all the choir of heaven and furniture of the earth, in a word all those bodies which compose the mighty frame of the world, have not any subsistence without a mind — that their *being is to be perceived or known*④; that consequently so long as they are not actually perceived by me, or do not exist in my mind or that of any other created spirit, they must either have no existence at all, or else subsist in the mind of some Eternal Spirit — it being perfectly unintelligible, and involving all the absurdity of abstraction, to attribute to any single part of them any existence independent of a spirit. To be convinced of which, the reader need only reflect, and try to separate in his own thoughts the *being* of a sensible thing from its *being perceived*⑤.

---

① repugnant: 令人厌恶反感的。

② For can there be...unperceived: 把可感物的存在与它的被感知分离,以为它们不被感知而存在,难道不是一种最好的抽象作用吗?

③ Light and colors...on the sense: 光、色、热、冷、外延和图形——一句话,我们看到的和感触到的东西——它们除了就是一些感觉、意念、观念或感官上的印象外,还会是什么呢?

④ Such I take...perceived or known: 我认为其中一个真理非常重要,即,天上的所有星宿,地上的一切成设,一句话,构成大宇宙的全部物体,在心灵之外没有任何存在;它们的存在就是被感知或被知道。

⑤ it being perfectly...independent of a spirit: 把事物的任何一部分赋予一种独立于精神外的存在,是完全不可理喻的,同时也包含了抽象的全部荒谬。

From what has been said it is evident there is not any other Substance than SPIRIT, or that which perceives.① But, for the fuller demonstration of this point, let it be considered the sensible qualities are color, figure, motion, smell, taste, etc, i.e. the ideas perceived by sense. Now, for an idea to exist in an unperceiving thing is a manifest contradiction; for to have an idea is all one as to perceive; that therefore wherein color, figure, etc. exist must perceive them; hence it is clear there can be no unthinking substance or *substratum* of those ideas②.

But, say you, though the ideas themselves do not exist without the mind, yet there may be things like them, whereof they are copies or resemblances, which things exist without the mind in an unthinking substance③. I answer, an idea can be like nothing but an idea; a color or figure can be like nothing but another color or figure. If we look but never so little into our own thoughts, we shall find it impossible for us to conceive a likeness except only between our ideas. Again, I ask whether those supposed originals or external things, of which our ideas are the pictures or representations, be themselves perceivable or no? If they are, then they are ideas and we have gained our point; but if you say they are not, I appeal to any one whether it be sense to assert a color is like something which is invisible; hard or soft, like something which is intangible; and so of the rest.

Brainstorming

1. If I look at the tree, I see a tree. If I see it through a mirror, am I seeing the tree of an image of it? If that's an image, how about seeing it through a pane of glass? What about seeing a part of it through an electron microscope, or through a telescope when it is five miles away, or in an x-ray, or on a computer screen?

2. If we had no visual or tactual sense-experiences but only experiences of hearing and smell, would we have been able to form the concept of a physical object? If you had never seen or touched a bell but only heard the ringing, would you be able to say, "The sound comes from a bell" or even "The sound comes from a physical object"?

3. I am the only observer about, and I see only the top half of a building. But the bottom half must be there even if I don't see it: How could it continue to stand there without the bottom half existing to support it? Would Berkeley have a reply?

4. "Nobody knows what physical objects are really like; we only know how they appear to us, not how they really are, what qualities they really have?" Comment.

5. Is belief in Berkeley's God just as satisfactory an explanation of the order of our sense-experience as is the belief in enduring physical objects? Defend your opinion.

---

① From what has been said…which perceives. 综上所述,显然,除了"精神"或感知者以外,再也没有任何别的"实体"。

② Hence it is clear…those ideas: 因此,显然那些观点不能有不思维的实体和基质。substratum: 基础,基质。

③ though the ideas…an unthinking substance: 虽然观念本身并不离开心灵而存在,但仍然可以有与观念相似的东西,而观念只是它们的摹本或肖像;这些东西则是可以离开心灵而存在于一个不思维的实体之中的。copies or resemblances: 摹本或相似物。

6. Can you ever have experiences you don't think you are having?

a. Someone is blindfolded and told that he will be branded with a red-hot poker. A piece of ice is pushed into his bare stomach, and he screams. Did he mistake the sensation of cold for one of warmth?

b. I have been suffering from a severe toothache. I get a tingling in my cheek, and for a moment I think it is the toothache again. Can I think I have it when I don't?

c. Is it possible to think that you feel a pain when you feel nothing at all, but only see blood on your knee?

Supplementary reading

In *A Treatise Concerning the Principles of Human Knowledge* Berkeley declares that his intention is to discover the principles that have led to doubt, uncertainty, absurdity, and contradiction in philosophy. In order to prepare the reader, he discusses two topics that lead to errors. First, he claims that the mind cannot conceive abstract ideas. We can't have an idea of some abstract thing that is common to many particular ideas and therefore has, at the same time, many different predicates and no predicates. Second, Berkeley declares that words, such as names, do not signify abstract ideas. With regard to ideas, he asserts, in the following passage from the introduction, that we can only think of particular things that have been perceived.

Introduction (excerpt)

Philosophy being nothing else but the study of wisdom and truth, it may with reason be expected that those who have spent most time and pains in it should enjoy a greater calm and serenity of mind, a greater clearness and evidence of knowledge, and be less disturbed with doubts and difficulties than other men. Yet so it is, we see the illiterate bulk of mankind that walk the high-road of plain common sense, and are governed by the dictates of nature, for the most part easy and undisturbed. To them nothing that is familiar appears unaccountable or difficult to comprehend. They complain not of any want of evidence in their senses, and are out of all danger of becoming Skeptics. But no sooner do we depart from sense and instinct to follow the light of a superior principle, to reason, meditate, and reflect on the nature of things, but a thousand scruples spring up in our minds concerning those things which before we seemed fully to comprehend. Prejudices and errors of sense do from all parts discover themselves to our view; and, endeavoring to correct these by reason, we are insensibly drawn into uncouth paradoxes, difficulties, and inconsistencies, which multiply and grow upon us as we advance in speculation, till at length, having wandered through many intricate mazes, we find ourselves just where we were, or, which is worse, sit down in a forlorn Skepticism.

The cause of this is thought to be the obscurity of things, or the natural weakness and imperfection of our understandings. It is said, the faculties we have are few, and those designed by nature for the support and comfort of life, and not to penetrate into the inward essence and constitution of things. Besides, the mind of man being finite, when it treats of things which partake of infinity, it is not to be wondered at if it run into absurdities and contradictions, out of which it is impossible it should ever extricate itself, it being of the nature of infinite not to be comprehended by that which is finite.

But, perhaps, we may be too partial to ourselves in placing the fault originally in our faculties, and not rather in the wrong use we make of them. It is a hard thing to suppose that right deductions from true principles should ever end in consequences which cannot be maintained or made consistent. We should believe that God has dealt more bountifully with the sons of men than to give them a strong desire for that knowledge which he had placed quite out of their reach. This were not agreeable to the wonted indulgent methods of Providence, which, whatever appetites it may have implanted in the creatures, doth usually furnish them with such means as, if rightly made use of, will not fail to satisfy them. Upon the whole, I am inclined to think that the far greater part, if not all, of those difficulties which have hitherto amused philosophers, and blocked up the way to knowledge, are entirely owing to ourselves — that we have first raised a dust and then complain we cannot see.

My purpose therefore is, to try if I can discover what those Principles are which have introduced all that doubtfulness and uncertainty, those absurdities and contradictions, into the several sects of philosophy; insomuch that the wisest men have thought our ignorance incurable, conceiving it to arise from the natural dullness and limitation of our faculties. And surely it is a work well deserving our pains to make a strict inquiry concerning the First Principles of Human Knowledge, to sift and examine them on all sides, especially since there may be some grounds to suspect that those lets and difficulties, which stay and embarrass the mind in its search after truth, do not spring from any darkness and intricacy in the objects, or natural defect in the understanding, so much as from false Principles which have been insisted on, and might have been avoided.

How difficult and discouraging so ever this attempt may seem, when I consider how many great and extraordinary men have gone before me in the like designs, yet I am not without some hopes — upon the consideration that the largest views are not always the clearest, and that he who is short-sighted will be obliged to draw the object nearer, and may, perhaps, by a close and narrow survey, discern that which had escaped far better eyes.

In order to prepare the mind of the reader for the easier conceiving what follows, it is proper to premise somewhat, by way of Introduction, concerning the nature and abuse of Language. But the unravelling this matter leads me in some measure to anticipate my design, by taking notice of what seems to have had a chief part in rendering speculation intricate and perplexed, and to have occasioned innumerable errors and difficulties in almost all parts of knowledge. And that is the opinion that the mind hath a power of framing abstract ideas or notions of things. He who is not a perfect stranger to the writings and disputes of philosophers must needs acknowledge that no small part of them are spent about abstract ideas. These are in a more especial manner thought to be the object of those sciences which go by the name of Logic and Metaphysics, and of all that which passes under the notion of the most abstracted and sublime learning, in all which one shall scarce find any question handled in such a manner as does not suppose their existence in the mind, and that it is well acquainted with them.

Famous quotations

He who says there is no such thing as an honest man, you may be sure is himself a knave①.
—— *Maxims Concerning Patriotism*

We have first raised a dust and then complain we cannot see②.
—— *Principles of Human Knowledge*, introduction, 3

(Tar water) is of nature so mild and benign and proportioned to the human constitution, as to warm without heating, to cheer but not inebriate③.
—— *Siris*, par. 217

Truth is the cry of all, but the game of the few④.
—— par. 368

If there were external bodies, it is impossible we could ever come to know it.⑤
—— *Principles of Human Knowledge*

An idea can be like nothing but an idea; a color or figure can be like nothing but another color or figure.⑥
—— *Principles of Human Knowledge*

Can a tree fall if there is nobody present to observe it? Objects only exists while there are perceived, according to Berkeley. However, the tree can fall over — because the tree, and the rest of the world, is always perceived by God.

---

① 谁总说世界无好人,你可以断定他本就是个歹徒。——《关于爱国主义的格言》
② 我们首先扬起了尘土,然后抱怨说看不见。——《人类知识原理》,导言第 3 节
③ (焦油水)性质平缓,柔和,与人类的体质相适应;温暖而不灼热,兴奋而不醉人。——《西利斯》,第 217 段。(这些话后来被诗人库珀盗用来赞美茶。)
④ 真理是全人类的呼声,却是少数人的游戏。——第 368 段
⑤ 假如有外部实体,我们也无从了解。——《人类知识原理》
⑥ 一个观念可以除了是一个观念外什么也不是;一种颜色或图形可以是除了另一种颜色或图形外什么也不像。——《人类知识原理》

Custom as Our Guide
—— Hume

Chapter 7

There is more to be learned from each page of David Hume than from the collected philosophical works of Hegel, Herbart and Schleiermacher taken together.

—— *Schopenhauer*

In this chapter
- Getting to know Hume
- peering into Hume's philosophical skepticism

David Hume

Born in Scotland, David Hume (1711—1776) was a precocious child who entered the University of Edinburgh at the age of 12. While still a student, he decided to pursue a career as a man of letters and setting out virtually all his philosophical ideas soon after graduation. In 1763 he was appointed to the Embassy in Paris, where he befriended the philosopher Jean-Jacques Rousseau[①]. Several years later, when he returned to his native Edinburg, he had a house built in the New Town and there enjoyed philosophical reflection and the company of friends and fellow citizens until his death. Throughout his life, Hume never married. He describes himself as "a man of mild dispositions, of command of temper, of an open, social and cheerful humor, capable of attachment, but little susceptible of enmity, and of great moderation in all my passions" (as is engraved on his "simple Roman tomb").

---

① 卢梭,见本书第 8 章。

Being one of the great skeptics of all time and a master stylist in any genre, Hume has exerted a major influence on the development of western thought since the mid-eighteenth century. Hume is said to have awaken Immanuel Kant from his "dogmatic slumbers"[①]. Charles Darwin[②] counted Hume as a central influence, as did "Darwin's bulldog" Thomas Henry Huxley[③]. The diverse directions in which these writers took what they gleaned from reading Hume reflect not only the richness of their sources but also the wide range of his empiricism. Today, philosophers still recognize Hume as a precursor of contemporary cognitive science, as well as one of the most thoroughgoing exponents of philosophical naturalism[④].

Distinctive insights[⑤]

A prominent figure in the skeptical philosophical tradition and a strong empiricist, Hume argues against the existence of innate ideas, concluding instead that humans have knowledge only of things they directly experience.

1. The Problem of Induction

The cornerstone of Hume's epistemology is the so-called Problem of Induction. It concerns the explanation of how we are able to make inductive inferences. Inductive inference is reasoning from the observed behavior of objects to their behavior when unobserved; as Hume says, it is a question of how things behave when they go "beyond the present testimony of the senses, and the records of our memory". Hume notices that we tend to believe that things behave in a regular manner; i.e., that patterns in the behavior of objects will persist into the future, and throughout the unobserved present. This persistence of regularities is sometimes called Uniformitarianism[⑥] or the Principle of the Uniformity of Nature.

Hume argues that we cannot rationally justify the claim that nature will continue to be uniform, as justification comes in only two varieties, and both of these are inadequate. First is the demonstrative reasoning. Hume says that the uniformity principle cannot be demonstrated, as it is "consistent and conceivable" that nature might stop being regular; second is the probable reasoning. Hume argues that we cannot hold that nature will continue to be uniform because it has been in the past, as this is using the very sort of reasoning (induction) that is under question: it would be circular reasoning. Thus no form of justification will rationally warrant our inductive inferences.

Hume's solution to this problem is to argue that, rather than reason, natural instinct

---

① 康德开始时是一位理性主义者,但休谟"将他从沉睡中唤醒",使他成为理性主义者以及经验主义者的综合体。
② 达尔文(1809—1882),英国生物学家,进化论的创始人。
③ 赫胥黎(1825—1895),英国生物学家。为捍卫达尔文的进化论,他自称为达尔文的"斗犬"。
④ 哲学自然主义通常是指继承唯物主义和实用主义衣钵、不探究自然界中超自然因素的哲学立场。
⑤ 休谟认为哲学是关于"人性"(包括知性、情感与道德)的科学。主张知识来源于经验,经验由两类知觉(印象与观念)所组成。首倡近代不可知论,对感觉之外的任何存在持怀疑态度,对外部世界的客观规律性和因果必然性持否定态度。
⑥ 均变论,否认灾变的发生,认为当今正在进行的地质过程也以同样的方式发生于地史时期,它们的速率和强度基本相同,主张"现在是解释过去的钥匙"的理论。

explains the human ability to make inductive inferences.

2. The Denying of the Necessary Connection of Cause and Effect①

Hume claims that our belief in cause-and-effect relationships between events is not grounded on reason, but rather arises merely by habit or custom. He believes that neither the senses nor reason can establish that one object (a cause) is connected together with another object (an effect) in such a way that the presence of the one entails the existence of the other. Experience reveals only that objects thought to be causally related are contiguous in time and space, and that the cause is prior to the effect, and that similar objects have been constantly associated in this way. He asks us to imagine what life would have been like for Adam, suddenly brought to life in the midst of the world. Adam would have been unable to make even the simplest predictions about the future behavior of objects. He would not have been able to predict what would happen "whenever someone on earth lets go of a rock". While we can grant that in every instance thus far when a rock was dropped on Earth it went down, this does not give us any reason to think that in the future, rocks will fall when in the same circumstances. It would give us reason only if we add as a premise that the future will resemble the past. But that isn't something that we can know based on past experience — all past experience could tell us is that in the past, the future has resembled the past. And yet we, endowed with these faculties, can not only make, but are unable to resist making, this and countless other such predictions.

What is the difference between ourselves and this putative Adam? Experience. We have experienced the constant conjunction (the invariant succession of paired objects of events) of particular causes and effects and, although our experience never includes even a glimpse of a causal connection, it does arouse in us an expectation that a particular event (a "cause") will be followed by another event (an "effect") previously and constantly associated with it. Regularities of experience give rise to these feelings, and thus determine the mind to transfer its attention from present impression to the idea of an absent but associated object. The idea of necessary connection is copied from these feelings. The idea has its foundation in the mind and is projected onto the world, but there is nonetheless such an idea. That there is an objective physical necessity to which this idea corresponds is an untestable hypothesis, nor would demonstrate that such necessary connections had held in the past guarantee that will hold in the future. Thus, while not denying that there may be physical necessity or that there is an idea of necessary connection, Hume remains a skeptic about causal necessity.

3. Impressions and Ideas②

In his *A Treatise of Human Nature*, Hume begins by examining the ways in which a

---

① 休谟提出"因果问题",认为人们之所以会认为某事情是因,某事情是果,是因为它们通常是伴随着发生,也就是因为时间上的连续性使然。但两件连接着发生的事情不一定有因果关系。他因此感到困惑:既然这种因果推断不是必然的,那么人类知识的可靠性和正当性又从何而来呢?"休谟问题"已成为认识论的核心问题,乃至今日仍然是科学哲学的中心论题。

② 休谟认为每个人都有知觉能力。知觉有两类:一是"印象"(Impressions),二是"观念"(Ideas)。印象是直接经验的材料。观念来自印象,是印象的复制。

human being perceives the world. He says that our perceptions are of two kinds: impressions, which are "all our sensations, passions and emotions as they make their first appearance in the soul"; and ideas, which are "the faint images of these (impressions) in thinking and reasoning". In other words he divides perceptions between strong and lively "impressions" or direct sensations and fainter "ideas," which are copied from impressions. Impressions and ideas may be either simple or complex and, Hume maintains, all simple ideas are derived from simple impressions. Impressions cause ideas but ideas do not cause impressions. We have a faculty of memory which retains ideas in the order in which they occur and a faculty of imagination which is able to rearrange ideas already derived from impressions to form the complex ideas.

For Hume the major difference between impressions and ideas is a difference in terms of degree of forcefulness, with impressions being the more vivid of the two kinds of perceptions. He gives credence only to claims which can be analyzed to show that they refer in the first instance to sense impressions. He therefore rejects all claims to knowledge of the existence of God, of the soul, and of substance regarded as a kind of colorless something which supports qualities because he can find no impressions of sense from which these concepts arise. He accounts for abstract or general ideas by in the first instance agreeing with Berkeley that ideas are always of particulars and not of abstracted generalities; he then points out that ideas that resemble one another become associated together so that one particular idea can "stand for" a group of ideas that have become associate.

4. Will and Freedom[①]

In his account of the will Hume claims that while all human actions are caused, they are nonetheless free. He argues that our ascriptions of causal connection have all the same foundation, namely, the observation of a "uniform and regular conjunction" of one object with another. Given that in the course of human affairs we observe "the same uniformity and regular operation of natural principles" found in the physical world, and that this uniformity results in an expectation of exactly the sort produced by physical regularities, it follows that there is no "negation of necessity and cause," or no liberty of indifference. The will, that internal impression we feel and are conscious of when we knowingly give rise to any action or thought, is an effect always linked (by constant conjunction and the resulting feeling of expectation) to some prior cause. But insofar as our actions are not forcibly constrained or hindered, we do remain free in another sense: we retain a liberty of spontaneity. Moreover, only freedom in this latter sense is consistent with morality. A liberty of indifference, the possibility of uncaused actions, would undercut moral assessment, for such assessments presuppose that actions are causally linked to motives.

Introductory remarks

The following is an excerpt from *Dialogues concerning Natural Religion*, Chapter V.

---

① 休谟认为"理性永远无法战胜情绪",即动机和行动之间没有因果关系。我们的意志不能操纵我们的行为。

Characters:

Pamphilus, a youth present during the dialogues. In a letter, he reconstructs the conversation of Demea, Philo, and Cleanthes in detail for his friend Hermippus. He serves as the narrator throughout the piece. Cleanthes seems to offer the strongest arguments at the end of the Dialogues. However, this could be out of loyalty to his teacher, as this does not seem to reflect Hume's own views on the topic. (When other pieces on religion by Hume are taken into consideration, it may be noted that they all end with apparently ironic statements reaffirming the truth of Christian religious views.)

Cleanthes, a theist — "an exponent of orthodox empiricism" — who presents a version of the teleological argument① for God's existence using the deductive paradigm.

Philo, according to the predominant view among scholars, probably representing a viewpoint similar to Hume's own, attacks Cleanthes's views on anthropomorphism and teleology; while not going as far as to deny the existence of god, Philo asserts that human reason is wholly inadequate to make any assumptions about the divine, whether through *a priori*② reasoning or observation of nature.

Demea, defending "the Cosmological argument③ and philosophical theism", he believes that instead of reason, people should base beliefs concerning God's nature through fideism. Demea rejects Cleanthes's "natural religion" for being too anthropomorphic. He also objects to the abandonment of the *a priori* arguments by Philo and Cleanthes (both of whom are empiricists). He perceives Philo to be "accepting an extreme form of skepticism."

Text

Dialogues Concerning Natural Religion④ (excerpt)

But to show you still more inconveniences, continued Philo, in your Anthropomorphism⑤, please to take a new survey of your principles. Like effects prove like causes. This is the experimental argument; and this, you say too, is the sole theological argument. Now, it is certain, that the liker the effects are which are seen, and the liker the causes which are inferred, the stronger is the argument. Every departure on either side diminishes the probability, and renders the experiment less conclusive. You cannot doubt of the principle; neither ought you to reject its consequences.

---

① 目的论,用目的或目的因解释世界的哲学学说。
② 先验的,先验推理。
③ 宇宙论,对宇宙整体的研究,并且延伸探讨至人在宇宙中的地位。
④ 《自然宗教对话录》,驳斥了当时欧洲盛行的宇宙设计论。宇宙设计论是当时宗教理论的中心支柱,对它的批判,客观上给予宗教本身以沉重的打击。
⑤ anthropomorphism:拟人论、拟人观。(神秘学里,常常把神、动物、植物、或非生物的东西赋予人的个性,谓之拟人论,或拟人观。)

Chapter 7 Custom as our Guide — Hume

All the new discoveries in astronomy, which prove the immense grandeur and magnificence of the works of Nature, are so many additional arguments for a Deity①, according to the true system of Theism; but, according to your hypothesis of experimental Theism, they become so many objections, by removing the effect still further from all resemblance to the effects of human art and contrivance. For, if Lucretius②, even following the old system of the world, could exclaim,

  Quis regere immensi summam, quis habere profundi
  Indu manu validas potis est moderanter habenas?
  Quis pariter coelos omnes convertere? et omnes
  Ignibus aetheriis terras suffire feraces?
  Omnibus inque locis esse omni tempore praesto?③

If Tully esteemed this reasoning so natural, as to put it into the mouth of his Epicurean④:
"Quibus enim oculis animi intueri potuit vester Plato
fabricam illam tanti operis, qua construi a Deo atque
aedificari mundum facit? quae molitio? quae ferramenta? qui
vectes? quae machinae? qui ministri tanti muneris fuerunt?
quemadmodum autem obedire et parere voluntati architecti
aer, ignis, aqua, terra potuerunt?"⑤

If this argument, I say, had any force in former ages, how much greater must it have at present, when the bounds of Nature are so infinitely enlarged, and such a magnificent scene is opened to us? It is still more unreasonable to form our idea of so unlimited a cause from our experience of the narrow productions of human design and invention.

The discoveries by microscopes, as they open a new universe in miniature, are still objections, according to you, arguments, according to me. The further we push our researches of this kind, we are still led to infer the universal cause of all to be vastly different from mankind, or from any object of human experience and observation.⑥

And what say you to the discoveries in anatomy, chemistry, botany? These surely are

---

① the Deity: 上帝,造物主。
② Lucretius: 卢克莱修(约 99—55 BC),古罗马哲学家。
③ 英文翻译:"Who can rule the sum, who hold in his hand with controlling force the strong reins, of the immeasurable deep? Who can at once make all the different heavens to roll and warm with ethereal fires all the fruitful earths, or be present in all places at all times":谁能控制这不可测量的究竟,谁能以统治的力量用手操持这不可测量的坚强的缰索? 谁能同时使一切不同的天体旋转,又用神秘的火温暖一切能够让生命生殖繁衍的地球,或者在一切时间存在于一切的地方?
④ 伊壁鸠鲁派,由伊壁鸠鲁创立。宣扬无神论,提倡寻求快乐和幸福。
⑤ 英文翻译:"For with what eyes of the mind could your Plato have beheld that workshop of such stupendous toil, in which he represents the world as having been put together and built by God? How was so vast an undertaking set about? What tools, what levers, what machines, what servants were employed in so great a work? How came air, fire, water, and earth to obey and submit to the architect's will?":用什么样的心灵的眼睛,你们的柏拉图看到如此伟大,由上帝结合在一起并建造而成的劳动工场? 如此伟大的任务是怎样开始的? 如此伟大的工作所用的是什么样的工具,什么样的杠杆,什么样的机器,什么样的工人? 空气、火、水、和泥土怎么会服从和听顺建筑师的意志?
⑥ The further we push ... human experience and observation:我们将这类研究推得愈远,愈能使我们推论出宇宙万物的普遍因与人类,或者与人类经验和观察的任何对象相差甚远。

no objections, replied Cleanthes; they only discover new instances of art and contrivance①. It is still the image of mind reflected on us from innumerable objects②. Add, a mind like the human, said Philo. I know of no other, replied Cleanthes. And the liker the better, insisted Philo. To be sure, said Cleanthes.

Now, Cleanthes, said Philo, with an air of alacrity and triumph, mark the consequences. First, By this method of reasoning, you renounce all claim to infinity in any of the attributes of the Deity. For, as the cause ought only to be proportioned to the effect, and the effect, so far as it falls under our cognizance, is not infinite; what pretensions have we, upon your suppositions, to ascribe that attribute to the Divine Being③? You will still insist, that, by removing him so much from all similarity to human creatures, we give in to the most arbitrary hypothesis, and at the same time weaken all proofs of his existence.④

Secondly, you have no reason, on your theory, for ascribing perfection to the Deity, even in his finite capacity, or for supposing him free from every error, mistake, or incoherence, in his undertakings. There are many inexplicable difficulties in the works of Nature, which, if we allow a perfect author to be proved a priori, are easily solved, and become only seeming difficulties, from the narrow capacity of man, who cannot trace infinite relations⑤. But according to your method of reasoning, these difficulties become all real; and perhaps will be insisted on, as new instances of likeness to human art and contrivance. At least, you must acknowledge, that it is impossible for us to tell, from our limited views, whether this system contains any great faults, or deserves any considerable praise, if compared to other possible, and even real systems. Could a peasant, if the Aeneid were read to him, pronounce that poem to be absolutely faultless, or even assign to it its proper rank among the productions of human wit, he, who had never seen any other production?⑥

But were this world ever so perfect a production, it must still remain uncertain, whether all the excellences of the work can justly be ascribed to the workman.⑦ If we survey a ship, what an exalted idea must we form of the ingenuity of the carpenter who framed so complicated, useful, and beautiful a machine? And what surprise must we feel, when we find him a stupid mechanic, who imitated others, and copied an art, which,

---

① contrivance：发明，设计，人工化痕迹。
② It is still the image of mind reflected on us from innumerable objects：这仍然是从无数的物体反映给我们的心灵的肖像。
③ the Divine Being：神，上帝。
④ ... weaken all proofs of his existence：削弱了关于神的存在的所有的证明。
⑤ There are many inexplicable difficulties... who cannot trace infinite relations：自然的作品中有许多不能解释的困难，假如我们承认完美的造物主是先验的，这些困难是容易解决的，只有就不能追究无限关系的人类的狭小能力而言，这些困难才俨然成为困难。
⑥ Could a peasant... who had never seen any other production：假如把《伊尼特》读给一个从未看过任何其他作品的农夫听，他能说那诗篇绝对完善无缺，甚或能为它在人类智慧的创作品中排定适当的地位吗？Aeneid：《伊尼特》，古罗马诗人维吉尔的代表作。
⑦ But were this world ever so perfect... be ascribed to the workman：但是假如这个世界确是十分完善的一个创造品，这个作品的所有的优点能否正当地归之于工匠，必然也还不能决定。

through a long succession of ages, after multiplied trials, mistakes, corrections, deliberations, and controversies, had been gradually improving? Many worlds might have been botched and bungled, throughout an eternity, ere this system was struck out; much labor lost, many fruitless trials made; and a slow, but continued improvement carried on during infinite ages in the art of world-making. In such subjects, who can determine, where the truth; nay, who can conjecture where the probability lies, amidst a great number of hypotheses which may be proposed, and a still greater which may be imagined?

And what shadow of an argument, continued Philo, can you produce, from your hypothesis, to prove the unity of the Deity? A great number of men join in building a house or ship, in rearing a city, in framing a commonwealth; why may not several deities combine in contriving and framing a world? This is only so much greater similarity to human affairs.① By sharing the work among several, we may so much further limit the attributes of each, and get rid of that extensive power and knowledge, which must be supposed in one deity, and which, according to you, can only serve to weaken the proof of his existence. And if such foolish, such vicious creatures as man, can yet often unite in framing and executing one plan, how much more those deities or demons, whom we may suppose several degrees more perfect!

To multiply causes without necessity, is indeed contrary to true Philosophy: but this principle applies not to the present case. Were one deity antecedently② proved by your theory, who were possessed of every attribute requisite to the production of the universe; it would be needless, I own, (though not absurd,) to suppose any other deity existent. But while it is still a question, whether all these attributes are united in one subject, or dispersed among several independent beings, by what phenomena in nature can we pretend to decide the controversy? Where we see a body raised in a scale, we are sure that there is in the opposite scale, however concealed from sight, some counterpoising weight equal to it; but it is still allowed to doubt, whether that weight be an aggregate of several distinct bodies, or one uniform united mass③. And if the weight requisite very much exceeds any thing which we have ever seen conjoined in any single body, the former supposition becomes still more probable and natural. An intelligent being of such vast power and capacity as is necessary to produce the universe, or, to speak in the language of ancient Philosophy, so prodigious an animal exceeds all analogy, and even comprehension.

But further, Cleanthes: men are mortal, and renew their species by generation; and this is common to all living creatures. The two great sexes of male and female, says Milton④, animate the world. Why must this circumstance, so universal, so essential, be

---

① A great number of men join in... similarity to human affairs: 很多的人可以合作来造一所房子、一只船、筑一座城、或组成一个国家,为什么不可以有几个神联合来设计和构造一个世界呢? 这才与人类事务更为相似。
② antecedently: 先前地;先时地。
③ Where we see a body raised in a scale... one uniform united mass: 我们看见物体在天秤的一端上被抬起来,我们就断定在天秤的另一端,虽然看不见,有某种等于这个物体的平衡的重量。但是那个重量是几个不同的物体的聚合体,还是一块完整的质料,仍然是可以怀疑的。aggregate: 聚合体。
④ 弥尔顿(1608~1674),英国诗人、政论家、民主斗士。

excluded from those numerous and limited deities? Behold, then, the theogony① of ancient times brought back upon us.

And why not become a perfect Anthropomorphite? Why not assert the deity or deities to be corporeal, and to have eyes, a nose, mouth, ears, &c. ? Epicurus maintained, that no man had ever seen reason but in a human figure; therefore the gods must have a human figure. And this argument, which is deservedly so much ridiculed by Cicero②, becomes, according to you, solid and Philosophical.

In a word, Cleanthes, a man who follows your hypothesis is able perhaps to assert, or conjecture, that the universe, sometime, arose from something like design: but beyond that position he cannot ascertain one single circumstance; and is left afterwards to fix every point of his theology by the utmost license of fancy and hypothesis. This world, for aught he knows, is very faulty and imperfect, compared to a superior standard; and was only the first rude essay of some infant deity, who afterwards abandoned it, ashamed of his lame performance: it is the work only of some dependent, inferior deity; and is the object of derision to his superiors: it is the production of old age and dotage in some superannuated deity; and ever since his death, has run on at adventures, from the first impulse and active force which it received from him. You justly give signs of horror, Demea, at these strange suppositions; but these, and a thousand more of the same kind, are Cleanthes's suppositions, not mine. From the moment the attributes of the Deity are supposed finite, all these have place. And I cannot, for my part, think that so wild and unsettled a system of theology is, in any respect, preferable to none at all.

These suppositions I absolutely disown③, cried Cleanthes: they strike me, however, with no horror, especially when proposed in that rambling④ way in which they drop from you. On the contrary, they give me pleasure, when I see, that, by the utmost indulgence of your imagination, you never get rid of the hypothesis of design in the universe, but are obliged at every turn to have recourse to it. To this concession I adhere steadily⑤; and this I regard as a sufficient foundation for religion.

Brainstorming

1. Which of the four characters in the Dialogue, do you believe, speaks for Hume? Why?

2. Does Hume believe in the existence of God? What is Anthropomorphism?

3. Explain Philo's arguments for the claim that the argument from design is not a real argument by analogy.

4. What is Hume's attitude implied in the reading passage toward cognition of cosmos?

---

① the theogony：神谱；叙述神统的史诗。
② 西塞罗(106—43 BC)，古罗马政治家、演说家、法学家和哲学家。
③ disown：否认；否认……权威性；否认……有效。
④ rambling：(言辞、文字)散漫芜杂的，不连贯的。
⑤ To this concession I adhere steadily：对于这个让步，我要牢牢地把握住。adhere to：坚持，遵守。

5. Who do you think won the argument between the present characters? Did anyone? Why do you think so?

6. Do you agree or disagree with the following reasoning: "The cause and the effect must be simultaneous, for the effect occurs at the very moment that the last condition (of a sufficient condition) is fulfilled. If there is even the slightest waiting period between it and the effect, there must be something else that has yet to occur before the effect can occur; otherwise, why wouldn't the effect occur immediately?"

Supplementary reading

Hume insists that philosophy cannot go beyond experience; and any hypothesis, that pretends to discover the ultimate original qualities of human nature, ought at first to be rejected as presumptuous and chimerical. Hume's neo-skeptical stance best manifests itself in the following reading.

An Enquiry Concerning Human Understanding[①](excerpt)

There is, indeed, a more mitigated skepticism or academical philosophy, which may be both durable and useful, and which may, in part, be the result of this Pyrrhonism[②], or excessive skepticism, when its undistinguished doubts are, in some measure, corrected by common sense and reflection. The greater part of mankind are naturally apt to be affirmative and dogmatical in their opinions; and while they see objects only on one side, and have no idea of any counter-poising argument, they throw themselves precipitately into the principles, to which they are inclined; nor have they any indulgence for those who entertain opposite sentiments. To hesitate or balance perplexes their understanding, checks their passion, and suspends their action. They are, therefore, impatient till they escape from a state, which to them is so uneasy: and they think, that they could never remove themselves far enough from it, by the violence of their affirmations and obstinacy of their belief. But could such dogmatical reasoners become sensible of the strange infirmities of human understanding, even in its most perfect state, and when most accurate and cautious in its determinations; such a reflection would naturally inspire them with more modesty and reserve, and diminish their fond opinion of themselves, and their prejudice against antagonists. The illiterate may reflect on the disposition of the learned, who, amidst all the advantages of study and reflection, are commonly still diffident in their determinations: and if any of the learned be inclined, from their natural temper, to haughtiness and obstinacy, a small tincture of Pyrrhonism might abate their pride, by showing them, that the few advantages, which they have attained over their fellows, are

---

① 《人类理解研究》，用大量的论说和例证，对印象、观念、知识和因果律等一系列问题提出了独特的见解。
② 皮浪主义。古希腊皮浪 Pyrrhon (c. 360—271 BC) 首先提出怀疑论的学说，因此怀疑论亦称皮浪主义 (Pyrrhonism)。皮浪认为由感觉与理性得来的知识都不可靠，事物是不可认识的，人们对任何事物都应存怀疑。

but inconsiderable, if compared with the universal perplexity and confusion, which is inherent in human nature. In general, there is a degree of doubt, and caution, and modesty, which, in all kinds of scrutiny and decision, ought for ever to accompany a just reasoner.

Another species of mitigated skepticism which may be of advantage to mankind, and which may be the natural result of the Pyrrhonian doubts and scruples, is the limitation of our enquiries to such subjects as are best adapted to the narrow capacity of human understanding. The imagination of man is naturally sublime, delighted with whatever is remote and extraordinary, and running, without control, into the most distant parts of space and time in order to avoid the objects, which custom has rendered too familiar to it. A correct Judgment observes a contrary method, and avoiding all distant and high enquiries, confines itself to common life, and to such subjects as fall under daily practice and experience; leaving the more sublime topics to the embellishment of poets and orators, or to the arts of priests and politicians. To bring us to so salutary a determination, nothing can be more serviceable, than to be once thoroughly convinced of the force of the Pyrrhonian doubt, and of the impossibility, that anything, but the strong power of natural instinct, could free us from it. Those who have a propensity to philosophy, will still continue their researches; because they reflect, that, besides the immediate pleasure attending such an occupation, philosophical decisions are nothing but the reflections of common life, methodized and corrected. But they will never be tempted to go beyond common life, so long as they consider the imperfection of those faculties which they employ, their narrow reach, and their inaccurate operations. While we cannot give a satisfactory reason, why we believe, after a thousand experiments, that a stone will fall, or fire burn; can we ever satisfy ourselves concerning any determination, which we may form, with regard to the origin of worlds, and the situation of nature, from, and to eternity?

This narrow limitation, indeed, of our enquiries, is, in every respect, so reasonable, that it suffices to make the slightest examination into the natural powers of the human mind and to compare them with their objects, in order to recommend it to us. We shall then find what are the proper subjects of science and enquiry.

It seems to me, that the only objects of the abstract science or of demonstration are quantity and number, and that all attempts to extend this more perfect species of knowledge beyond these bounds are mere sophistry and illusion. As the component parts of quantity and number are entirely similar, their relations become intricate and involved; and nothing can be more curious, as well as useful, than to trace, by a variety of mediums, their equality or inequality, through their different appearances. But as all other ideas are clearly distinct and different from each other, we can never advance farther, by our utmost scrutiny, than to observe this diversity, and, by an obvious reflection, pronounce one thing not to be another. Or if there be any difficulty in these decisions, it proceeds entirely from the undeterminate meaning of words, which is corrected by juster definitions. That the square of the hypothenuse is equal to the squares of the other two sides, cannot be known, let the terms be ever so exactly defined, without a train of reasoning and enquiry. But to convince us of this proposition, that where there is no property, there can be no injustice, it is only necessary to define the terms, and explain injustice to be a violation of property. This proposition is, indeed, nothing but a more imperfect definition. It is the same case with all those pretended syllogistical reasonings, which may be found in every other branch of learning, except the sciences of quantity and number; and these may safely, I think, be pronounced the only proper objects of knowledge and demonstration.

All other enquiries of men regard only matter of fact and existence; and these are evidently incapable of demonstration. Whatever is may not be. No negation of a fact can involve a contradiction. The non-existence of any being, without exception, is as clear and distinct an idea as its existence. The proposition, which affirms it not to be, however false, is no less conceivable and intelligible, than that which affirms it to be. The case is different with the sciences, properly so called. Every proposition, which is not true, is there confused and unintelligible. That the cube root of 64 is equal to the half of 10, is a false proposition, and can never be distinctly conceived. But that Caesar, or the angel Gabriel, or any being never existed, may be a false proposition, but still is perfectly conceivable, and implies no contradiction.

The existence, therefore, of any being can only be proved by arguments from its cause or its effect; and these arguments are founded entirely on experience. If we reason a priori, anything may appear able to produce anything. The falling of a pebble may, for aught we know, extinguish the sun; or the wish of a man control the planets in their orbits. It is only experience, which teaches us the nature and bounds of cause and effect, and enables us to infer the existence of one object from that of another 1. Such is the foundation of moral reasoning, which forms the greater part of human knowledge, and is the source of all human action and behavior.

Moral reasonings are either concerning particular or general facts. All deliberations in life regard the former; as also all disquisitions in history, chronology, geography, and astronomy.

The sciences, which treat of general facts, are politics, natural philosophy, physic, chemistry, &c. where the qualities, causes and effects of a whole species of objects are enquired into.

Divinity or Theology, as it proves the existence of a Deity, and the immortality of souls, is composed partly of reasonings concerning particular, partly concerning general facts. It has a foundation in reason, so far as it is supported by experience. But its best and most solid foundation is faith and divine revelation.

Morals and criticism are not so properly objects of the understanding as of taste and sentiment. Beauty, whether moral or natural, is felt, more properly than perceived. Or if we reason concerning it, and endeavor to fix its standard, we regard a new fact, to wit, the general tastes of mankind, or some such fact, which may be the object of reasoning and enquiry.

When we run over libraries, persuaded of these principles, what havoc must we make? If we take in our hand any volume; of divinity or school metaphysics, for instance; let us ask, Does it contain any abstract reasoning concerning quantity or number? No. Does it contain any experimental reasoning concerning matter of fact and existence?

No. Commit it then to the flames: for it can contain nothing but sophistry and illusion.

Famous quotations

Custom, then, is the great guide of human life①.
—— *An Enquiry Concerning Human Understanding* (1748), sec. 5. pt. 1

Avarice, the spur of industry, is so obstinate a passion, and works its way through so many real dangers and difficulties, that it is not likely to be scared by a imaginary danger, which is so small that it scarcely admits of calculation②.
—— *Essays* (1741—1742), *Of Civil Liberty*

Beauty in things exists in the mind which contemplates them③.
—— *Of Tragedy*

No testimony is sufficient to establish a miracle, unless the testimony be of such a kind that its falsehood would be more miraculous than the fact which it endeavors to establish④.
—— *Of Miracles*

Never literary attempt was more unfortunate than my Treatise of Human Nature. It fell dead-born from the Press⑤.
—— *My Own Life*, ch. 1

Opposing one species of superstition to another, set them a quarrelling; while we ourselves, during their fury and contention, happily make our escape into the calm, tough obscure, regions of philosophy⑥.
—— *The Natural History of Religion*, xv

Science supplies us with ever more detailed information about the world. However, according to Hume, science deals with theories only, and can never yield a "law of nature".

---

① 习俗是人生的伟大的向导。——《人类理智研究》,(1748),第 5 节第 1 部分。
② 贪欲作为勤劳的动力,是一种非常固执的情怀,它能经受现实中的千难万险;至于意想中的危险,简直可以忽略不计,贪欲决不会为之吓倒。——《论说文集》(1741—1742 年),《论平民自由》
③ 外界事物中的美存在于思考这些事物的心灵之中。——《论悲剧》
④ 任何声明都不足以造就奇迹,除非这种声明的虚假性比它所力求确立的事实显得更为神奇。——《论奇迹》
⑤ 任何著述都不会像我的《人性论》这样生不逢时。它是在出版社作为死胎生下来的。——《自传》(1777),第 1 章
⑥ 用一种迷信反对另一种迷信,挑起它们之间的争吵;就在它们愤怒相争之时,我们自己却欣然溜进了平静但又深奥的哲学领域。——《宗教的自然史》(1757 年),第 15 节

Society Corrupts
—— Rousseau

Chapter 8

The last age had exhausted all its powers in giving a grace and nobleness to our mutual appetites, and in raising them into a higher class and order than seemed justly to belong to them. Through Rousseau, your masters are resolved to destroy these aristocratic prejudices.

—— *Edmund Burke*

In this chapter
- Getting to know Rousseau
- Appreciating Rousseau's political doctrines
- Looking at the proposed social contract

Jean Jacques Rousseau

  Born into a Calvinist family in Geneva, Rousseau (1712—1778) was largely a self-educated man. His mother died a few days after his birth, and his father fled home leaving him in the care of an uncle. After he moved to France as a teenager, he worked first as a composer, a tutor and then switched to philosophy. In 1750 after he was awarded a prize by the Academy of Dijon① for an essay on "*Whether the restoration of the sciences and*

---

① 第戎学院。

the arts has had a purifying effect on morals", a work now known as his first *Discourse*, he became well known. But because his ideas caused tremendous controversy, his books were banned in Switzerland and in France as well, and warrants were issued for his arrest. Thereafter throughout much of his life he had to move from place to place, eventually settling in Paris in 1770, where he lived until his death at the age of 66.

Being popularly thought to be the champion of an attitude that saw virtue in natural things and "the noble savage" as the ideal human being, Rousseau has been widely influential. His profound insight can be found in almost every trace of modern philosophy today; his writing has an intense and personal quality that compellingly transmits his vision of a society in which each person is able to be fulfilled, happy and free. His philosophy thus has marked a radical shift in the history of Western philosophy, in part because of its vitality and passion but also because it focuses on issues of freedom and human relationships that are of perennial interest as well as being difficult, perhaps impossible to resolve.

Distinctive insights①

Rousseau holds that freedom is supremely important and his whole theory is designed to secure it for everyone; not, however, in the form of a removal of all constraints but as a positive freedom to participate in the activity of legislating for the common good. For him it is law rather than anarchy that sets people free. He investigates the principles underlying this freedom, examining "men as they are" and "laws as they can be". He seeks to elucidate a form of political association which, he writes, "will defend and protect with the whole common force the person and goods of each associate, and in which each, while uniting himself with all, may still obey himself alone, and remain as free as before".

1. The General Will②

Rousseau distinguishes between what he calls "the will of all③" which is totality of individual centered wishes and the General Will, which is arrived at only when each citizen reflects on what will produce the good of all. The General Will must be general not only in its origins but also in its application: "What makes the will general is not the number of citizens concerned but the common interest by which they are united... the sovereign knows only the nation as a whole④." Rousseau maintains that the General Will is always right. This is not to say that the actual deliberations of the people are always right but that when every citizen is adequately informed and deliberates rationally for the general good then the conclusions arrived at will be right. Moreover, the enactment of the

---

① 卢梭批判文明所造成的罪恶和人类不平等的起源。主张人生而自由、平等,私有制是人类不平等的根源,以及社会契约说。

② 公共意志,指社会全体成员基于共同利益、共同目的、共同幸福而形成的共同意志。是卢梭政治和道德哲学思想的核心。

③ 全体意志。公共意志"只考虑公共的利益",它与全体意志(Will of all)不同,全体意志"只不过是个别意志的总和而已。"

④ 选自卢梭 *The Social Contract*,第二部,第4章

General Will is a culmination and fulfillment of freedom, for the initial contract that establishes the collective sovereign person is freely entered into by its members who then put themselves under laws of their own making. As subject to the sovereign the citizen participates in the making of legislation; as an individual he or she is recipient of rights thereby allocated: "Sovereign and subjects", Rousseau says, "are simply the same people in different respects." We compel ourselves to be free.

2. The Social Contract

In *The Social Contract*① Rousseau suggests that the structure of the society in general is that of the family writ large. The ruler of the society is like the father of a family and people yield up their freedom to the ruler as children yield to a father, in order to preserve their safety. Might, he says, does not create right. We obey only legitimate might. The contract made between ruler and people should be one that entails reciprocal rights and obligations. Individuals together become a collective moral body, a kind of dispersed self which, in its wholeness, is the sovereign power. The sovereign is a moral concept, a rational abstraction which is the basis of the equality and freedom of the people it comprises. It transforms natural liberty into civil liberty through which a moral will can be expressed. The social contract, too, is an abstraction: it is a concept that describes the kind of association that obtains in a state or civil society rather than any specific agreement drawn up at some particular time and place.

With account of the practical role of the legislator and the introduction of the concept of the general will, Rousseau attempts to give us a foundation for good government by presenting a solution to the conflicts between the particular and the universal, the individual and the citizen, and the actual and the moral. Individuals, freely agreeing to a social pact and giving up their rights to the community, are assured of the liberties and equality of political citizenship found in the contract. While the individual is naturally good, he must always guard against being dominated or dominating. It is only through being a citizen that the individual can fully realize his freedom and exercise his moral rights and duties.

3. Society Corrupts

In *The Discourse on the Origin of Inequality*②(1755), Rousseau presents us with an almost idyllic view of humanity. They are fundamentally good since they are endowed with innate virtue, and the attributes of compassion and empathy. But private property quickly follows on the division of labor, and humans find themselves alienated from each other by the class divisions engendered. Once the previous state of innocence is disrupted and the power of reason begins to distance themselves from nature, people become detached from their natural virtues. The imposition of civil society on the state of nature therefore entails a move away from virtue toward vice, and from idyllic happiness toward misery.

---

① 《社会契约论》一译《民约论》,论述社会公约、主权、政府和政治等问题。主张全体社会成员协议,订立社会契约是一切合法权利的基础,因而,国家只应该是自由的人民所订立的社会契约的产物。

② 《论人类不平等的起源和基础》,描述人类自然状态,导致人类进入文明社会的因素以及社会状态中人类的不平等、政治奴役和道德堕落。

4. Evils of Education

In the book entitled *Emile*, or *On Education*①, Rousseau expanded on his theme that education is responsible for corrupting the state of nature and perpetuating the evils of modern society. By trying to analyze the principles underlying a natural process maturing of a child growing up in the country from infancy to adulthood, he affirms his belief in a natural human goodness, albeit one that is vulnerable to vice and error. Moreover, he advocates a quiet and gentle nurturing that is related to the needs of each stage of a child's development and one that is especially sympathetic to the thought that "nature wants children to be children before being men." As the child matures, he believes, relationships with others begin to be more important; moral and political awareness follows and eventually the individual becomes fully social human being who is well able, if his education has spared him unnatural stimulations and tensions, to exercise his natural powers to the full within a community of rational beings.

Introductory remarks

One of the most quoted remarks in the whole of political philosophy is the sentence with which Rousseau opens Chapter 1 of *The Social Contract*. "Man is born free and everywhere he is in chains." The chains he refers to are not those of a particular despotic rule but of legitimate government in general and his chief concern is to discover a justification for submitting to this kind of bondage. While arguing that the ruler is the people's agent, not its master, he claims that laws should be derived from the people's general will. Yet in preaching subservience to the impersonal state he comes close to defining freedom as the recognition of necessity. The following selection is taken from *The Social Contract*, Book 1, Ch. 6., in which Rousseau expresses his views on the rights, liberty and equality of all people. It remains a classic of political theory and one of the most influential works of abstract political thought in the western tradition.

Text

The Social Contract or Principles of Political Right (excerpt)

I MEAN to inquire if, in the civil order, there can be any sure an legitimate rule of administration, men being taken as they are and laws as they might be. In this inquiry I shall endeavor always to unite what right sanctions with what is prescribed by interest, in order that justice and utility may in no case be divided.②

---

① 《爱弥儿》或《论教育》,对孩子的教育提出"回归自然",认为教育能恢复人的天性,教育应该顺应儿童的本性,让他们的本性得到自由的发展。

② In this inquiry...may in no case be divided:在这一研究中,我将努力把权利所许可的和利益所要求的结合在一起,以便使正义与功利二者不致有分歧。

I enter upon my task without proving the importance of the subject. I shall be asked if I am a prince or a legislator, to write on politics. I answer that I am neither, and that is why I do so. If I were a prince or a legislator, I should not waste time in saying what wants doing; I should do it, or hold my peace.①

As I was born a citizen of a free State, and a member of the Sovereign, I feel that, however feeble the influence my voice can have on public affairs, the right of voting on them makes it my duty to study them②: and I am happy, when I reflect upon governments, to find my inquiries always furnish me with new reasons for loving that of my own country.

1. SUBJECT OF THE FIRST BOOK

MAN is born free; and everywhere he is in chains. One thinks himself the master of others, and still remains a greater slave than they. How did this change come about? I do not know. What can make it legitimate? That question I think I can answer.

If I took into account only force, and the effects derived from it, I should say: "As long as a people is compelled to obey, and obeys, it does well; as soon as it can shake off the yoke, and shakes it off, it does still better③; for, regaining its liberty by the same right as took it away, either it is justified in resuming it, or there was no justification for those who took it away." But the social order is a sacred right which is the basis of all other rights. Nevertheless, this right does not come from nature, and must therefore be founded on conventions. Before coming to that, I have to prove what I have just asserted.

2. THE FIRST SOCIETIES

THE most ancient of all societies, and the only one that is natural, is the family: and even so the children remain attached to the father only so long as they need him for their preservation. As soon as this need ceases, the natural bond is dissolved. The children, released from the obedience they owed to the father, and the father, released from the care he owed his children, return equally to independence. If they remain united, they continue so no longer naturally, but voluntarily; and the family itself is then maintained only by convention.

This common liberty results from the nature of man. His first law is to provide for his own preservation, his first cares are those which he owes to himself; and, as soon as he reaches years of discretion, he is the sole judge of the proper means of preserving himself, and consequently becomes his own master.

The family then may be called the first model of political societies④: the ruler corresponds to the father, and the people to the children; and all, being born free and

---

① If I were a prince... or hold my peace. 假如我是个君主或立法者,我不会浪费自己的时间来空谈应该做什么事;我会去做那些事情,否则,我会保持沉默。

② As I was born a citizen... my duty to study them: 生为一个自由国家的公民,主权国的一员,不管我的呼声在公共事务中的影响多么微弱,对公共事务的投票权就足以使我有义务去研究它们。

③ As long as a people... and shakes it off, it does still better: 当人民被迫服从而服从时,他们做得对;但是,一旦人民可以打破自己身上的桎梏而打破它时,他们就做得更对。shake off the yoke: 挣脱枷锁。yoke: 枷锁,束缚。

④ the first model of political societies: 政治社会的原始模型。

equal, alienate① their liberty only for their own advantage. The whole difference is that, in the family, the love of the father for his children repays him for the care he takes of them, while, in the State, the pleasure of commanding takes the place of the love which the chief cannot have for the peoples under him.

Grotius denies that all human power is established in favor of the governed②, and quotes slavery as an example. His usual method of reasoning is constantly to establish right by fact. It would be possible to employ a more logical method, but none could be more favorable to tyrants.

It is then, according to Grotius, doubtful whether the human race belongs to a hundred men, or that hundred men to the human race: and, throughout his book, he seems to incline to the former alternative, which is also the view of Hobbes③. On this showing, the human species is divided into so many herds of cattle, each with its ruler, who keeps guard over them for the purpose of devouring them.

As a shepherd is of a nature superior to that of his flock, the shepherds of men, i.e., their rulers, are of a nature superior to that of the peoples under them. Thus, Philo tells us, the Emperor Caligula reasoned, concluding equally well either that kings were gods, or that men were beasts.④

The reasoning of Caligula agrees with that of Hobbes and Grotius. Aristotle, before any of them, had said that men are by no means equal naturally, but that some are born for slavery, and others for dominion.

Aristotle was right; but he took the effect for the cause. Nothing can be more certain than that every man born in slavery is born for slavery. Slaves lose everything in their chains, even the desire of escaping from them: they love their servitude⑤, as the comrades of Ulysses⑥ loved their brutish condition. If then there are slaves by nature, it is because there have been slaves against nature. Force made the first slaves, and their cowardice perpetuated the condition.

I have said nothing of King Adam, or Emperor Noah⑦, father of the three great monarchs who shared out the universe, like the children of Saturn⑧, whom some scholars have recognized in them. I trust to getting due thanks for my moderation; for, being a

---

① alienate：转让(财产)等。
② Grotius denies that all human power is established in favor of the governed：格老秀斯否认人类一切权力都应该是为了有利于被统治者而建立的。格老秀斯(1583—1645)，荷兰人文主义，国际法学创始人。
③ It is then, according to Grotius...which is also the view of Hobbes：根据格老秀斯来看，究竟全人类是属于某一百个人，亦或那一百个人是属于全人类，仍是个疑问；而且他的整部著作似乎都倾向于前一种见解；而这也正是霍布斯的看法。霍布斯(1588—1679)，英国哲学家。
④ Philo tells us...or that men were beasts：据斐洛的记载，卡利古拉皇帝便是这样推理的，他从这种类比竟然做出结论说：君王都是神明，或者说，人民都是畜性。Philo：斐洛(20 BC—40 AD)，古犹太神秘主义哲学家；卡利古拉皇帝(公元12—41)，是罗马帝国第三位皇帝。
⑤ servitude：奴役；束缚。
⑥ Ulysses：尤利西斯，希腊神。
⑦ 诺亚王。诺亚，《圣经》中人物，诺亚方舟(Noah'ark)的主人。十分虔诚地信奉上帝。
⑧ 萨杜恩，罗马神话中的农业之神。

direct descendant of one of these princes, perhaps of the eldest branch, how do I know that a verification of titles might not leave me the legitimate king of the human race? In any case, there can be no doubt that Adam was sovereign of the world, as Robinson Crusoe was of his island, as long as he was its only inhabitant①; and this empire had the advantage that the monarch, safe on his throne, had no rebellions, wars, or conspirators② to fear.

3. THE RIGHT OF THE STRONGEST

THE strongest is never strong enough to be always the master, unless he transforms strength into right, and obedience into duty. Hence the right of the strongest, which, though to all seeming meant ironically, is really laid down as a fundamental principle. But are we never to have an explanation of this phrase? Force is a physical power, and I fail to see what moral effect it can have. To yield to force is an act of necessity, not of will — at the most, an act of prudence. In what sense can it be a duty③?

Suppose for a moment that this so-called "right" exists. I maintain that the sole result is a mass of inexplicable④ nonsense. For, if force creates right, the effect changes with the cause: every force that is greater than the first succeeds to its right. As soon as it is possible to disobey with impunity, disobedience is legitimate; and, the strongest being always in the right, the only thing that matters is to act so as to become the strongest.⑤ But what kind of right is that which perishes when force fails? If we must obey perforce, there is no need to obey because we ought; and if we are not forced to obey, we are under no obligation to do so. Clearly, the word "right" adds nothing to force: in this connection, it means absolutely nothing.

Obey the powers that be. If this means yield to force, it is a good precept, but superfluous: I can answer for its never being violated. All power comes from God, I admit; but so does all sickness: does that mean that we are forbidden to call in the doctor?⑥ A brigand surprises me at the edge of a wood: must I not merely surrender my purse on compulsion; but, even if I could withhold it, am I in conscience bound to give it up? For certainly the pistol he holds is also a power.

Let us then admit that force does not create right, and that we are obliged to obey only legitimate powers. In that case, my original question recurs.⑦

---

① In any case...he was its only inhabitant: 无论如何,人们决不会反对亚当曾是全世界的主权者,正如鲁滨逊只要是他那荒岛上的唯一居民,便是岛上的主权者一样。

② conspirators: 阴谋家,谋反者。

③ To yield to force is an act...can it be a duty: 向强力屈服,只是一种必要的行为,而不是一种意志的行为;它最多也不过是一种明智的行为而已。在哪种意义上,它才可能是一种义务呢?

④ inexplicable: 无法说明的;费解的。

⑤ As soon as it is possible...so as to become the strongest: 只要人们不服从而又能不受惩罚,人们就可以合法地不再服从;而且,既然最强者总是有理的,所以问题就只在于怎样做才能使自己成为最强者。

⑥ All power comes from God...we are forbidden to call in the doctor: 一切权力都来自上帝,这一点我承认;可是一切疾病也都来自上帝。难道这就是说,应该禁止人去请医生吗?

⑦ Let us then admit that...my original question recurs: 那么,就让我们承认:强力并不构成权利,而人们只是对合法的权力才有服从的义务。这样,就重新回到我起初的问题上来。

Brainstorming

1. Illustrate the statement "Man is born free; and everywhere he is in chains".
2. How does human society transit from natural society to political society according to Rousseau?
3. What is the basis of legitimate powers?
4. Why can't the social order established on the basis of power?
5. Is Rousseau right when he compares the structure of society in general to that of a large family? Why?
6. Where do rights come from? And why do we let others rule us?
7. Would your prescriptions for a good society be the same as or similar to those you would prescribe for a good person?

Supplementary reading

Emile, or *On Education* is a treatise on the nature of education and of man, which is divided into five books. Book One, from which our present reading is taken, discusses not only Rousseau's fundamental philosophy but also outlines how one would have to raise a child to conform with that philosophy. Rousseau begins with the early physical and emotional development of the infant and the child.

On Education[①] (excerpt)

Everything is good as it leaves the hands of the Author of things, everything degenerates in the hands of man. He forces one soil to nourish the products of another, one tree to bear the fruits of another. He mixes and confuses the climates, the elements, the seasons. He mutilates his dog, his horse, his slave. He turns everything upside down, he disfigures everything, he loves deformities, monsters. He wants nothing as nature made it, not even man himself. For him man must be trained like a saddle-horse; he must be shaped according to the fashion, like trees in his garden.

Without this everything would be even worse; our species was not made to remain only half-finished. Under existing conditions a man left to himself from birth would be the most disfigured of all. Prejudice, authority, necessity, example — all the social conditions in which we find ourselves submerged — would stifle nature in him and put nothing in its place. Human nature would be like a seedling that chance had sown in the midst of the highway, bent this way and that and soon crushed by the passers-by.

It is you whom I address, tender, foresighted mother — you who know how to stay away from the busy highway and protect the growing seedling from the impact of human opinion! Cultivate and water the young plant before it dies; its fruit will one day be your

---

① 《爱弥儿》,或《论教育》,书中提出了"回归自然"的主张,认为教育能恢复人的天性,教育应该顺应儿童的本性,让其得到自由的发展。

delight. Early on, form an enclosure around your child's soul. Someone else can mark its circumference, but you alone must build the fence.

Plants are fashioned by cultivation, man by education. If a man were born tall and strong, his size and strength would be of no good to him until he had learned to use them; they would even harm him by preventing others from wanting to assist him. Left to himself he would die of misery before he knew his needs. We lament the helplessness of infancy; we fail to perceive that the human race would have perished had not man begun by being a child.

We are born weak, we need strength; we are born lacking everything, we need aid; we are born stupid, we need judgment. All that we lack at birth and that we need when we are grown is given by education.

This education comes to us from nature, from men, or from things. The inner growth of our organs and faculties is the education of nature, the use we learn to make of this growth is the education of men, and what we gain by our experience of our surroundings is the education of things.

Thus we are each taught by three masters. The pupil in whom their diverse lessons conflict is poorly raised and will never be in harmony with himself; he in whom they all agree on the same points and tend towards the same ends goes straight to his goal and lives consistently. The latter is well raised.

Now of these three factors in education, the education of nature is wholly beyond our control; that of things is only partly in our power; the education of men is the only one of which we are truly the master. And even here our power is largely illusory, for who can hope to direct every word and action of all those who surround a child?

As much therefore as education is an art, it is almost impossible that it succeed, since the coordination necessary to its success depends on no one person. All one can do by one's own efforts is to more or less approach the goal. One needs luck to attain it.

What is this goal? It is the goal of nature, which has just been proved. Since the coordination of the three educations is necessary to their perfection, the two that we can control must follow the lead of that which is beyond our control. Perhaps this word Nature has too vague a meaning. Let us try to define it.

Nature, we are told, is merely habit. What does this signify? Are there not habits formed under compulsion, habits which never stifle nature? Such, for example, is the habit of plants that have had their vertical direction altered. Once given liberty, the plant keeps the shape it was forced into. And yet for all that, the sap has not changed its original direction, and any new growth the plant makes will be vertical. It is the same with the inclinations of man. As long as we stay in the same condition we will keep those inclinations that result from habit and which are the least natural to us. But as soon as the situation changes, habit ceases and nature reasserts itself. Education is certainly only a habit, for there are people who forget or lose their education and others who keep it. Whence comes this difference? If we restrict the name of nature to those habits that conform to nature, we can spare ourselves any confusion.

Famous quotations

Man is born free, and everywhere he is in chains①.

—— *The Social Contract*, ch. 1

The first man who, having fenced in a piece of land, said, "This is mine," and found people naive enough to believe him, that man was the true founder of civil society②.

—— The *Discourse on the Origin of Inequality*

The strongest is never strong enough to be always the master, unless he transforms strength into right, and obedience into duty.③

—— *The Social Contract*, ch. 1

Everything is good as it leaves the hands of the Author, everything degenerates in the hand of man.④

—— *Emile*, or *On Education*, Book I

Conscience is the voice of the soul; the passions are the voice of the body.⑤

—— *Emile*, or *On Education*, Book III

To renounce liberty is to renounce being a man, to surrender the rights of humanity and even its duties.⑥

—— *The Social Contract*, ch. 4

Adam and Eve represent the kind of perfect "natural" humans that Rousseau thought predated society. Because they ate of the forbidden fruit, they underwent the "fall". Rousseau says that we, like them, are corrupted by knowledge, becoming even more selfish and unhappy.

---

① 人生来是自由的,但无处不受限制。——《社会契约论》,第1章。
② 谁第一个把一块地圈起来说,"这是我的",而且发现人们居然天真地相信了他的话,这个人就是文明社会的真正奠基人。——《论人类社会不平等的起源和基础》
③ 即使是最强者也决不会强得足以永远做主人,除非他把自己的强力转化为权利,把服从转化为义务。——《社会契约论》,第1章。
④ 一切事物离开造物主时都是完美的;一切落入人手中的事物便腐化堕落了。——《论教育》,第一部
⑤ 良心是灵魂的声音,欲望是身体的呼喊。——《论教育》,第三部
⑥ 放弃自由是放弃成为一个人,是向与生俱来的权利甚至义务投降。——《社会契约论》,第4章。

The Starry Heavens above and the Moral Law within
—— Kant

Chapter 9

He was indifferent to nothing worth knowing. No cabal, no sect, no prejudice, no desire for fame could ever tempt him in the slightest away from broadening and illuminating the truth. He incited and gently forced others to think for themselves; despotism was foreign to his mind. This man, whom I name with the greatest gratitude and respect, was Immanuel Kant.
—— John Herder

In this chapter
- Glimpsing Descartes' life
- Surveying Kant's transcendental idealism
- Appreciating Kant's categorical imperative

Immanuel Kant

German philosopher Immanuel Kant (1724—1804) was born into a family of financially struggling artisans. He lived and worked his whole life in the cosmopolitan Baltic port city of Konigsberg, then the part of Prussia. Kant studied philosophy, physics, and mathematics at the University of Konigsberg, and taught a variety of subjects at the same institution for the next 27 years.

Kant's work is highly original and wide-ranging. It was produced at a crucial time in the development of philosophy when there was tension between the continental allegiance to rational thought and the British espousal of sense experience. In his *Critiques* he attempts a synthesis of these two themes and thereby has changed the course of philosophy. Kant's philosophy has influenced almost every area of thought, his work still being an important reference point for contemporary philosophers today, especially in the branches of metaphysics and epistemology. Though he never left his native province, he became internationally famous ranking with Plato and Aristotle as one of the most important philosophers in Western culture.

Distinctive insights[①]

Kant thought it was "scandalous" that in more than 2,000 years of philosophical thought, nobody had been able to produce an argument to prove that there really is a world out there, external to us. He recognized the strength of the empiricist claim that sense experience is the source of all our beliefs but could not accept its skeptical conclusion that those beliefs cannot be justified. At the same time he rejected the rationalist claim that factual truths about what does and does not exist can be conclusively established by the use of reason alone. His ideas are as follows:

1. Kant's Copernican Revolution

Kant claims to have created a "Copernican Revolution" in philosophy. This involves two interconnected foundations of his "critical philosophy": the epistemology of transcendental idealism and the moral philosophy of the autonomy of practical reason. These teachings place the active, rational human subject at the center of the cognitive and moral world. In other words, the revolution is the inversion of the traditional relation between the subject of knowledge and the object of that knowledge. By proposing that the observed objects affect the observing subject, he holds that the subject's constitution affects the way that the objects are observed. Following this transcendental idealism theory, he arrives at the point that the possibility of knowledge is thus to be found in the structure of the subject itself, instead of in an objective reality from which nothing can be said.

2. The Synthetic vs. Analytic[②] **and *a Priori vs a Posteriori***[③].

All judgments, said Kant, can be divided into two kinds, which he called *analytic* and *synthetic*. In analytic judgments the predicate repeats all or part of what was already in the subject, in synthetic judgments the predicate says something over and above what was in the subject. Analytic judgments are of the form "All A is A"; synthetic judgments are of the form "All A is B." "All bachelors are bachelors" is analytic, so is "All bachelors are

---

① 康德思想分为"前批判时期"与"批判时期"。前批判时期以自然科学的研究为主进行哲学探究,提出关于太阳系起源的星云假说。批判时期主要"批判"地研究人的认识能力及其范围与限度,将世界划分为"现象界"与"自在之物"世界;人的认识分为"感性"、"知性"、"理性";人的认识只能达到"现象"。在自在之物世界中,上帝、自由、灵魂等为超自然的东西,属信仰范围,它们的存在是为了适应道德的需要。在政治上,同情法国革命,主张自由平等。在教育上,认为应重视儿童天性,养成儿童自觉遵守纪律的习惯。

② Synthetic:综合命题,指主词和谓词没有蕴含关系,其正确性必须根据经验事实来验证。Analytic:分析命题相对综合命题,是谓词包含在主词中的命题,只需分析谓词和主词的关系就能判断该命题真假,且分析命题的判断是必然的。

③ *a priori*:先验指无须经验或先于经验获得的知识,通常与后验知识相比较。*a posteriori*:后验意指"在经验之后"。

unmarried," when you substitute the definition of "bachelor," an unmarried man, for the word and get "All unmarried men are unmarried men," which is analytic. On the other hand, "All bachelors are tall" is not analytic but synthetic (and this one is false).

Analytic propositions can also take the form "All AB is A"; in which only a defining characteristic instead of the whole definition, appears in the predicate. Thus, "All triangles are three-sided" and "All fathers are male" are both analytic, although the predicate term contains only a part of the definition. The statement is still true entirely by virtue of the meanings of the words in it: all fathers are male, because anyone who was not a male would not be called a father (as we use the word "father").

Kant further introduces another pair of terms, "*a priori*" and "*a posteriori*." These terms do not deal with the propositions themselves (as "analytic" and "synthetic" do) but with our knowledge of them. An *a priori* truth is one that can be known "independently of experience" — which isn't to say that we didn't have to learn it at some time or that we didn't need to have experience of learning the words, but only that we don't have to discover it inductively, by amassing instances, as we do with laws of nature. All analytic statements are knowable *a priori*: we need only to know the meanings of the terms in order to know whether they're true; we don't have to look to nature. By contrast, "All apples are sweet" is knowable only *a posteriori* — that is, after (posterior to) people have had experience of tasting the apples. And the same, of course, is true for laws about the temperature at which water freezes, lead melts, and so on — all of which have to be established in a case-by-case basis through sense-experience. Laws of nature are all *a posteriori*: only experience is qualified to serve either as confirmation or as refutation to these laws.

3. Time and Consciousness

Kant wants to demonstrate that there is an external, material world, the existence of which cannot be doubted. His argument begins as follows: in order for something to exist, it must be determinable in time, that is, we must be able to say when it exists and for how long. But how does this work in the case of my own consciousness?

Although consciousness seems to be constantly changing with a continuous flow of sensations and thoughts, we can use the word "now" to refer to what is currently happening in our consciousness. But "now" is not a determinate time or date. Every time I say "now", consciousness is different.

Here lies the problem: what makes it possible to specify the "when" of my own existence? We cannot experience time itself, directly, rather, we experience time through things that move, change, or stay the same. Consider the hands of a clock, constantly moving slowly around. The moving hands are useless for determining time on their own—they need reference objects against which the change can be reflected, such as the numbers on a clock face. Every resource I have for measuring my constantly changing "now" is found in material objects outside me in space (including my own physical body). Saying that I exist requires a determinate point in time, and this, in turn, requires an actually existing outside world in which time takes place. My level of certainty about the existence of consciousness, which Descartes believed was absolute certain.

4. Intuitions and Concepts

Kant split knowledge into intuitions, gained from direct sensibility of the world, and concepts, which come indirectly from our understanding. Some of our knowledge — both of sensibility and understanding — comes from empirical evidence, while some is known as *a priori*. In his famous work *Critique of Pure Reason*①, Kant argues that our experience of the world involves two elements. The first is what he calls "sensibility" — our ability to be directly acquainted with particular things in space and time, such as this book you are reading now. The second is what he calls the "understanding", our ability to have and use concepts. For Kant, a concept is an indirect acquaintance with things as examples of a type of thing, such as the concept of "cow" in general. Without concepts we would not know our intuition was a cow; without intuition we would never know that there were cows at all. Each of these elements has, in turn, two sides. In sensibility, there is my intuition of a particular thing in space and time (like the cow) and my intuition of space and time as such (my acquaintance with what space and time are like in general). In understanding, there is my concept of some type of thing (cows) and my concept of a "thing" as such (substance). A concept such as substance defines what it means to be a thing in general rather than defining some type of thing like a cow. My intuition of a cow and the concept of a cow are empirical, for how could I know anything about cows unless I had come across them in the world? But my intuition of space and time and the concept of substance are *a priori*, meaning that they are known before or independently of any experience.

The fact that Kant locates the *a priori* even within our intuitions of the world was important for 20th-century phenomenologists such as Edmund Husserl and Martin Heidegger, who sought to examine objects of experience independently of any assumptions we may have about them.

5. The Hypothetical Imperative vs the Categorical Imperative②

Kant's ethics was expounded in the *Critique of Practical Reason*. While theoretical reason is concerned with knowledge, practical reason is concerned with will, or self-determination. Kant believes that there is only one human reason, but after it decides what it can know, it must determine how it shall act. Thus the freedom of the will determines how one shall lead his life. And the basic, reasonable principle of a free morality (a morality that one is free to choose) is some universal and necessary law which follows. This principle is called by Kant the "Categorical Imperative," which states that a man should act in a way that is acceptable and applicable to all people.

Moral value, according to Kant, is determined ultimately by the nature of intention of the agent, which in turn is determined by the nature of what he calls the general maxim

---

① 《纯粹理性批判》(1781),阐述了纯粹经验基于经验带给人类知识,但是实践经验不是基于经验,而是"先验",它假设了人类的自由意志,上帝和道德。所谓"纯粹理性",是指独立于一切经验的理性;而所谓"批判",则是指对这种纯粹思辨的理性进行一种考察,以便弄清楚人类知识的来源、范围与界限。

② 假言命令,把一个可能行为的实践必然性,看作是达到人之所愿望的,至少是可能愿望的另一目的的手段。它是有条件的,即认为善行是到达偏好和利益的手段。至上命令,亦称"无上命令",是康德的伦理学原则。康德认为至上命令是普遍的、先验的、永恒不变的,是人人都必须无条件遵守的一种意志或行动准则。

or subjective principle underlying a person's action. One follows a hypothetical imperative when one's maxim does not presume an unconditional end, a goal (like the fulfillment of duty) that one should have irrespective of all sensible desires, but rather a "material end" dependent on contingent inclinations (e.g., the directive "get this," in order to feel happy). In contrast, a categorical imperative is a directive saying what ought to be done from the perspective of pure reason alone; it is categorical because what this perspective commands is not contingent on sensible circumstances and it always carries overriding value. The general formula of the categorical imperative is to act only according to those maxims that can be consistently willed as a universal law — something said to be impossible for maxims aimed merely at material ends. In accepting this imperative, we are doubly self-determined, for we are not only determining our action freely, as Kant believes humans do in all exercises of the faculty of choice; we are also accepting a principle whose content is determined by that which is absolutely essential to us as agents, namely our pure practical reason. We thus are following our own law and so have autonomy when we accept the categorical imperative; otherwise we fall into heteronomy, or the (free) acceptance of principles whose content is determined independently of the essential nature of our own ultimate being, which is rational.

Kant regards accepting the categorical imperative as tantamount to respecting rational nature as an end in itself, and to willing as if we were legislating a kingdom of ends. This is to will that the world become a "systematic union of different rational beings through common laws," i.e., laws that respect and fulfill the freedom of all rational beings. Although there is only one fundamental principle of morality, there are still different types of specific duties. One basic distinction is between strict duty and imperfect duty. Duties of justice, of respecting in action the rights of others, or the duty not to violate the dignity of persons as rational agents, are strict because they allow no exception for one's inclination. A perfect duty is one that requires a specific action (e.g. keeping a promise), whereas an imperfect duty, such as the duty to perfect oneself or to help others, cannot be completely discharged or demanded by right by someone else, and so one has considerable latitude in deciding when and how it is to be respected. A meritorious duty involves going beyond what is strictly demanded and thereby generating an obligation in others, as when one is extraordinarily helpful to others and "merits" their gratitude.

Introductory remarks

Kant is one of the first philosophers to develop and integrate aesthetic theory into a unified and comprehensive philosophical system, utilizing ideas that played an integral role throughout his philosophy. The following selection from Kant's *Critique of Judgment*[①] offers a penetrating analysis of our experience of the beautiful and the sublime.

---

① 《判断力批判》(1790),辩证地表述了康德的自然观,即在认识论和伦理学之间建构一反思判断,并试图寻求道德界与自由王国两个分割世界的沟通。

It also discusses the objectivity of taste, aesthetic disinterestedness, the relation of art and nature, the role of imagination, genius and originality, the limits of representation, and the connection between morality and the aesthetics.

Text

First Moment of the Judgment of Taste:

Moment of Quality①

The definition of taste here relied upon is that it is the faculty of estimating the beautiful. But the discovery of what is required for calling an object beautiful must be reserved for the analysis of judgments of taste②. In my search for the moments to which attention is paid by this judgment in its reflection, I have followed the guidance of the logical functions of judging (for a judgment of taste always involves a reference to understanding). I have brought the moment of quality first under review, because this is what the aesthetic judgment on the beautiful looks to in the first instance.

1. The Judgment of Taste is Aesthetic

If we wish to discern whether anything is beautiful or not, we do not refer the representation of it to the object by means of understanding with a view to cognition, but by means of the imagination (acting perhaps in conjunction with understanding) we refer the representation to the subject and its feeling of pleasure or displeasure.③ The judgment of taste, therefore, is not a cognitive judgment, and so not logical, but is aesthetic—which means that it is one whose determining ground cannot be other than subjective④. Every reference of representations is capable of being objective, even that of sensations (in which case it signifies the real in an empirical representation). The one exception to this is the feeling of pleasure or displeasure. This denotes nothing in the object, but is a feeling which the subject has of itself and of the manner in which it is affected by the representation.

To apprehend a regular and appropriate building with one's cognitive faculties, be the mode of representation clear or confused, is quite a different thing from being conscious of this representation with an accompanying sensation of delight⑤. Here the

---

① First Moment of the Judgment of Taste: Moment of Quality: 鉴赏判断的第一个契机：质的契机。moment: 关键性的，决定性的东西。

② But the discovery of what is... of judgments of taste: 判定一定对象为美时所要求的是些什么呢，这必须从分析鉴赏判断才能发现。

③ If we wish to... feeling of pleasure or displeasure: 为了判别某一对象是美或不美，我们不是把它的表象凭借悟性速系于客体以求得知识，而是凭借想象力（或者想象力和悟性相结合），将表象连系于主体和它的快感和非快感。representation: 表象；cognition: 认知。

④ it is one whose determining ground cannot be other than subjective: 它的判定标准只能是主观的，不可能是别的。

⑤ To apprehend a regular and appropriate building... sensation of delight: 比起用自己的认知能力去了解一座常规的合适的建筑物（不管它是在清晰的或模糊的表象形态里），用愉快的感觉去意识这个表象是全然不同的。

representation is referred wholly to the subject, and what is more to its feeling of life—under the name of the feeling of pleasure or displeasure—and this forms the basis of a quite separate faculty of discriminating and estimating, that contributes nothing to knowledge. All it does is to compare the given representation in the subject with the entire faculty of representations of which the mind is conscious in the feeling of its state. Given representations in a judgment may be empirical, and so aesthetic; but the judgment which is pronounced by their means is logical, provided it refers them to the object[①]. Conversely, be the given representations even rational, but referred in a judgment solely to the subject (to its feeling), they are always to that extent aesthetic[②].

2. The Delight Which Determines the Judgment of Taste is Independent of All Interest

The delight which we connect with the representation of the real existence of an object is called interest. Such a delight, therefore, always involves a reference to the faculty of desire, either as its determining ground, or else as necessarily implicated with its determining ground.[③] Now, where the question is whether something is beautiful, we do not want to know, whether we, or any one else, are, or even could be, concerned in the real existence of the thing, but rather what estimate we form of it on mere contemplation (intuition or reflection). If any one asks me whether I consider that the palace I see before me is beautiful, I may, perhaps, reply that I do not care for things of that sort that are merely made to be gaped at. Or I may reply in the same strain as that Iroquois Sachem who said that nothing in Paris pleased him better than the eating-houses. I may even go a step further and inveigh with the vigor of a Rousseau against the vigor of a great against the vanity of the people on such superfluous things[④]. Or, in fine, I may quite easily persuade myself that if I found myself on an uninhabited island, without hope of ever again coming among men, and could conjure such a palace into existence by a mere wish, I should still not trouble to do so, so long as I had a hut there that was comfortable enough for me. All this may be admitted and approved; only it is not the point now at issue. All one wants to know is whether the mere representation of the object is to my liking, no matter how indifferent I may be to the real existence of the object of this representation. It is quite plain that in order to say that the object is beautiful, and to show that I have taste, everything turns on the meaning which I can give to this representation, and not on any factor which makes me dependent on the real existence of the object. Every one must allow that a judgment on the beautiful which is tinged with the slightest

---

① Given representations in a judgment... it refers them to the object：在一个判断里面给定的诸表象可能是从经验得来的(因此也是审美的)，但是因此而下的那个判断若在判断时只是连系于客体，那么这个判断就是逻辑方面的了。

② Conversely, be the given representations... they are always to that extent aesthetic：与此相反，如果这些一定的表象尽管是属于纯理性的，而在一个判断里却只是连系于主体(它的情感)，那么它们就因此在任何时候都是审美的了。

③ Such a delight, therefore, always involves... with its determining ground：这种快感常常和欲望能力有关，或是作为它的规定根据，或是作为和它的规定根据必然地连结着的因素。

④ I may, perhaps, reply that I do not care for... the vanity of the people on such superfluous things：我固然可以说：我不爱这一类徒然让人为之瞠目惊奇的事物，或是，像那位易洛魁族的沙赫姆那样来答复，他在巴黎没有感到比小食店使他更满意的东西；此外我还可以照卢梭的样子骂大人物们的虚荣浮华，不惜把人民的血汗浪费在这些无用的东西上面。inveigh：猛烈抨击，强烈抗议；superfluous：多余的，奢侈浪费的。

interest, is very partial and not a pure judgment of taste①. One must not be in the least prepossessed in favor of the real existence of the thing, but must preserve complete indifference in this respect, in order to play the part of judge in matters of taste.

This proposition, which is of the utmost importance, cannot be better explained than by contrasting the pure disinterested delight which appears in the judgment of taste with that allied to an interest—especially if we can also assure ourselves that there are no other kinds of interest beyond those presently to be mentioned.

A judgment upon an object of our delight may be wholly disinterested but withal② very interesting, i.e., it relies on no interest, but it produces one. Of this kind are all pure moral judgments. But, of themselves judgments of taste do not even set up any interest whatsoever. Only in society is it interesting to have taste—a point which will be explained in the sequel.

3. Delight in the Agreeable is Coupled with Interest.

That is agreeable which the senses find pleasing in sensation. This at once affords a convenient opportunity for condemning and directing particular attention to a prevalent confusion of the double meaning of which the word sensation is capable. All delight (as is said or thought) is itself sensation (of a pleasure). Consequently everything that pleases, and for the very reason that it pleases, is agreeable—and according to its different degrees, or its relations to other agreeable sensations, is attractive, charming, delicious, enjoyable, etc. But if this is conceded, then impressions of sense, which determine inclination, or principles of reason, which determine the will, or mere contemplated forms of intuition, which determine judgment, are all on a par in everything relevant to their effect upon the feeling of pleasure③, for this would be agreeableness in the sensation of one's state; and since, in the last resort, all the elaborate work of our faculties must issue in and unite in the practical as its goal, we could credit our faculties with no other appreciation of things and the worth of things, than that consisting in the gratification which they promise. How this is attained is in the end immaterial; and, as the choice of the means is here the only thing that can make a difference, men might indeed blame one another for folly or imprudence④, but never for baseness or wickedness; for they are all, each according to his own way of looking at things, pursuing one goal, which for each is the gratification in question.

When a modification of the feeling of pleasure or displeasure is termed sensation, this expression is given quite a different meaning to that which it bears when I call the representation of a thing (through sense as a receptivity pertaining to the faculty of knowledge) sensation.⑤ For

---

① Every one must allow that... not a pure judgment of taste: 每个人必须承认, 一个关于美的判断, 只要夹杂着极少的利益得失在里面, 就会有偏爱而不是纯粹的欣赏判断了。

② withal: 依然, 仍然。

③ But if this is conceded... the feeling of pleasure: 承认了这一点, 那么决定倾向性的诸感官印象, 或决定意志的理性原则, 或决定判断力的直观反省形式, 在相关快乐感觉效果的所有事情上便全然同一了。concede: 承认; 承认……为真(正确); on a par: (和……)同等, 同价

④ folly or imprudence: 愚蠢或鲁莽的行为。

⑤ When a modification of the feeling of pleasure... faculty of knowledge) sensation: 如果快乐及不快的情绪的改变被称为感觉, 那么这个名称是和我把一件事物的表象(经由感官, 作为隶属于认识的感受性)命名为感觉是完全两回事。pertaining to: 从属于, 附属于。

in the latter case the representation is referred to the object, but in the former it is referred solely to the subject and is not available for any cognition, not even for that by which the subject cognizes itself.

Now in the above definition the word sensation is used to denote an objective representation of sense; and, to avoid continually running the risk of misinterpretation, we shall call that which must always remain purely subjective, and is absolutely incapable of forming a representation of an object, by the familiar name of feeling①. The green color of the meadows belongs to objective sensation, as the perception of an object of sense; but its agreeableness to subjective sensation, by which no object is represented; i. e., to feeling, through which the object is regarded as an object of delight (which involves no cognition of the object).

Now, that a judgment on an object by which its agreeableness is affirmed, expresses an interest in it, is evident from the fact that through sensation it provokes a desire for similar objects, consequently the delight presupposes, not the simple judgment about it, but the bearing its real existence has upon my state so far as affected by such an object. Hence we do not merely say of the agreeable that it pleases, but that it gratifies. I do not accord it a simple approval, but inclination is aroused by it, and where agreeableness is of the liveliest type a judgment on the character of the object is so entirely out of place that those who are always intent only on enjoyment (for that is the word used to denote intensity of gratification) would fain dispense with all judgment②.

Brainstorming

1. Why does Kant call aesthetic judgments "judgments of taste"? How can one reach the pure judgment?
2. According to Kant, what is the essence of beauty? Where does the delight at beauty arise?
3. What does "sensation" mean? Why is it important?
4. How can you understand the proverb: "beauty is in the eye of the beholder"?
5. Why do we value art? Or what is it about art that we value, apart from the pleasure it gives?
6. Why should we have any less of all obligations to justify our aesthetic judgments than we have to justify our factual or moral judgments?

Supplementary reading

Kant is known for his theory that there is a single moral obligation, which he calls

---

① to avoid continually running the risk...by the familiar name of feeling：为避免误解，我们用熟悉的情感一词来称呼那种一直是纯粹主观的，并且根本不能形成一件物品的表象的东西。

② those who are always intent...would fain dispense with all judgment：那些一直寻求享乐的人们（享乐这一词意即强烈的满足感），是乐于放弃一切批判的。

the *Categorical Imperative*, from which all other moral obligations are generated. He believes that the moral law is a principle of reason itself, and is not based on contingent facts about the world. Accordingly he believes that moral obligation applies to all and only rational agents. For Kant it is also an unconditional obligation, which is formulated in three ways as follows in the first section of *Groundwork of the Metaphysic of Morals*.

The Categorical Imperative[①]

Nothing in the world — indeed nothing beyond the world — can possibly be conceived which could be called good without qualification except a good will. Intelligence, wit, judgment, and the other talents of the mind, however they may be named, or courage, resoluteness, and perseverance as qualities if temperament, are doubtless in many respects good and desirable. But they can become extremely bad and harmful if the will, which is to make use of these gifts of mature and which in its special constitution is called character, is not good. It is the same with the gifts of fortune. Power, riches, honor, even health, general well-being, and the contentment with one's condition which is called happiness, make for pride and even arrogance if there is not a good will to correct their influence on the mind and on its principles of action so as to make it universally comfortable to its end. It need hardly be mentioned that the sight of being adorned with no feature of a pure and good will, yet enjoying uninterrupted prosperity, can never give pleasure to a rational impartial observer. Thus the good will seems to constitute the indispensable condition even of worthiness to be happy...

(Thus the first proposition of morality is to have moral worth an action must be done from duty.) The second proposition is: An action performed from duty does not have its moral worth in the purpose which is to be achieved through it but in the maxim by which it is determined. Its moral value, therefore, does not depend on the realization of the object of the action but merely on the principle of volition by which the action is done, without any regard to the objects of the faculty of desire. From the preceding discussion it is clean that he purposes we may have for our actions and their effects as ends and incentives of the will cannot give the actions any unconditional and moral worth. Wherein, then, can this worth lie, if it is not in the will in relation to its hoped-for effect? It can lie nowhere else than in the principle of the will, irrespective of the ends which can be realized by such action. For the will stands, as it were, at the crossroads halfway between it's a priori principle which is formal and it's a posteriori incentive which is material. Since it must be determined by something, if it is done from duty, it must be determined by the formal principle of volition as such every material principle has been withdrawn from it.

The third principle is a consequence of the two preceding. I would express as

---

① 至上命令,亦称"无上命令",是康德的伦理学原则。康德认为任何人在任何时间和地点,以及在任何条件下,都必须遵守一种意志或行动的准则,这种准则同时也能成为所有人都应奉行的"普遍的立法原则"或普遍的道德规范。康德把这种"无条件的"行为原则称作"至上命令",并认为至上命令是普遍的、先验的、永恒不变的。

follows: Duty is the necessity of an action executed from respect for law. I can certainly have an inclination to the object as an effect of the proposed action, but I can never have respect for it precisely because it is a mere effect and not an activity of a will. Similarity, I can have no respect for any inclination whatsoever, whether my own or that of another: in the former case I can even love it, i. e. see it as favorable to my own advantage. But that which is connected with my will merely as ground and not as consequence, that which does it serve my inclination but overpowers it or at least excludes it from being considered in making a choice — in a word, law itself — can be an object of respect and thus a command. Now as an act from duty wholly excludes the influence of inclination and therewith every object of the will, nothing remains which can determine the will objectively except the law, and nothing subjectively except pre respect for this practical law. This subjective element is the maxim that I ought to follow such a law even if it thwarts all my inclinations.

Thus the moral worth of an action does not lie in the effect which is expected from it or in any way principle of action which has to borrow its motive from this expected effect. For all these effects (agreeableness if my own condition, indeed even the promotion of the happiness of others) could be brought about through other causes and would not require the will of a rational being, while the highest and unconditional good can be found only in such a will. Therefore, the preeminent good can consist only in the conception of the law in itself (which can be only present in a rational being) so far as this conception and not the hoped-for effect is the determining ground of the will. This preeminent good, which we call moral, is already present in the person who acts according to this conception, and we do not have to look for it first in the result.

But what kind of a law can that be, the conception of which must determine the will without reference to the expected result? Under this condition alone the will can be called absolutely good without qualification. Since I have robbed the will if all impulses which could come to it from obedience to any law, nothing remains to serve as a principle of the will except universal conformity of its action to law as such. That is, I should never act in such a way that I could not also will that my maxim should be a universal law. Mere conformity to law as such (without assuming any particular law applicable to certain actions) serve as the principle of the will, and it must serve as such a principle if duty is not to be a vain delusion and chimerical concept. The common reason of mankind in its practical judgments is in perfect agreement with this and has this principle constantly in view...

I do not, therefore, need any penetrating acuteness in order to discern what I have to do in order that my volition may be morally good. Inexperienced in the course of the world, incapable of being prepared for all its contingencies, I ask myself only: Can I will that my maxim become a universal law? If not, it must be rejected, not because of any disadvantages accruing to myself or even to others, but because it cannot enter as a principle into a possible universal legislation, and reason extorts from me an immediate respect for such legislation. I do not as yet discern on what it is grounded (a question the philosopher may investigate), but I at least understand that it is an estimation of the worth which far outweighs all the worth if the necessity if my actions from pure respect for the practical law constitutes duty. To duty every other motive must give place, because duty is the condition of a will good in itself, whose worth transcends everything...

There is, therefore, only one categorical imperative. It is: Act only according to that maxim by which you can at the same time will that it should become a universal law.

Now if all imperatives of duty can be derived from this one imperative as a principle, we can at least show what we understand by the concept if duty and what it means, even though it remain undecided whether that which is called duty is an empty concept or not.

Famous quotations

Morality is not properly the doctrine of how we may make ourselves happy, but how we may make ourselves worthy of happiness①.

—— *Critique of Practical Reason*

Two things fill the mind with ever new and increasing admiration and awe, the oftener and the more steadily we reflect on them: the starry heavens above and the moral law within②.

—— *Critique of Pure Reason*, conclusion

I am never to act otherwise than so that I could also will that my maxim should become a universal law③.

—— *Groundwork of the metaphysics of morals*, sec. 1

Finally, there is an imperative which commands a certain conduct immediately, without having as its condition any other purpose to be attained by it. This imperative is Categorical — This imperative may be called that of Morality④.

—— sec. 2

In Kant's moral theory, the categorical imperative is the absolute moral law understood as a duty by any rational creature.

---

① 道德并不是专门指导我们如何取得幸福的原理,而是使我们如何堪与幸福相称的原理。——《实践理性批判》

② 有两样东西使我心中不断充满崇拜和敬畏,使我越来越不断地进行思考:头顶的星空和心中的道德律。——《纯粹理性批判》结束语

③ 我必须这样行动,而不能采用另一种方式,因为我要求我的行为准则成为一种普遍的法则。——《道德的形而上学论》,第1节

④ 最后,有一种紧迫的责任心要求我们迅速做出某种行动,而不以其他任何目的作为先决条件。这种责任是绝对的——这种责任可称为道德法则。——第2节

Greatest Good of the Greatest Number
—— Mill

Chapter 10

I should say that from about 1860—65 or thereabouts he (John Mill) ruled England in the region of thought as very few men ever did: I do not expect to see anything like it again.

—— Henry Sidgwick

In this chapter
- Getting to know John Stuart Mill
- Laying out Mill's utilitarian doctrines
- Appreciating Mill's political philosophy

John Stuart Mill

　　Mill (1806—1873) was born into an intellectually privileged family in London, the son of the well-known political theorist James Mill. When young he was notably precocious and received a remarkably thorough education at home. Later he turned out to be, as his father had hoped, an effective spokesman for the utilitarian outlook that had been developed by his father's friend Jeremy Bentham (1748—1832). After years of intense study, Mill suffered a psychological breakdown at 20. He left the university to work for the East India Company where he stayed until his retirement, as it gave him a living and time to write. Mill developed a very close relationship with Harriet Taylor and eventually married her. As a feminist, Taylor greatly influenced his thinking, and inspired his late work the Subjection of Woman, in which he strongly advocates women's suffrage.

Mill is regarded as one of the most outstanding thinkers of the nineteenth century. Rather than an ivory tower philosophy dealing with the most abstract of philosophical topics, he is one of enduring interest because it reflects how a fine mind struggles with and attempts to synthesize important intellectual and cultural movements. His work has contributed to many areas of philosophy, including logic, metaphysics, and epistemology. His ideas, especially his utilitarian-inspired philosophy are hugely influential in social, political, philosophical, and economic thinking well into the 20th century.

Distinctive insights[①]

Mill writes on many topics, but his most widely known doctrines are to be found in his two short books: *On Liberty* (1859) and *Utilitarianism* (1863). His main ideas are as follows:

1. Distinction between Happiness and Contentment

Mill's famous formulation of utilitarianism is known as the "greatest-happiness principle". It holds that one must always act so as to produce the greatest happiness for the greatest number of people, within reason. While he agrees with Bentham[②] that pleasure is intrinsically valuable, he argues with Bentham that not all pleasures are qualitatively equal. Some, he says, are just better than others: the "higher" intellectual and moral pleasures are certainly to be valued superior to the "lower" physical forms of pleasure. He distinguishes between happiness and contentment, claiming that the former is of higher value than the latter, a belief wittily encapsulated in the statement that "it is better to be a human being dissatisfied than a pig satisfied; better to be Socrates dissatisfied than a fool satisfied. And if the fool, or the pig, is of a different opinion, it is because they only know their own side of the question." This is, perhaps, in direct contrast with Bentham's statement that "Pushpin is as good as Poetry". Mill's argument is that the "simple pleasures" tend to be preferred by people who have no experience with high art, and are therefore not in a proper position to judge. Thus, while Mill agrees with Bentham that people seek to maximize their pleasures, unlike Bentham he also holds that not all ends are selfish, and that pleasures are not only quantitatively but also qualitatively distinct.

2. The Harm Principle

Mill places the individual, rather than society, at the center of his utilitarian philosophy. He strongly defends the so-called "harm principle", which says that the only legitimate reason for anyone, including governments, to limit a person's freedom is to prevent harm to others. That is to say, each individual ought to be free to think and act as he wishes, so long as his actions do not harm others. If the action is self-regarding, or, if

---

① 穆勒的哲学思想接近休谟的经验论和孔德的实证论,认为感觉是唯一的实在。在道德和政治观念上是功利主义者,拥护边沁的学说。在政治经济学上,主张在保存资本主义所有制下,通过分配关系的改革,实现社会改良。对逻辑归纳法有一定贡献。

② 边沁(1748—1832),英国功利主义哲学家、经济学家和社会改革者。

it only directly affects the person undertaking the action, then society has no right to intervene, even if it feels the actor is harming himself. He does argue, however, that individuals are prevented from doing lasting, serious harm to themselves or their property by the harm principle. Because no one exists in isolation, harm done to oneself also harms others, and destroying property deprives the community as well as oneself.

Mill sees any restriction of the individual's freedom to pursue happiness as a tyranny, whether this is the collective tyranny of the majority (through democratic election) or a singular rule of a despot. He therefore suggests practical measures to restrict the power of society over the individual, and to protect the rights of the individual to free expression.

Social liberty, in Mill's view, means putting limits on the ruler's power so that he would not be able to use his power on his own wishes and make decisions which can harm society. That is to say, people should have the right to have a say in the government's decisions. He claims that social liberty was "the nature and limits of the power that can be legitimately exercised by society over the individual". It was attempted in two ways: by obtaining recognition of certain immunities, called liberties or rights; and by establishment of a system of constitutional checks.

3. The Laissez-faire① Economic Policy

Mill supports the laissez faire economic policies that had been defended by earlier economists such as David Ricardo②, as his overall concern is here as else where with self development. He sees the system of wages that had developed in the industrial revolution as one which robbed the workers of any interest in the goods that they were producing. He therefore attempts to make the radical proposal that the whole wage system be abolished, and that it be replaced by a cooperative system in which the producers would act in combinations, collectively owning the capital necessary for carrying on their operations, and working under managers who would be responsible overall to them. He believes that profits in the long run would tend to diminish and that the formation of new capital would thereby come to an end. This would bring industry to a halt and population to a stationary level. The result would be a relatively static form of society, in which, Mill hopes, people's thoughts would turn from concerns of self-interest to more socially and humanly worthy ends. In such society, many of our present problems would disappear.

4. Legislating for Liberty

While Mill is respectful of the teachings of religious leaders such as Jesus, he holds that the institutions of government and of economy, like those of religion should all be subjected to criticism based on the principle of utility: Do they contribute to human welfare? Are there any alternatives that could do better? For Mill, government is not a matter of natural rights or social contract, as in many forms of liberalism. Forms of government, according to him, are to be evaluated in terms of their capacity to enable

---

① laissez-faire：放任政策；不干涉主义。
② 李嘉图 (1772—1823)，英国古典经济学家。

each person to exercise and develop in his or her own way their capacities for higher forms of human happiness. Such development will be an end for each individual, but also a means for society as a whole to develop and to make life better for all. Mill thus argues that a free-market economy has many benefits but that the defects, in terms of poverty for many resulting from private ownership of the means of production may imply that we should institute the alternative of socialism or public ownership of the means of production. He similarly argues for the utility of liberty as a social institution: under such a social order individuality will be encouraged, and this individuality in turn tends to produce innovations in knowledge, technology, and morality that contribute significantly to improving the general welfare. Conversely, institutions and traditions that stifle individuality, as religious institutions often do, should gradually be reformed, and democratic representative government with a legal system of rights should be set up to defend individuals from the tyranny of public opinion and of the majority.

5. Status of Women

Among the things for which Mill campaigns are women's rights, women's suffrage, and equal access for women to education and to occupations. *The Subjection of Women*[①] shows how Mill appeals to both the patent injustice of contemporary familial arrangements and to the negative moral impact of those arrangements on the people within them. In particular, he discusses the ways in which the subordination of women negatively affects not only the women, but also the men and children in the family. This subordination stunts the moral and intellectual development of women by restricting their field of activities, pushing them either into self-sacrifice or into selfishness and pettiness. Men, to the contrary, either become brutal through their relationships with women or turn away from projects of self-improvement to pursue the social "consideration" that women desire. He was therefore led to the conclusion that women's votes are needed precisely to check the pursuit of male self-interest. More generally, equality is essential if the interest of the family as such is to be served, rather than making the family serve male-interest as had hitherto been the case. Changing the relation between men and women to one of equality will force both parties to curb their self-interest and broaden their social sympathies to include others. Thus, women's suffrage is an essential step toward the moral improvement of humankind.

Introductory remarks

Mill believes that human happiness is the only thing which is intrinsically valuable — that it is the one thing that every human being wants, and that our desire for happiness is the root behind all other desires. For example, we may want a bicycle, or an education, or a chocolate cake, but we want these things because we believe they will make us happy.

---

① 《女性的屈从》(1869)。该书为当时英国妇女所处的无权地位大声疾呼,批评了当时的政治和社会制度,要求给予妇女同男人平等的受教育权、工作权和选举权。

Therefore, the right conduct is that which tends to maximize happiness.

Mill's book *Utilitarianism*① is a philosophical defense of utilitarianism in ethics. The original book is divided into five chapters: namely, 1. General Remarks; 2. What Utilitarianism Is; 3. Of the Ultimate Sanction of the Principle of Utility; 4. Of What Sort of Proof the Principle of Utility is Susceptible; and 5. On the Connection between Justice and Utility. The following selection is taken from the second chapter, in which Mill attempts to clarify the utilitarian standard in order to formulate a single ethical principle, that is, human happiness is the only thing which is intrinsically valuable, and right conduct is that which tends to maximize happiness.

Text

What Utilitarianism Is (excerpt)

The creed which accepts as the foundation of morals, Utility, or the Greatest Happiness Principle, holds that actions are right in proportion as they tend to promote happiness, wrong as they tend to produce the reverse of happiness②. By happiness is intended pleasure, and the absence of pain; by unhappiness, pain, and the privation of pleasure. To give a clear view of the moral standard set up by the theory, much more requires to be said; in particular, what things it includes in the ideas of pain and pleasure; and to what extent this is left an open question③. But these supplementary explanations do not affect the theory of life on which this theory of morality is grounded—namely, that pleasure, and freedom from pain, are the only things desirable as ends; and that all desirable things (which are as numerous in the utilitarian as in any other scheme) are desirable either for the pleasure inherent in themselves, or as means to the promotion of pleasure and the prevention of pain.

Now, such a theory of life excites in many minds, and among them in some of the most estimable in feeling and purpose, inveterate dislike④. To suppose that life has (as they express it) no higher end than pleasure—no better and nobler object of desire and pursuit—they designate as utterly mean and grovelling; as a doctrine worthy only of swine, to whom the followers of Epicurus were, at a very early period, contemptuously likened; and modern holders of the doctrine are occasionally made the subject of equally

---

① 《功利主义》(1861),穆勒一方面继承了边沁的功利原则,认为最大幸福是任何行为的目的,但另一方面,却反对边沁的快乐只有量的区别的主张。边沁的功利主义重视当事人的功利,而穆勒则更重视的是总体功利。

② The creed which... happiness. 把"功利"或"最大幸福"作为道德基础的信仰认为:正确的行动和促进幸福的程度成比例;错误的行动则和导致不幸成比例。

③ what things it includes... question:痛苦和快乐的概念所包含的内容及其程度这一问题还悬而未决。

④ Such a theory of life... inveterate dislike:这样的生活理论引起了许多人的思考,包括那些在感情上和目的上最值得尊敬的人士的根深蒂固的反感。inveterate:根深蒂固的。

polite comparisons by its German, French, and English assailants①.

When thus attacked, the Epicureans have always answered, that it is not they, but their accusers, who represent human nature in a degrading light; since the accusation supposes human beings to be capable of no pleasures except those of which swine are capable②. If this supposition were true, the charge could not be gainsaid, but would then be no longer an imputation③; for if the sources of pleasure were precisely the same to human beings and to swine, the rule of life which is good enough for the one would be good enough for the other. The comparison of the Epicurean life to that of beasts is felt as degrading, precisely because a beast's pleasures do not satisfy a human being's conceptions of happiness④. Human beings have faculties more elevated than the animal appetites, and when once made conscious of them, do not regard anything as happiness which does not include their gratification. I do not, indeed, consider the Epicureans to have been by any means faultless in drawing out their scheme of consequences from the utilitarian principle⑤. To do this in any sufficient manner, many Stoic, as well as Christian elements require to be included⑥. But there is no known Epicurean theory of life which does not assign to the pleasures of the intellect, of the feelings and imagination, and of the moral sentiments, a much higher value as pleasures than to those of mere sensation. It must be admitted, however, that utilitarian writers in general have placed the superiority of mental over bodily pleasures chiefly in the greater permanency, safety, uncostliness, etc., of the former — that is, in their circumstantial advantages rather than in their intrinsic nature⑦. And on all these points utilitarians have fully proved their case; but they might have taken the other, and, as it may be called, higher ground, with entire consistency. It is quite compatible with the principle of utility to recognize the fact, that some kinds of pleasure are more desirable and more valuable than others. It would be absurd that while, in estimating all other things, quality is considered as well as quantity,

---

① as a doctrine worthy... German, French, and English assailants：猪是早期对伊壁鸠鲁信徒们的鄙夷比喻；伊壁鸠鲁学说的现代信奉者，也不时被德国、法国和英国的攻击者们用于类似文雅比喻的主体。Epicurus：伊壁鸠鲁（c. 341—270 B. C.）是古希腊唯物主义哲学家，伊壁鸠鲁学派创始人。contemptuously：鄙夷地；assailants：攻击者。

② When thus attacked... swine are capable：遭到这样的抨击时，伊壁鸠鲁主义者总是回敬道，既然这些谴责者假设人类除了猪能感到的快感外别无其他快乐，那么不是他们，而是这些攻击者自己贬低了人的本性。

③ If this supposition... an imputation：如果该假设成立，对伊壁鸠鲁主义者的攻击虽然不能被否定，却不再是一种诋毁。gainsay：否定；imputation：诋毁。

④ The comparison... conception of happiness：将伊壁鸠鲁主义式生活比作野兽的生活是对人的贬低，因为野兽的快感不能满足人们对幸福的种种看法。

⑤ ... the Epicureans to have... the utilitarian principle：伊壁鸠鲁主义者从功利主义原则得到其结构框架的做法是无懈可击的。

⑥ To do this... require to be included：为了充分做到这一点，需要将基督教以及斯多葛派的许多观点包括在内。Stoic：斯多葛学派，由芝诺（Zeno c. 336-264 B. C.）于公元前 300 年左右在雅典创立。

⑦ It must be admitted... rather than in their intrinsic nature：必须承认，功利主义论述者一般将精神快乐置于肉体快乐之上，主要认为前者更具有持久性、安全性、节俭性等特点，换言之，主要考虑其外部的有利因素，而不是内在的本质。place the superiority of... over...：将……置于重要地位。

the estimation of pleasures should be supposed to depend on quantity alone①.

If I am asked, what I mean by difference of quality in pleasures, or what makes one pleasure more valuable than another, merely as a pleasure, except its being greater in amount, there is but one possible answer. Of two pleasures, if there be one to which all or almost all who have experience of both give a decided preference, irrespective of any feeling of moral obligation to prefer it, that is the more desirable pleasure. If one of the two is, by those who are competently acquainted with both, placed so far above the other that they prefer it, even though knowing it to be attended with a greater amount of discontent②, and would not resign it for any quantity of the other pleasure which their nature is capable of, we are justified in ascribing to the preferred enjoyment a superiority in quality, so far outweighing quantity as to render it, in comparison, of small account.

Now it is an unquestionable fact that those who are equally acquainted with, and equally capable of appreciating and enjoying, both, do give a most marked preference to the manner of existence which employs their higher faculties③. Few human creatures would consent to be changed into any of the lower animals, for a promise of the fullest allowance of a beast's pleasures④; no intelligent human being would consent to be a fool, no instructed person would be an ignoramus⑤, no person of feeling and conscience would be selfish and base⑥, even though they should be persuaded that the fool, the dunce, or the rascal is better satisfied with his lot than they are with theirs. They would not resign what they possess more than he for the most complete satisfaction of all the desires which they have in common with him. If they ever fancy they would, it is only in cases of unhappiness so extreme, that to escape from it they would exchange their lot for almost any other, however undesirable in their own eyes. A being of higher faculties requires more to make him happy, is capable probably of more acute suffering, and certainly accessible to it at more points, than one of an inferior type⑦; but in spite of these liabilities, he can never really wish to sink into what he feels to be a lower grade of existence...

I have dwelt on this point, as being a necessary part of a perfectly just conception of Utility or Happiness, considered as the directive rule of human conduct. But it is by no means an indispensable condition to the acceptance of the utilitarian standard; for that standard is not the agent's own greatest happiness, but the greatest amount of happiness

---

① It would be absurd... depend on quantity alone 在评价其他所有事物时一并考虑质量和数量,而评价快乐时却只依赖数量,这样的做法将会是荒诞的

② If one of the two is... with a greater amount of discontent:如果对两种快乐都十分熟悉的人对其中之一的估价远远高于另外一种,即便知道前者会带来更多的不愉快而选择前者....。be acquainted with:对……熟悉。

③ Now it is an unquestionable... employs their higher faculties:那些熟悉并且能够欣赏和享受两种快乐的人明显地喜欢那种可运用其高等官能的生活方式,这已是一个不容置疑的事实。

④ the fullest allowance of a beast's pleasures:动物的全部快感。allowance:限额;定量。

⑤ an ignoramus:浑噩无知的人;笨蛋。

⑥ be selfish and base:自私和卑鄙。base:卑劣的;卑怯的;可鄙的。

⑦ A being of higher faculties... than one of an inferior type:与只有低等官能的人相比,一个具有高等官能的人需要更多的东西来使自己快乐,可能会感觉到更为剧烈的痛苦,而且肯定在更多方面受到痛苦的影响。

altogether; and if it may possibly be doubted whether a noble character is always the happier for its nobleness, there can be no doubt that it makes other people happier, and that the world in general is immensely a gainer by it①. Utilitarianism, therefore, could only attain its end by the general cultivation of nobleness of character, even if each individual were only benefited by the nobleness of others, and his own, so far as happiness is concerned, were a sheer deduction from the benefit. But the bare enunciation of such an absurdity as this last, renders refutation superfluous...

According to the greatest happiness principle, as above explained, the ultimate end, with reference to and for the sake of which all other things are desirable—whether we are considering our own good or that of other people is an existence exempt as far as possible from pain, and as rich as possible in enjoyments, both in point of quantity and quality; the test of quality and the rule for measuring it against quantity being the preference felt by those who, in their opportunities of experience, to which must be added their habits of self-consciousness and self-observation, are best furnished with the means of comparison②. This, being according to the utilitarian opinion the end of human action, is necessarily also the standard of morality, which may accordingly be defined "the rules and precepts for human conduct," by the observance of which an existence such as has been described might be, to the greatest extent possible, wecured to all mankind; and not to them only, but, so far as the nature of things admits, to the whole sentient creation...

Brainstorming

1. Can pleasure or happiness be measured? How does Mill define happiness? How does this affect utility as a measuring device?

2. Is happiness our only goal? Can we — and should we — be motivated by a desire to promote the greatest happiness?

3. Do you agree with Mill's claim that "It's better to be a human being dissatisfied than a pig satisfied; better to be Socrates dissatisfied than a fool satisfied?" Why or why not?

4. Does utilitarianism justify unethical actions?

5. Pamela is walking through the forest when she happens upon a man who is about to kill five people. He tells her that if she kills one of those people, he will let the other four go free. Pamela has reason to believe he will keep his promise. What would Mill say she should do, and why? If you disagree with Mill, explain why.

6. Evaluate the following:

a. Happiness is good independently of who has it. We should work to achieve the good. Therefore, I should work to achieve your good as well as my own.

---

① if it may possibly be doubted...immensely a gainer by it: 如果有人可能怀疑一个高尚角色是否因其高尚性而更为幸福，那么，毫无疑问的是，他使其他人更为幸福，而且世界从整体上讲，会因其存在而大为受益。

② in their opportunities of experience...means of comparison: 有人在其经验机会中拥有最好的比较手段，除此之外还需加上他们的自我意识和自我观察习惯。

b. "Why is it immoral to produce a value and keep it, but moral to give it away? And if it is not moral for you to keep a value when you give it, are they not selfish and vicious when they take it? Does virtue consist of serving vice?"

Supplementary reading

In 1859 John Stuart Mill published what many consider the most important and persuasive defense of personal freedom and individuality in his essay, *On Liberty*①. Mill argues that society has no right to interfere in the affairs of the individual beyond what is required for the protection of others.

Limited Government: The Utilitarian Approach (excerpt)

A time, however, came, in the progress of human affairs, when men ceased to think it a necessity dependent power, opposed in interest to themselves. It appeared to them much better that the various magistrates of the state should be their tenants or delegates, revocable at their pleasure. In that way alone, it seemed, could they have complete security that the powers of government would never be abused to their disadvantage. By degrees this new demand for elective and temporary rulers became the prominent object of the exertions if the popular party, wherever any such party existed; and superseded, to a considerable extent, the previous efforts to limit the power of rules. As the struggle proceeded for making the ruling power emanate from the periodical choice of the ruled, some persons began to think that too much importance had been attached to the limitation of the power itself. That (it might seem) was a resource against rulers whose interests were habitually opposed to those of the people.

What was now wanted was, that the rulers should be identified with the people; that their interest and will should be the interest and will of the nation. The nation did not need to be protected against its own will. There was no fear of its tyrannizing over itself. Let the rulers be effectually responsible to it, promptly removable by it, and it could afford to trust them with power of which it could itself dictate the use to be made. Their power was but the nation's power, concentrated, and in a form convenient for exercises.

But in political and philosophical theories, as well as in persons, success discloses faults and infirmities which failure might have concealed from observation. The notion that the people have no need to limit their power over themselves, might seem axiomatic when popular government was a thing only dreamed about, or read of having existing at some distant period of past. Neither was that notion necessarily disturbed by such temporary aberrations as those of the French Revolution, the worst of which were the work of a usurping few, and which, in any case, belonged not to the permanent working

---

① 《论自由》(1859)，从自由主义观点出发，反对绝对的个人自由，认为在不侵犯他人自由的基础上，个人有完全的行动自由，他人不能干涉。但当一个人的行为危害到他人利益时，应受社会的惩罚。

of popular institutions, but to a sudden and convulsive outbreak against monarchical and aristocratic despotism. In time, however, a democratic republic came to occupy a large portion of the earth's surface, and made itself felt as one of the most powerful members of the community of nations; and elective and responsible government became subject to the observations and criticism which wait upon a great existing fact.

It was now perceived that such phrases as "self-government", and the "power of the people over themselves", do not express the true state of the case. The "people" who exercise the power are not always the same people with those over whom it is exercised; and the "self-government" spoken of is not the government of each by himself, but of each by all the rest. The will of the people, moreover, practically means the will of the most numerous or the most active part of the people; the majority, or those who succeed in making themselves accepted as the majority: the people, consequently may desire to oppress a part of their number, and precautions are as much needed against this as against any other abuse of power. The limitation, therefore, of the power of government over individuals loses none of its importance when the holders of power are regularly accountable to the community, that is, to the strongest party therein. This view of things, recommending itself equally to the intelligence of thinkers and to the inclination of those important classes in European society to whose real or supposed interests democracy is adverse, has had no difficulty in establishing itself; and in political speculations "the tyranny of the majority" is now generally included among the evils against which society requires to be on its safeguard.

Like other tyrannies, the tyranny of the majority was at first, and is still vulgarly, held in dread chiefly as operating through the acts of the public authorities. But reflecting persons perceived that when society is itself the tyrant — society collectively over the separate individuals who compose it — its means of tyrannizing are not restricted to the acts which it may do by the hands of its political functionaries. Society can and does execute its own mandates; and if it issues wrong mandates instead of right, or any mandates at all in things with which it ought not to meddle, it practices a social tyranny more formidable than many kinds of political oppression, since, though not usually upheld by such extreme penalties, it leaves fewer means of escape, penetrating much more deeply into the details of life, and enslaving the soul itself.

Protection, therefore, against the tyranny magistrate is not enough: there needs protection also against the tyranny of the prevailing opinion and feeling; against the tendency of society to impose, by other means than civil penalties, its own ideas and practices as rules of conduct on those who dissent from them; to fetter the development, and if possible, prevent the formation, of any individually not in harmony with its ways, and compel all characters to fashion themselves upon the model of its own. There is a limit to the legitimate interference of collective opinion with individual independence; and to find that limit, and maintain it against encroachment, is as indispensable to a good condition of human affairs, as protection against political despotism...

But there is a sphere of action in which society, as distinguished from the individual, has, if any, only an indirect interest; comprehending all that portion of a person's life and conduct which affects only himself, or if it also affects others, only with their free, voluntary, and undeceived consent and participation. When I say only himself, I mean directly, and in the first instance; for whatever affects himself, may affect others through himself; and the objection which may be grounded on this contingency, will receive consideration in the sequel.

This, then, is the appropriate region of human liberty. It comprises, first, the inward domain of consciousness; demanding liberty of conscience in the most comprehensive sense; liberty of thought and feeling; absolute freedom of opinion and sentiment on all subjects, practical or speculative, scientific, moral, or theological. The liberty of expressing and publishing opinions may seem to fall under a different principle, since it belongs to that part of the conduct of an individual which concerns other people; but, being almost of as much importance as the liberty of thought itself, and resting in great part on the same reason, is practically inseparable from it. Secondly, the principle requires liberty of tastes and pursuits; of framing the plan of our life to suit our own character; of doing as we like, subject to such consequences as may follow: without impediment from our fellow-creatures, so long as what we do does not harm them, even though they should think our conduct foolish, perverse, or wrong. Thirdly, from this liberty of each individual, follows the liberty, within the same limits, of combination among individuals; freedom to unite for any purpose not involving harm to others: the persons combining being supposed to be of full age, and not forced or deceived.

No society in which these liberties are not, on the whole, respected, is free, whatever may be its form of government; and none is completely free in which they do not exist absolute and unqualified. The only freedom which deserves the name, is that of pursuing our own good in our own way, so long as we do not attempt to deprive others of theirs, or impede their efforts to obtain it. Each is the proper guardian of his own health, whether bodily, or mental and spiritual...

Famous quotations

Ask yourself whether you are happy, and you cease to be so①.

—— *Autobiography*, ch. 5

As often as a study is cultivated by narrow minds, they will draw from it narrow conclusions②.

—— *Auguste Comte and Positivism*, p. 82

The sole end for which mankind is warranted, individually or collectively, in interfering with the liberty of action of any of their number, is self-protection.③

—— *On Liberty*, ch. 1

---

① 问你自己是否幸福,你就不会再这样。——《自传》,第 5 章
② 由心地狭隘的人所从事的研究往往只得出狭隘的结论。——《奥古斯特·孔德与实证主义》,第 82 页。
③ 保障人类在个人或集体的事物上有权干预任何一个成员的行动自由的唯一宗旨乃是自我保护。——《论自由》,第 1 章

If all mankind minus one, were of one opinion, and only one person were of the contrary opinion, mankind would be no more justified in silencing that one person, than he, if he had the power, would be justified in silencing mankind.①

—— ch. 2

The liberty of the individual must be thus far limited; he must not make himself a nuisance to other people.②

—— ch. 3

Everyone who receives the protection of society owes a return for the benefit.③

—— ch. 4

Liberty consists in doing what one desires.④

—— ch. 5

The great majority of those who speak of perfectibility as a dream, do so because they feel that it is one which would afford them no pleasure if it were realized⑤.

—— *Speech on Perfectibility*

The moral regeneration of mankind will only really commence, when the most fundamental of the social relations (marriage) is placed under the rule of equal justice, and when human beings learn to cultivate their strongest sympathy with an equal in rights and cultivation⑥.

—— ch. 4

The kind-hearted Samaritan helps his enemy in a biblical parable that demonstrates Mill's golden rule: to do as one would be done by, and to love one's neighbor as oneself. This spirit constitutes the ideal perfection of utilitarian morality, and by doing so, Mill believes, the overall level of happiness of society would be greatly enhanced.

---

① 如果除一人外所有人的意见是一致的,只有一人持相反的意见,那么压制这个人的意见如同一个有权势的人压制群众的呼声一样是不正当的。——第 2 章

② 对于个人自由务必如此加以限制:他必须使自己不会成为害群之马。——第 3 章

③ 凡是接受社会保护的人应当给社会以报答。——第 4 章

④ 自由即是按照自己的意愿去工作。——第 5 章

⑤ 有些人把完美的境界称为梦想,其中的大多数人之所以这样说是因为他们认为这种境界一旦实现,也不会给他们带来什么好处。——《关于完美境界的讲演》

⑥ 当最根本的社会关系(婚姻)被置于平等公正的控制之下,当人类懂得培育自己对权利平等和教育平等的强烈同情心时,人类的道德复兴才会真正开始。——第 4 章

Truth and Usefulness
—— James

Chapter 11

It has sometimes crossed my mind that James wanted to be a poet and an artist, and that there lay in him, beneath the ocean of metaphysics, a lost Atlantis of fine arts; and that he really hated philosophy and all its works, and pursued them only as Hercules might spin or as a prince in a fairy tale sorts seeds for an evil dragon, or as anyone might patiently do some careful work for which he had no aptitude.

—— *John J. Chapman*

In this chapter
- Glimpsing James' life
- Surveying James' basic pragmatic doctrines
- Assessing determinism

William James

Born and brought up in a wealthy and intellectual family in New York City, William James (1842—1910) was the eldest of five children. His father was a famously eccentric theologian, and his brother Henry became a well-known author. His real schooling took place in the family home where intelligent and learned friends frequently came to engage in discussions on a wide range of topics. He attended schools in Switzerland, Germany, France and England, and later attended Harvard as a medical student. But his studies at Harvard were interrupted by poor health and depression resulting from the overwork during his childhood. He eventually graduated in 1872 and took a teaching post at Harvard until his retirement there in 1907.

James interacted with a wide array of writers and scholars throughout his life. Being the major American philosopher of his day, he adopted and developed the pragmatic philosophy. His influential works on the young science of psychology, educational psychology, psychology of religious experience and mysticism, and on the philosophy of pragmatism, have been collected in a massive nineteen-volume critical edition, which can be seen as an imaginative vestibule into the 20th century. His ideas resonate in the work of many contemporary philosophers such as Royce, Husserl, Dewey, and Wittgenstein.

Distinctive insights[①]

William James was the major American philosopher of his day. He adopts and has developed the philosophy of pragmatism, first expounded by his fellow American Charles Sanders Peirce. At the heart of his thought is an acceptance of the plurality, flux and indefiniteness of all things and a candid, common-sense attitude towards every aspect of ordinary human experience. His main ideas are as follows:

1. Truth and Goodness

James maintains that if an idea "works" it is a true idea; in so far as it makes a difference to life it is meaningful. The truth of an idea depends on how useful it is; that is to say, whether or not it does what it requires of it. If an idea does not contradict the known facts, such as law and science, and it does provide a means of predicting things accurately enough for our purposes, then there can be no reason not to consider it true. Therefore, truth for James, is not a fixed and unchanging absolute that is independent of human cognition of it but is invented or created by means of human activity. Moreover, truth and goodness are closely connected: what is true turns out to be what is good. James's ultimate concern is a moral one. He wants to proclaim a philosophical method for living well as the beings we manifestly are.

2. The Stream of Thought[②]

James holds that the individual's personal viewpoint and attitude are of major importance in philosophy. His own writings reveal how brilliantly gifted he was in articulating with clarity and grace the precise "feel" of inward experiences. His famous work, *the Principles of Psychology*, amply exhibits his conviction that it is experience rather than theory, abstractions and traditional philosophy that is the key to a practical understanding of ourselves and the world. In the *Principles* he gives an account of mental

---

① 詹姆斯将皮尔士提出的实用主义基本思想系统化。自称其哲学为彻底经验论，它的任务是把贝克莱的思想贯穿到底。曾创用信仰意志一语。是机能心理学创始人之一，并与丹麦朗格先后提出詹姆斯—朗格情绪说。他提出的意识流概念在现代西方哲学、心理学、美学、文学艺术等方面有广泛影响。

② 意识流，指人的"原始的感觉混沌"（即人的内省经验）。詹姆士认为意识是不断流动的，每个人都可以根据自己的兴趣，从连续性的意识流中把他所注意的那一部分挑选出来，构成他自己的世界；每个人所谓的事物，只是他自己从意识流中划分出来的片断。

states, maintaining that they are engendered by physical states but that they also affect physical changes. He refuses to subscribe to a traditional dualism of the physical and mental but at the same time would not allow that the mental was reducible to the physical. Throughout the Principles his aim is to give a full description by means of introspective observation of mental states and activities, maintaining that the mind must be seen as an instrument for realizing purposes. Analysis of thought, or consciousness, James says, shows that every mental state belongs to a personal consciousness; that thought is continuous in the sense that even though one may sleep or lose consciousness, one's waking consciousness links back to one's pre-sleep consciousness; that thought is always changing in the sense that there are no identical recurring states; and consciousness is able to be selective of its objects. These claims are backed up by descriptions which are wonderfully perspicuous, apt and detailed.

3. The Will to Believe[①]

"The Will to Believe" is aimed at defending our right, in certain cases, to adopt a belief even without prior evidence of its truth, in particular, our right to adopt religious belief even if we lack sufficient evidence of its truth. James' central argument in "The Will to Believe" focuses on the idea that for certain beliefs, their truth, or at least our access to evidence of the truth, depends crucially on our first adopting them as beliefs on insufficient evidence (e.g., sometimes it is only through believing upon insufficient evidence that I can do something, or that I will come to possess the confidence I need to do it). James then argues that in virtue of this dependency, that a believer is rational in adopting a belief of this limited sort even if they are lacking sufficient evidence of the belief's truth before adopting it. James then extends this result into a defense of a believer's right to religious belief even upon insufficient evidence on the grounds that religious belief is dependent in this way.

4. James-Lange Theory of Emotion[②]

This theory combined the ideas of William James and Danish physiologist Carl Lange, who largely independently arrived at the same conclusion. According to them, we have experiences, as a result, our autonomic nervous system creates physiological events such as muscular tension, heart rate increases, perspiration, dryness of the mouth, etc. This theory proposes that emotions happen as a result of these, rather than being the cause of them. The sequence thus is as follows: Event ⇒ arousal ⇒ interpretation ⇒ emotion. The bodily sensation prepares us for action, as in the Fight-or-Flight reaction. Emotions grab our attention and at least attenuate slower cognitive processing.

---

① 信仰意志,指将幻想视同实在的主观愿望。詹姆斯认为人们的行为往往不为理智所支配,而为信仰所决定。人们信仰的东西往往是他们从主观愿望和意向出发而信以为真的东西。只要人们具有信仰意志,信仰这些东西(如上帝的存在、灵魂不朽等)而得到精神上的满足或安慰,那么这些东西就是真实的。信仰意志无法证明,无法推翻,因而宗教必须永远存在。

② 詹姆斯—朗格情绪(1884),由詹姆斯和丹麦朗格(Carl Georg Lange, 1834—1900)在19世纪后期提出。认为情绪是生理变化(如脉搏、血液循环、呼吸等)的主观经验,没有生理变化,便没有情绪体验。詹姆斯说:"我们因为哭,所以愁,因为动手打,所以生气;并不是我们愁了才哭,生气了才打。"此说反对传统的情绪先于并导致身体的变化的情绪学说。

Introductory remarks

James holds a world view in line with pragmatism. His *Pragmaticism*: *A New Name for Some Old Way of Thinking*① consists of eight chapters, declaring that the value of any truth was utterly dependent upon its use to the person who holds it. Our present reading is an excerpt taken from Chapter II *What Pragmatism Means*, in which James explains the pragmatic method and its consequences, advocating its usefulness in understanding what we take to be true belief. He holds that to have a belief is to have certain rules for action. Any and every notion has its own set of practical consequences.

Text

What Pragmatism Means (excerpt)

There is absolutely nothing new in the pragmatic method. Socrates was an adept at it. Aristotle used it methodically. Locke, Berkeley and Hume made momentous contributions to truth by its means. Shadworth Hodgson keeps insisting that realities are only what they are 'known-as.' But these forerunners of pragmatism used it in fragments: they were preluders only. Not until in our time has it generalized itself, become conscious of a universal mission, pretended to a conquering destiny. I believe in that destiny, and I hope I may end by inspiring you with my belief.

Pragmatism represents a perfectly familiar attitude in philosophy, the empiricist attitude, but it represents it, as it seems to me, both in a more radical and in a less objectionable form than it has ever yet assumed. A pragmatist turns his back resolutely and once for all upon a lot of inveterate habits dear to professional philosophers. He turns away from abstraction and insufficiency, from verbal solutions, from bad *a priori* reasons, from fixed principles, closed systems, and pretended absolutes and origins.② He turns towards concreteness and adequacy, towards facts, towards action, and towards power. That means the empiricist temper regnant, and the rationalist temper sincerely given up.③ It means the open air and possibilities of nature, as against dogma, artificiality and the pretence of finality in truth.

At the same time it does not stand for any special results. It is a method only. But the general triumph of that method would mean an enormous change in what I called in my last lecture the 'temperament' of philosophy. Teachers of the ultra-rationalistic type would be frozen out, much as the courtier type is frozen out in republics, as the

---

① 《实用主义：旧的思维方法之新名称》。

② A pragmatist turns his... pretended absolutes and origins: 实用主义坚决、断然地抛弃了职业哲学家的许多积习。它避免了由于仅在字面纠结、抽劣的先验理由、墨守成规的原则、故步自封的体系，以及矫饰的绝对和本原所导致的抽象的不恰当的研究方法。inveterate: 根深蒂固的，顽固不化的；

③ That means the empiricist... sincerely given up. 这意味着经验主义气质占了统治地位，而理性主义气质却老老实实地甘拜下风。regnant: 占优势的；强大的。

ultramontane type of priest is frozen out in protestant lands①. Science and metaphysics would come much nearer together, would in fact work absolutely hand in hand.

Metaphysics has usually followed a very primitive kind of quest. You know how men have always hankered② after unlawful magic, and you know what a great part, in magic, words have always played. If you have his name, or the formula of incantation that binds him, you can control the spirit, genie, afrite, or whatever the power may be. Solomon knew the names of all the spirits, and having their names, he held them subject to his will③. So the universe has always appeared to the natural mind as a kind of enigma④, of which the key must be sought in the shape of some illuminating or power—bringing word or name. That word names the universe's principle, and to possess it is, after a fashion, to possess the universe itself. 'God,' 'Matter,' 'Reason,' 'the Absolute,' 'Energy,' are so many solving names. You can rest when you have them. You are at the end of your metaphysical quest.

But if you follow the pragmatic method, you cannot look on any such word as closing your quest. You must bring out of each word its practical cash-value⑤, set it at work within the stream of your experience. It appears less as a solution, then, than as a program for more work, and more particularly as an indication of the ways in which existing realities may be changed. Theories thus become instruments, not answers to enigmas, in which we can rest. We don't lie back upon them, we move forward, and, on occasion, make nature over again by their aid⑥. Pragmatism unstiffens all our theories, limbers them up⑦ and sets each one at work. Being nothing essentially new, it harmonizes with many ancient philosophic tendencies. It agrees with nominalism for instance, in always appealing to particulars; with utilitarianism in emphasizing practical aspects; with positivism in its disdain for verbal solutions, useless questions, and metaphysical abstractions.⑧

All these, you see, are anti-intellectualist tendencies. Against rationalism as a pretension and a method, pragmatism is fully armed and militant⑨. But, at the outset, at

---

① Teachers of the ultra-rationalistic... in protestant lands: 极端理性主义倡导者们会遭到排斥,就像朝廷宦官在共和国里会被排斥一样,主张教皇绝对权力的神父在基督新教国家中会被排斥一样。ultra-rationalistic: 极端理性的,超理性的; courtier: 弄臣;ultramontane: 教皇至上论的;教皇绝对权利主义的。
② hanker: 渴望,热切希望。
③ If you have his name... subject to his will: 要是你们知道那些妖魔鬼怪的名字,或知道制服它们的符咒,你们就能控制住这些妖魔鬼怪或其他任何邪恶力量了。所罗门知道所有魔神的名字。正因如此,他能使他们服从他的意旨。incantation: 咒语,符咒;afrite: =afreet,阿拉伯神话中的恶魔,巨神;solomon: 所罗门,古以色列王国国王大卫之子,以智慧著称。
④ enigma: 费解的事物,未弄清楚的情况,令人困惑的处境。
⑤ cash-value: 兑现价值。
⑥ Theories thus become instruments... make nature over again by their aid: 因此理论成为我们可以依赖的工具,而不是谜语的答案。我们并不向后靠,依赖这种工具,而是向前进,有时借助这种工具去重新改变自然。
⑦ limber... up: 使……柔软。
⑧ It agrees with nominalism... and metaphysical abstractions: 比如在殊相问题上,实用主义和唯名主义一致;在强调实践方面,它和功利主义一致;在鄙弃一切字面纠缠、无用途问题和抽象的形而上学方面,它与实证主义一致。nominalism: 唯名论;disdain: 鄙视,鄙弃;positivism: 实证主义。
⑨ Against rationalism as a pretension... armed and militant: 实用主义全副武装,坚决反对把理性主义作为一种矫饰和方法。

least, it stands for no particular results. It has no dogmas, and no doctrines save its method. As the young Italian pragmatist Papini has well said, it lies in the midst of our theories, like a corridor in a hotel①. Innumerable chambers open out of it. In one you may find a man writing an atheistic volume; in the next someone on his knees praying for faith and strength; in a third a chemist investigating a body's properties. In a fourth a system of idealistic metaphysics is being excogitated②; in a fifth the impossibility of metaphysics is being shown. But they all own the corridor, and all must pass through it if they want a practicable way of getting into or out of their respective rooms.

No particular results then, so far, but only an attitude of orientation, is what the pragmatic method means. The attitude of looking away from first things, principles, 'categories,' supposed necessities; and of looking towards last things, fruits, consequences, facts.

So much for the pragmatic method! You may say that I have been praising it rather than explaining it to you, but I shall presently explain it abundantly enough by showing how it works on some familiar problems. Meanwhile the word pragmatism has come to be used in a still wider sense, as meaning also a certain theory of truth. I mean to give a whole lecture to the statement of that theory, after first paving the way, so I can be very brief now. But brevity is hard to follow, so I ask for your redoubled attention for a quarter of an hour. If much remains obscure, I hope to make it clearer in the later lectures.

Brainstorming

1. According to William James, what kind of attitude is the "empiricist attitude"?
2. How to understand the sentence "it lies in the midst of our theories, like a corridor in a hotel"? What kind of Pragmatism's characteristic does it show?
3. What is the pragmatic method after all according to William James?
4. How Pragmatism works on some familiar problems?
5. James holds that there are times when we may legitimately allow our will, or what he calls our "passionate nature" — the total complex of our needs, interests, feelings and desires to influence what we believe, in this sense, what functions can religion serve today? Can human beings flourish, psychologically and socially, without religion, in his eyes?

Supplementary reading

For James, one cannot draw a conclusion, fix a belief, or hold to a moral or religious maxim unless all suggestions of an alternative position are explored. The following reading stresses the irreducibility of ambiguity, the presence of chance, and the desirability of tentativeness in our judgment.

---

① As the young Italian pragmatist Papini... like a corridor in a hotel: 意大利年轻的实用主义帕皮尼说得好,实用主义置身我们的各种理论之中,就象旅馆里的一条走廊。Papini: 帕皮尼(1881—1956),意大利诗人、作家。

② excogitate: 探索,对……深思熟虑。

The Dilemma of Determinism(excerpt)

To begin, I must suppose you are acquainted with all the usual arguments on the subject. I cannot stop to take up the old proofs from causation, from statistics, from the certainty with which we can foretell one another's conduct, from the fixity of character, and all the rest. But there are two words which usually encumber these classical arguments, and which we must immediately dispose of if we are to make any progress. One is the eulogistic word freedom, and the other is the opprobrious word chance.

The word "chance" I wish to keep, but I wish to get rid of the word "freedom". Its eulogistic associations have so far overshadowed all the rest of its meaning that both parties claim the sole right to use it, and determinists today insist that they alone are freedom's champions. Old-fashioned determinism was what we may call hard determinism. It did not shrink from such words as fatality, bondage and the like. Nowadays, we have a soft determinism which abhors harsh words, and, repudiating fatality, necessity, and even predetermination, says that its real name is freedom, for freedom is only necessity understood, and bondage to the highest is identical with true freedom.

Now, all this is a quagmire of evasion under which the real issue of fast has been entirely smothered. . . But there is a problem, an issue of fact and not of words, an issue of the most momentous importance, which is often decided without discussion in one sentence, — nay, in one clause of a sentence, — by those very writers who spin out whole chapters in their efforts to show what "true" freedom is; and that is the question of determinism, about which we are to talk tonight.

Fortunately, no ambiguities hang about this word or about its opposite, indeterminism. Both designate an outward way in which things may happen, and their cold and mathematical sound has no sentimental associations that can bribe our partiality either way in advance. Now, evidence of an external kind to decide between determinism and indeterminism is, as I intimated a while back, strictly impossible to find. Let us look at the difference them and see for ourselves. What does determinism profess?

It professes that those parts of the universe already laid down absolutely appoint and decree what the other parts shall be. The future has no ambiguous possibilities hidden in its womb: the part we call the present is compatible with only one totality. Any other future complement than the one fixed from eternity is impossible. The whole is in each and every part, and welds it with the rest into an absolute unity, an iron block, in which there can be no equivocation or shadow of turning.

Indeterminism, on the contrary, says that the parts have a certain amount of loose play on one another, so that the laying down of one of them does not necessarily determine what the others shall be. It admits that possibilities may in excess of actualities, and that things not yet revealed to our knowledge may really in themselves be ambiguous. Of two alternative futures which we conceive, both may now be really possible; and the one becomes impossible only at the very moment when the other excludes it by becoming real itself. Indeterminism thus denies the world to be one unbending unit of fact. It says there is a certain ultimate pluralism in it; and, so saying, it corroborates our ordinary unsophisticated view of things. To that view, actualities seem to float in a wider sea of possibilities from out of which they are chosen; and somewhere, indeterminism says, such possibilities exists, and form a path of truth.

Determinism, on the contrary, says they exist nowhere, and that necessity on the one hand and impossibility on the other are the sole categories of the real. Possibilities that fail to get realized are, for determinism, pure illusions: they never were possibilities at all. There is nothing inchoate, it says, about this universe of ours, all that was or is or shall be actual in it having been from eternity virtually there. The cloud of alternatives our minds escort this mass actuality withal is a cloud of sheer deceptions, to which "impossibilities" is the only name that rightfully belongs.

The issue, it will be seen, is a perfectly sharp one, which no eulogistic terminology can smear over or wipe out. The truth must lie with one side or the other, and its lying with one side makes the other false.

The question relates solely to the existence of possibilities, in the strict sense of the term, as things that may, but need not, be. Both sides admit that a volition, for instance, had occurred. The indeterminists say another volition might have occurred in its place; the determinists swear that nothing could possibly have occurred in its place. Now, can science be called in to tell us which of these two point-blank contradicters of each other is right? Science professes to draw no conclusions but such as are based on matters of fact, things that have actually happened; but how can any amount of assurance that something actually happened give us the least grain of information as to whether another thing might or might not have happened in its place? Only facts can be proved by other facts. With things that are possibilities and not facts, facts have no concern. If we have no other evidence than the evidence of existing facts, the possibility-question must remain a mystery never to be cleared up…

The sting of the word "chance" seems to lie in the assumption that it means something positive, and that if anything happens by chance, it must be something of an intrinsically irrational and preposterous sort. Now, chance means nothing of the kind. It is a purely negative and relative term, giving us no information about that of which it is predicated, except that it happens to be disconnected with something else — not controlled, secured or necessitated by other things in advance of its own actual presence. As this point is the most subtle one of the whole lecture, and at the same time the point on which all the rest hinges, I beg you to pay particular attention to it. What I say is that it tells us nothing about what a thing may in itself to call it "chance". It may be lucidity, transparency, fitness incarnate, matching the whole system of other things, when it has once befallen, in an unimaginably perfect way. All you mean by calling it "chance" is that this is not guaranteed, that it may also fall out otherwise.

Famous quotations

The moral flabbiness born of the bitch-godness SUCCESS. That — with the squalid cash

Chapter 11 Truth and Usefulness —— James

interpretation put on the word success — is our national disease①.
—— *Letter to H. G. Wells*, 11 Sept. 1906

Real culture lives by sympathies and admirations, not by dislikes and distains; under all misleading wrappings it pounces unerringly upon the human core②.
—— *Memories and Studies* (1911), *The Social Value of the College-Bred*

I think you will practically recognize the two types of mental make-up that I mean if I head the columns by the title "tender-mined" and "tough-minded" respectively③.
—— *Pragmatism*

Habit is... the enormous flywheel of society, its most precious conservative agent. It alone is what keeps us within the bounds of ordinance④.
—— *The Principle of Psychology*, ch. 4

Genius... means little more than the faculty of perceiving in an unhabitual way⑤.
—— ch. 19

The art of being wise is the art of knowing what to overlook⑥.
—— ch. 22

Waking consciousness, as we call it, it but one special type of consciousness, whilst all about it, parted from it by the flimsiest of screens, there lie potential forms of consciousness entirely different⑦.
—— *Varieties of Religious experience*

Be not afraid of life. Believe that life is worth living, and your belief will help create the fact⑧.
—— *The Will to Believe*. *Is Life Worth Living*?

The man engenders truth upon reality. The idea of a flat earth served well as a "truth" for several thousand years, despite the fact that Earth is a sphere. Thus, James claims that an idea's usefulness determines its truthfulness.

---

① 道德上的薄弱起源于对"成功"这位女财神的崇拜。以肮脏的金钱来解释"成功"这个词,这便是我们民族的疾患。——《致 H. G. 威尔斯》,1906 年 9 月 11 日。

② 真正的文化以同情和赞美为生,而不是以憎恶和轻蔑为生;在各种使人误解的包装下,它正确无误地奔向人类的内心。——《回忆与研究》,科班出身者的社会价值

③ 我认为实际上你会认识到人有两种心理属性,那就是我给专栏分别加上的标题:"理想型"和"务实型"。——《实用主义》

④ 习俗是……社会的巨大飞轮,是最难得的稳定力量。唯有它才能使我们都保持在传统习俗的范围之内。——《心理学原理》,第 4 章

⑤ 天才……不过是以一种非常规的方式观察事物的能力。——第 19 章

⑥ 智慧的艺术就是懂得该宽容什么的艺术。——第 22 章

⑦ 觉醒的意识,我们这样称呼它,只不过是艺术的一种特殊类型,而在这种意识周围,被极脆弱的屏障所隔开的是完全不同的各种潜在的意识形式。——《宗教体验种种》

⑧ 别害怕生活。要相信生活有自身价值。这种信念会帮助你创造现实。——《要深信不疑》,"生活有意义吗?"

Overturning Old Values
—— Nietzsche
Chapter 12

The degree of introspection achieved by Nietzsche had never been achieved by anyone.
—— Sigmund Freud

In this chapter
- Glimpsing the life of Nietzsche
- Appreciating Nietzsche's voluntarism and his philosophy of life
- Reevaluating Christian values

Friedrich Wilhelm Nietzsche

Born to a religious family in a small town in the Prussian province of Saxony, Nietzsche (1844—1900) was brought up by his mother, grandmother, and two aunts. His early education emphasized religion and classical languages and literature. At the age of 24, before he had even received his doctorate, he became a professor at Basel University. During his early years there he became intensely involved with the composer Richard Wagner, who influenced him strongly until Wagner's anti-semitism forced him to end their relationship. Owing to the deterioration of his health, Nietzsche had to resign his professorship after a decade at Basel, and spent the next ten years traveling in Europe. But he never recovered. He died at the age of 56.

Nietzsche was a radical and highly original thinker. He was prophetic, poetic and profoundly critical of philosophy as he found it. Much of his philosophy is a sustained attack on the belief that there is an objective world structure that is independent of any human apprehension of it. The arresting style and intensity of his writing have made his ideas extremely attractive. His short sentences have a poetic intensity that forces one to dwell on them and a vitality that is almost a physical presence on the page. His influence remains substantial within and beyond philosophy, notably in existentialism, nihilism and postmodernism. His style and radical questioning of the value and objectivity of truth have resulted in much commentary and interpretation from numerous philosophers. He has been called the philosopher's philosopher and also the non-philosopher's philosopher.

Distinctive insights[①]

Nietzsche's central idea is that man is something to be surpassed. "With a hammer", he attempts to shatter many of the most cherished views of the Western philosophical tradition, especially in relation to the three linked ideas in particular. They are, first, the idea of "man" or human nature; second, the idea we have of God; and third, the idea we have about morality, or ethics. His systematic theory could be summarized as follows:

1. Revaluation of all values[②]

Nietzsche indisputably insists upon the interpretive character of all human thought; and he calls for "new philosophers" who would follow him in engaging in more self-conscious and intellectually responsible attempts to assess and improve upon prevailing interpretations of human life. Deeply concerned with the present morality, Nietzsche asserts that Christianity, not merely as a religion but also as the predominant moral system of the Western world, in fact inverts nature, and is "hostile to life". As "the religion of pity", Christianity elevates the weak over the strong, exalting that which is "ill-constituted and weak" at the expense of that which is full of life and vitality. Thus, he makes much of the need for a revaluation of all accepted traditional values, and for attention to the problems of the nature, status, and standards of value and evaluation.

Like the existentialists, Nietzsche maintains that we make rather than discover values and meanings and that this making is brought about through actions which, cannot be justified or grounded in reasons. We have to separate ourselves from the meaningless flux of things and demand of ourselves what we can. By rejecting existing conventions we create new ideas and new values, and by exerting a "will to power" that embraces suffering as a means to rich experience we accept "truth" to fulfil the yearnings of the heart rather than the dictates of reason. This does not mean that Nietzsche is without respect for reason; indeed, he esteems it highly. But he regards the work of reason as well as the acquisition of scientific knowledge as a means to the supremely important end of

---

① 尼采否定传统的哲学、宗教、伦理道德观念,提出"重新估定一切价值"。其哲学大致包括强力意志说、永恒轮回说、超人说、反理性主义说和非道德说等方面。认为自然界与社会中的决定力量是意志,历史的进程就是强力意志实现其自身的过程,人生的目的在于发挥强力、"扩张自我"。认为超人是历史的创造者,群众只是超人实现其强力意志的工具。主张艺术是强力意志的一种表现形式,艺术家即高度扩张自我、表现自我的人。

② 重估一切价值。尼采认为,人类必须抛弃前所具有的唯理性价值观,崇尚非理性观念,弘扬人的生命力与本能的冲动,从这里出发去创造新观念与新标准。

ascribing values and creating fresh perspectives. He urges his readers to work to understand how accepted values become firmly established; how, for instance, the practices of fasting and celibacy became so important in Christianity and how a transvaluation of these values might come about through the actions of those with a will to power who can simply command change in the words, "It shall be thus." Such persons will be beyond their own time and therefore, in spite of their strength, will be lonely, abused and misunderstood by many. They will realize that there is no God while affirming existence and embracing and welcoming every pain as well as joy of life.

2. God is Dead①

Nietzsche is strongly critical of Christianity, though he has some respect for Jesus. While he acknowledges that some religions have played significant roles in great cultures (in ancient Greece and ancient Israel, for instance), he holds that the central doctrines of the Judaeo-Christian religious tradition are no longer intellectually credible. This is the event he calls the "death of God" — both a cultural event—the waning and impending demise of the "Christian-moral" interpretation of life and the world — and also a philosophical development: the abandonment of anything like the God-hypothesis (all demi-divine absolutes included). It represents a crisis in Western civilization because the metaphysical doctrines in question formed the basis for an entire world view, including an ethical system and a specific sense of the meaning of life.

The danger facing Western culture at this juncture, he claims, is that "nihilism②", a loss of faith in the value of anything, will become prevalent. But Nietzsche believes the death of God also represents a unique opportunity; for with the decline of the old dogmas we are in a position to propose new values and create new ideas to express a much stronger, healthier, more beautiful and more life-affirming attitude to life than Christianity has ever offered.

3. Will to Power③

In place of this cluster of traditional ontological categories and interpretations, Nietzsche conceives the world in terms of an interplay of forces without any inherent structure or final end. It ceaselessly organizes and reorganizes itself, as the fundamental disposition he calls "will to power" gives rise to successive arrays of power relationships.

On one level, the will to power is a psychological insight: our fundamental drive is for power as realized in independence and dominance. This will is stronger than the will to survive, as martyrs willingly die for a cause if they feel that associating themselves with that cause gives them greater power, and it is stronger than the will to sex, as monks

---

① 尼采的"上帝死了"并非指基督教的耶稣已死,而是基督教"死了",即基督教的各种道德观念死了。因此所谓"上帝死了"乃是尼采严厉批判西方传统的基督教道德观念的一种有力而新颖的表达方式。

② 虚无主义,源出拉丁文 nihil(虚无)一词。尼采把历史传统和道德原则的否定叫做虚无主义。

③ 强力意志,亦作"权力意志",用来描述生命特征。尼采认为生命的特征并非消极地求生存,也非对真理的追求,而是不断超越自身,具有不断自我创造,增强并释放力量以支配和驱使他物为自己的目的服务的意志,是一种"贪得无厌的表现权力的欲望,或运用权力作为创造的本能"。强力意志被视为存在的最高原则,宇宙的本原,及最高的价值尺度,是评价人类一切精神文化价值的标准。

willingly renounce sex for the sake of a greater cause. While the will to power can manifest itself through violence and physical dominance, Nietzsche is more interested in the sublimated will to power, where people turn their will to power inward and pursue self-mastery rather than mastery over others.

On a deeper level, the will to power explains the fundamental, changing aspect of reality. In Nietzsche's view, everything is in flux, and there is no such thing as fixed being. Matter is always moving and changing, as are ideas, knowledge, truth, and everything else. The will to power is the fundamental engine of this change. The universe is primarily made up not of facts or things but rather wills. "This world is the will to power — and nothing besides," as he claims; "and you yourself are also this will to power — and nothing besides!" The idea of the human soul or ego is just a grammatical fiction. What we call "I" is really a chaotic jumble of competing wills, constantly struggling to overcome one another. Because change is a fundamental aspect of life, Nietzsche considers any point of view that takes reality to be fixed and objective, be it religious, scientific, or philosophical, as life denying. A truly life-affirming philosophy embraces change and recognizes in the will to power that change is the only constant in the world.

4. Eternal Return[①]

Nietzsche's idea of the eternal return (or eternal recurrence) underscores this conception of a world without beginning or end. It involves a supreme affirmation of life. He first introduces this idea to express that time is cyclical and that we will live every moment of our lives over and over an infinite number of times, each time exactly the same. In other words, each passing moment is not fleeting but rather echoes for all eternity. He also entertains his doctrine of the eternal recurrence with distinctive metaphysical notions. Nietzsche contends that there is no such thing as being, for everything is always changing, always in a state of becoming. Because nothing is fixed, there are no "things" that we can distinguish and set apart from other "things". All of reality is intertwined, such that we cannot pass judgment on one aspect of reality without passing judgment on all of reality. In other words, we cannot feel regret for one aspect of our lives and joy for another because these two aspects of our lives cannot properly be distinguished from one another. Thus, for Nietzsche eternal return means that the life one has now is the only one has, and that one has it forever. In recognizing this, he concludes since we are faced with the simple choice of saying *yes* or *no* to all life, we should be able to embrace the eternal recurrence and live in affirmation with the yes-saying attitude.

5. Master-morality versus Slave-morality

Nietzsche insists that moralities as well as other traditional modes of valuation ought to be assessed in the perspective of life. Seeing Christian morality as an attempt to deny all those characteristics associating with healthy life, he argues that it is contrary to the

---

① "永恒轮回",亦译"永恒重现",指强力意志永恒地生成、变化、再生的不断肯定自身、循环流转的特征。尼采认为强力意志是世界的本质,它是"一种不知满足、不知厌倦的力量",是一种"永远在自我创造、永远在自我摧毁的力量",同时,它又是"一种常住不变的力量,永不变大变小、永不消耗,只是流转异形,总量不变"。

enhancement of life, reflecting the all-too-human needs and weaknesses and fears of less favored human groups and types.

Distinguishing between "master" and "slave" moralities, he finds the latter to have become the dominant type of morality in the modern world, which he regards as a "herd-animal morality," or slave-morality, and which is well suited to the requirements and vulnerabilities of the mediocre, but stultifying and detrimental to the development of human potentiality. The Christian concept of sin, he believes, makes us ashamed of our instincts and sexuality; the concept of faith discourages our curiosity and natural skepticism while the concept of pity encourages us to value and cherish weakness. Accordingly, he draws attention to the origins and functions of this type of morality (as a social-control mechanism and device by which the weak defend and avenge and assert themselves against the actually or potentially stronger). Since Christian morality springs from resentment for life and those who enjoy it, and seeks to overthrow health and strength with its life-denying ethics, he further suggests the desirability of a "higher morality" for the exceptions, in which the contrast of the basic "slave/herd morality" categories of "good and evil" would be replaced by categories more akin to the "good and bad" contrast characteristic of "master morality," with a revised and variable content better attuned to the conditions and attainable qualities of the enhanced forms of life such exceptional human beings can achieve.

6. The Overman versus the Last Man

Nietzsche's concept of the Ubermensch, or Overman, permeates much of his work. His conception of such a person, male or female, is not so much of someone who is in some sense superior in breeding and endowment, but of a person who confronts all the possible terrors and wretchedness of life and still joyously affirms it. Otherwise he or she is a Last Man.

Nietzsche advocates rigorous self-discipline and a voluntary exposure to suffering in order to exercise the will to power that can overcome the kind of submissive mediocrity he sees as characteristic of most people's lives. He regards the will to power as the very essence of all our strivings and cruelties that are a necessary though never admirable component of any life. Moreover the will to power as exercised by the Ubermensch was not simply a pitting of oneself against the pain and bitterness of life in order to preserve oneself but an effort to master all adversity and continually make a new and higher density for oneself. In Nietzsche's universe God is dead and there is no limit to what humankind alone might set itself to achieve. His advice is to follow one's highest ideals and to act on them at each moment in order to be an Overman in a world that will recur repeatedly through all eternity.

Introductory remarks

The Birth of Tragedy was Nietzsche's first philosophical work. It is divided into twenty-five chapters and a forward. The first fifteen chapters deal with the nature of Greek Tragedy, which Nietzsche claims, was born when the Apollonian worldview met the Dionysian. The last ten chapters use the Greek model to understand the state of modern culture, both its decline and its possible rebirth.

The following reading is an excerpt taken from the first part of *The Birth of Tragedy*. At the outset Nietzsche describes the tension between two opposing forces during an artistic creation: the "Apollonian" and the "Dionysian"—both are necessary in the creation. The former is a life-and-form-giving force, as identified by Nietzsche, and it is characterized by measured restraint and detachment, which reinforces a strong sense of self, while the latter is the Greek god of wine and music, as regarded by him, and is a frenzy of self-forgetting in which the self gives way to a primal unity where individuals are at one with others and with nature. Without the Apollonian, the Dionysian lacks the firm and structure to make a coherent piece of art, and without the Dionysian, the Apollonian lacks the necessary vitality and passion. Although they are diametrically opposed, they are also intimately intertwined. Notice the tone of this reading is very inspirational.

Text

The Birth of Tragedy① (excerpt)

Much will have been gained for aesthetics once we have succeeded in apprehending directly — rather than merely ascertaining — that art owes its continuous evolution to the Apollonian — Dionysian② duality, even as the propagation of the species depends on the duality of the sexes, their constant conflicts and periodic acts of reconciliation. I have borrowed my adjectives from the Greeks, who developed their mystical doctrines of art through plausible embodiments, not through purely conceptual means. It is by those two art sponsoring deities, Apollo and Dionysus, that we are made to recognize the tremendous split, as regards both origins and objectives, between the plastic, Apollonian arts and the non-visual art of music inspired by Dionysus③. The two creative tendencies developed alongside one another, usually in fierce opposition, each by its taunts forcing the other to more energetic production, both perpetuating in a discordant concord that agon which the term art but feebly denominates; until at last, by the thaumaturgy of an Hellenic act of will, the pair accepted the yoke of marriage and, in this condition, begot Attic tragedy, which exhibits the salient features of both parents④.

---

① 《悲剧的诞生》,推崇希腊神话中的酒神狄奥尼索斯,认为日神阿波罗代表理性、形式与限制,而酒神则象征无限奔放的生命力,两者搭配才能形成希腊悲剧。
② Apollonian — Dionysian:日神精神与酒神精神。尼采认为两种精神不断冲突、调和产生希腊悲剧。
③ Apollo and Dionysus...non-visual art of music inspired by Dionysus:我们认为,在希腊世界里,按照根源和目标来说,在日神的造型艺术和酒神的非造型的音乐艺术之间存在着极大的对立。
④ by the thaumaturgy...of both parents:由于希腊"意志"的一个形而上的奇迹行为,它们才彼此结合起来,而通过这种结合,终于产生了阿提刻悲剧这种既是酒神的又是日神的艺术作品。thaumaturgy:魔术,奇术;Hellenic:希腊式的;Attic tragedy:阿提刻悲剧;salient features:显著特征。

To reach a closer understanding of both these tendencies, let us begin by viewing them as the separate art realms of dream and intoxication, two physiological phenomena standing toward one another in much the same relationship as the Apollonian and Dionysian. It was in a dream, according to Lucretius①, that the marvelous gods and goddesses first presented themselves to the minds of men. That great sculptor, Phidias, beheld in a dream the entrancing bodies of more than human beings, and likewise, if anyone had asked the Greek poets about the mystery of poetic creation, they too would have referred him to dreams and instructed him much as Hans Sachs instructs us in Die Meistersinger②:

> The poet's task is this, my friend,
> to read his dreams and comprehend.
> The truest human fancy seems
> to be revealed to us in dreams:
> all poems and versification
> are but true dreams' interpretation.

The fair illusion of the dream sphere, in the production of which every man proves himself an accomplished artist, is a precondition not only of all plastic art, but even, as we shall see presently, of a wide range of poetry. Here we enjoy an immediate apprehension of form, all shapes speak to us directly, nothing seems indifferent or redundant. Despite the high intensity with which these dream realities exist for us, we still have a residual sensation that they are illusions; at least such has been my experience③ — and the frequency, not to say normality, of the experience is borne out in many passages of the poets. Men of philosophical disposition are known for their constant premonition that our everyday reality, too, is an illusion, hiding another, totally different kind of reality. It was Schopenhauer who considered the ability to view at certain times all men and things as mere phantoms or dream images to be the true mark of philosophic talent. The person who is responsive to the stimuli of art behaves toward the reality of dream much the way the philosopher behaves toward the reality of existence④: he observes exactly and enjoys his observations, for it is by these images that he interprets life, by these processes that he rehearses it. Nor is it by pleasant images only that such plausible connections are made: the whole divine comedy of life, including its somber aspects, its sudden balkings, impish accidents, anxious expectations, moves past him, not

---

① Lucretius: 卢克莱修(99—55 BC), 古罗马哲学家。
② That great sculptor, Phidias...instructs us in Die Meistersinger: 伟大的雕刻家菲狄亚斯是在梦中看见超人灵物优美的四肢结构。如果要探究诗歌创作的秘密, 希腊诗人同样会提醒人们注意梦, 如同汉斯·萨克斯在《名歌手》中教导的那样。菲狄亚斯(480—430 B.C.), 古希腊雕刻家、画家和建筑师; 萨克斯(1494—1576), 德国十六世纪著名诗人、工匠歌手。Die Meistersinger:《名歌手》, 即《纽伦堡的名歌手》(Die Meistersinger von Nürnberg), 德国作曲家瓦格纳的三幕歌剧。
③ Despite the high intensity... at least such has been my experience: 即使在梦的现实最活跃时, 我们仍然对它的外观有朦胧的感觉。至少这是我的经验。residual: 残余的。
④ It was Schopenhauer who considered...toward the reality of existence: 叔本华指出, 一个人间或把人们和万物当作纯粹幻影和梦象这种才能是哲学天赋的真正标志。正如哲学家面向存在的现实一样, 艺术上敏感的人面向梦的现实。

quite like a shadow play — for it is he himself, after all, who lives and suffers through these scenes — yet never without giving a fleeting sense of illusion; and I imagine that many persons have reassured themselves amidst the perils of dream by calling out, "It is a dream! I want it to go on." I have even heard of people spinning out the causality of one and the same dream over three or more successive nights. All these facts clearly bear witness that our innermost being, the common substratum of humanity, experiences dreams with deep delight and a sense of real necessity. This deep and happy sense of the necessity of dream experiences was expressed by the Greeks in the image of Apollo①. Apollo is at once the god of all plastic powers and the soothsaying god. He who is etymologically the "lucent" one, the god of light, reigns also over the fair illusion of our inner world of fantasy. The perfection of these conditions in contrast to our imperfectly understood waking reality, as well as our profound awareness of nature's healing powers during the interval of sleep and dream, furnishes a symbolic analogue to the soothsaying faculty and quite generally to the arts, which make life possible and worth living. But the image of Apollo must incorporate that thin line which the dream image may not cross, under penalty of becoming pathological, of imposing itself on us as crass reality: a discreet limitation, a freedom from all extravagant urges, the sapient tranquility of the plastic god. His eye must be sun-like, in keeping with his origin. Even at those moments when he is angry and ill-tempered there lies upon him the consecration of fair illusion. In an eccentric way one might say of Apollo what Schopenhauer says, in the first part of *The World as Will and Idea*, of man caught in the veil of Maya②: "Even as on an immense, raging sea, assailed by huge wave crests, a man sits in a little rowboat trusting his frail craft, so, amidst the furious torments of this world, the individual sits tranquilly, supported by the principium individuationis and relying on it."③ One might say that the unshakable confidence in that principle has received its most magnificent expression in Apollo, and that Apollo himself may be regarded as the marvelous divine image of the principium individuationis, whose looks and gestures radiate the full delight, wisdom, and beauty of "illusion"...

Not only does the bond between man and man come to be forged once more by the magic of the Dionysian rite, but nature itself, long alienated or subjugated, rises again to celebrate the reconciliation with her prodigal son, man.④ The earth offers its gifts

---

① All these facts clearly bear witness... expressed by the Greeks in the image of Apollo：所有事实清楚地证明，我们最内在的本质，我们所有人共同的深层基础，带着深刻的喜悦和愉快的必要性，亲身经验着梦。希腊人在他们的日神身上表达了这种经验梦的愉快的必要性。

② the veil of Maya：摩耶的面纱。摩耶是印度哲学和美学中的一个词汇，意为"幻"，是印度宗教哲学中一个十分重要的概念。

③ Even as on an immense, raging sea... individuationis and relying on it：喧腾的大海无边无际，翻卷着咆哮的巨浪，一人坐于船中，托身于这叶扁舟；同样地，孤独的人平静地置身于苦难世界之中，信赖个体化原理。（源自叔本华《作为意志和表象的世界》第一卷）

④ Not only does the bond between... reconciliation with her prodigal son, man. 在酒神的魔力下，不但人与人重新团结，而且长期疏远、被奴役的大自然也重新庆祝她与她的浪子——人类和解的节日。Dionysian rite：酒神祭。alienated：疏远；subjugated：屈从的；prodigal：挥霍者；浪荡子。

voluntarily, and the savage beasts of mountain and desert approach in peace. The chariot of Dionysus is bedecked with flowers and garlands; panthers and tigers stride beneath his yoke. If one were to convert Beethoven's "*Paean to Joy*"① into a painting, and refuse to curb the imagination when that multitude prostrates② itself reverently in the dust, one might form some apprehension of Dionysian ritual. Now the slave emerges as a freeman; all the rigid, hostile walls which either necessity or despotism has erected between men are shattered. Now that the gospel of universal harmony is sounded, each individual becomes not only reconciled to his fellow but actually at one with him — as though the veil of Maya had been torn apart and there remained only shreds floating before the vision of mystical Oneness. Man now expresses himself through song and dance as the member of a higher community; he has forgotten how to walk, how to speak, and is on the brink of taking wing as he dances. Each of his gestures betokens enchantment; through him sounds a supernatural power, the same power which makes the animals speak and the earth render up milk and honey.③

He feels himself to be godlike and strides with the same elation and ecstasy as the gods he has seen in his dreams. No longer the artist, he has himself become a work of art: the productive power of the whole universe is now manifest in his transport, to the glorious satisfaction of the primordial One④. The finest clay, the most precious marble-man-is here kneaded and hewn, and the chisel blows of the Dionysian world artist are accompanied by the cry of the Eleusinian mystagogues⑤: "Do you fall on your knees, multitudes, do you divine your creator?"

Brainstorming

1. How do Apollo and Dionysus differ in their conception of boundaries?
2. What is the mythical story of Dionysus's suffering?
3. What is the distinction between the two art worlds of dreams and drunkenness?
4. Does Nietzsche's Dionysian man resemble Shakespeare's Hamlet? And in what way?
5. Why is language unable to render the cosmic symbolism of music?
6. What is Nietzsche's definition of art? What art does he consider to be degenerate, and why?

Supplementary reading

The name of Nietzsche's prophet, Zarathustra, is an alternative name for the ancient

---

① Beethoven's "*Paean to Joy*": 贝多芬的《欢乐颂》。
② prostrate: 俯卧；拜倒。
③ Each of his gestures betokens enchantment...render up milk and honey: 他的神态表明他着了魔。就象此刻野兽开口说话、大地流出牛奶和蜂蜜一样，超自然的奇迹也在人身上出现。
④ the primordial One: 太一，古代表示世界本原的哲学范畴。
⑤ the Eleusinian mystagogues: 厄琉息斯的秘密仪式。

Persian prophet Zoroaster. The book *Thus Spoke Zarathustra* begins by telling us that at the age of 30, Zarathustra goes to live in the mountains. For ten years he took great delight in the solitude, but one dawn, he wakes up to find that he is tired of the wisdom he has accumulated alone on the mountain. So he decides to descend to the marketplace to share his wisdom with the rest of humankind. When he reaches the town, Zarathustra sees that there is a crowd gathered around a tightrope walker who is about to perform, and he joins them.

In opening his book in this unusual way, Nietzsche describes such a man — the overman, who confronts all the possible terrors and wretchednesss of life and still joyously affirms it.

Thus Spoke Zarathustra[①](excerpt)

When Zarathustra arrived at the edge of the forest, he came upon a town. Many people had gathered there in the marketplace to see a tightrope walker who had promised a performance. The crowd, believing that Zarathustra was the ringmaster who comes to introduce the tightrope walker, gathered around to listen. And Zarathustra spoke to the people:

I teach you the Overman! Mankind is something to be overcome. What have you done to overcome mankind?

All beings so far have created something beyond themselves. Do you want to be the ebb of that great tide, and revert back to the beast rather than overcome mankind? What is the ape to a man? A laughing-stock, a thing of shame. And just so shall a man be to the Overman: a laughing-stock, a thing of shame. You have evolved from worm to man, but much within you is still worm. Once you were apes, yet even now man is more of an ape than any of the apes.

Even the wisest among you is only a confusion and hybrid of plant and phantom. But do I ask you to become phantoms or plants?

Behold, I teach you the Overman! The Overman is the meaning of the earth. Let your will say: The Overman shall be the meaning of the earth! I beg of you my brothers, remain true to the earth, and believe not those who speak to you of otherworldly hopes! Poisoners are they, whether they know it or not. Despisers of life are they, decaying ones and poisoned ones themselves, of whom the earth is weary: so away with them!

Once blasphemy against God was the greatest blasphemy; but God died, and those blasphemers died along with him. Now to blaspheme against the earth is the greatest sin, and to rank love for the Unknowable higher than the meaning of the earth!

Once the soul looked contemptuously upon the body, and then that contempt was the supreme thing: — the soul wished the body lean, monstrous, and famished. Thus it

---

① 《查拉图斯特拉如是说》(1883—1885),通过散文诗体裁,假托古波斯宗教家查拉图斯特拉修行多年后下降人世传经布道的传奇故事,叙述作者的哲学和伦理思想,表现了作者本人的痛苦、欢乐、期望等人生体验。

thought to escape from the body and the earth. But that soul was itself lean, monstrous, and famished; and cruelty was the delight of this soul! So my brothers, tell me: What does your body say about your soul? Is not your soul poverty and filth and wretched contentment?

In truth, man is a polluted river. One must be a sea to receive a polluted river without becoming defiled. I teach you the Overman! He is that sea; in him your great contempt can go under.

What is the greatest thing you can experience? It is the hour of your greatest contempt. The hour in which even your happiness becomes loathsome to you, and so also your reason and virtue.

The hour when you say: What good is my happiness? It is poverty and filth and wretched contentment. But my happiness should justify existence itself!

The hour when you say: What good is my reason? Does it long for knowledge as the lion for his prey? It is poverty and filth and wretched contentment!

The hour when you say: What good is my virtue? It has not yet driven me mad! How weary I am of my good and my evil! It is all poverty and filth and wretched contentment!

The hour when you say: What good is my justice? I do not see that I am filled with fire and burning coals. But the just are filled with fire and burning coals!

The hour when you say: What good is my pity? Is not pity the cross on which he is nailed who loves man? But my pity is no crucifixion!

Have you ever spoken like this? Have you ever cried like this? Ah! If only I had heard you cry this way!

It is not your sin — it is your moderation that cries to heaven; your very sparingness in sin cries to heaven!

Where is the lightning to lick you with its tongue? Where is the madness with which you should be cleansed?

Behold, I teach you the Overman! He is that lightning, he is that madness!

And while Zarathustra was speaking in this way, someone in the crowd interrupted: "We've heard enough about the tightrope walker; now it's time to see him!" And while the crowd laughed at Zarathustra, the tightrope walker, believing that he had been given his cue, began his performance.

Zarathustra, however, looked at the people and wondered. Then he spoke thus: Man is a rope stretched between the animal and the Overman — a rope over an abyss.

A dangerous crossing, a dangerous wayfaring, a dangerous looking-back, a dangerous trembling and halting.

What is great in man is that he is a bridge and not a goal: what is lovable in man is that he is an over-going and a down-going.

I love those that know not how to live except as down-goers, for they are the over-goers.

I love the great despisers, because they are the great adorers, and arrows of longing for the other shore.

I love those who do not first seek a reason beyond the stars for going down and being sacrifices, but sacrifice themselves to the earth, that the earth may become the Overman's.

I love him who lives in order to know, and seeks to know in order that the Overman may hereafter live. Thus he seeks his own down-going.

I love him who labors and invents, that he may build the house for the Overman, and prepare for him earth, animal, and plant: for thus he seeks his own down-going.

I love him who loves his virtue: for virtue is the will to down-going, and an arrow of longing.

I love him who reserves no share of spirit for himself, but wants to be wholly the spirit of his virtue: thus he walks as spirit over the bridge.

I love him who makes his virtue his inclination and destiny: thus, for the sake of his virtue, he is willing to live on, or live no more.

I love him who desires not too many virtues. One virtue is more of a virtue than two, because it is more of a knot for one's destiny to cling to.

I love him whose soul is lavish, who wants no thanks and does not give back: for he always gives, and desires not to keep for himself.

I love him who is ashamed when the dice fall in his favor, and who then asks: "Am I a cheat?" — for he wants to perish.

I love him who scatters golden words in advance of his deeds, and always does more than he promises: for he seeks his own down-going.

I love him who justifies the future ones, and redeems the past ones: for he is willing to perish through the present ones.

I love him who chastens his God, because he loves his God: for he must perish through the wrath of his God.

I love him whose soul is deep even in the wounding, and may perish through a small matter: thus he goes willingly over the bridge.

I love him whose soul is so overfull that he forgets himself, and all things are in him: thus all things become his down-going.

I love him who is of a free spirit and a free heart: thus is his head only the bowels of his heart; his heart, however, causes his down-going.

I love all who are like heavy drops falling one by one out of the dark cloud that lowers over man: they herald the coming of the lightning, and perish as heralds.

Lo, I am a herald of the lightning, and a heavy drop out of the cloud: the lightning, however, is the Overman!

Famous quotations

I teach you the superman. Man is something to be surpassed[①].

—— *Thus Spoke Zarathustra. Prologue*

---

① 我教你们做超人。人是必须被超越的。

Man is a rope stretched between the animal and the Superman — a rope over an abyss①.

—— *Thus Spoke Zarathustra. Prologue*

What I understand by "philosopher": a terrible explosive in the presence of which everything is in danger.②

—— *Ecce Homo*

God is dead; but considering the state the species Man is in, there will perhaps be caves, for ages yet, in which his shadow will be shown.③

—— *The Gay Science*, III, 108

Believe me! The secret of reaping the greatest fruitfulness and the greatest enjoyment from life is to live dangerously!④

—— IV, 283

It is not the strength but the duration of great sentiments that makes great men⑤.

—— *Beyond Good and Evil*, IV. 72

One will rarely err if extreme actions be ascribed to vanity, ordinary actions to habit, and mean actions to fear.⑥

—— *Human, All Too Human*, 7

Wit is the epitaph of an emotion.⑦

—— 202

At the base of all these aristocratic races the predator is not to be mistaken, the splendorous blond beast, avidly rampant for plunder and victory.⑧

—— *On the Genealogy of Morality*, I, 11

For Nietzsche the Ubermench (Overman) is someone of enormous strength and independence in mind and body, like Napoleon and Socrates.

---

① 人是连接动物与超人之间的绳索———根跨越深渊的绳索。——同上
② 就我所理解的哲学家而言,他是使一切事物处于危险之中的令人畏惧的炸药。——《看啦！这人》
③ 上帝死了,可是正如人类所处情况那样,也许还存在千年的洞穴,上帝的影子在那里显现。——《快乐的科学》,第3章,第108节
④ 请相信我！从生活中索取最大成果,享受最大欢乐的秘密在于一种充满风险的生活。——第4章,第283节。
⑤ 造就伟人的不是力量,而是持久的伟大情感。——《善恶之彼岸》,第4章,第72节。
⑥ 如果人们把极端的行动归于虚荣,把平庸的行动归于习惯,把卑劣的行动归于恐惧,那么人便很少犯错误。——《人性,太人性化了》,第7节
⑦ 理智是感情死亡的墓志铭。——第202节
⑧ 在一切种族高贵的地区有一种猛兽不可不察,它外表漂亮,披着金发,却是一种到处游荡寻找猎物,求胜心切的凶残动物。——《道德的世系》(又译《道德体系论》),第1章,第11节

Anatomy Is Destiny
—— Freud

Chapter 13

If often he was wrong and at times, absurd, / to us he is no more a person / now but a whole climate of opinion / under whom we conduct our different lives....

—— W. H. Auden

In this chapter
- Getting to know Freud
- Appreciating Freudian psychoanalytic ideas
- Examining Freudian method of interpreting dreams

Sigmund Freud

Born into a poor Jewish family in a small town in Freiburg, Freud (1856—1939) turned out to be an outstanding pupil in high school. Young Freud loved literature and was proficient in German, French, Italian, Spanish, Hebrew, Latin and Greek. In 1881, he successfully completed his medical studies in the University of Vienna and began his medical career. Several years later he resigned his hospital post and set up in private practice specializing in "nervous disorders", while in the meantime developing his theory psychoanalysis. Having suffered from cancer in severe pain, Freud persuaded his friend and doctor to help him commit suicide in 1939.

Being the founder of psychoanalysis, Freud was also a prolific essayist, drawing on psychoanalysis to contribute to the interpretation and critique of culture. Despite the fact that some of his theories have been marginalized within psychology departments, his innovative treatment of human actions, dreams, and indeed of cultural artifacts as invariably possessing implicit symbolic significance has proven to be extraordinarily influential within the humanities, and has had massive implications for a wide variety of fields, including anthropology, semiotics, and artistic creativity and appreciation in addition to psychology. Indeed, his language, whether specifying divisions of the mind, types of disorder, or the structure of experience, has become the language in which we describe and understand ourselves and others.

Distinctive insights①

Notwithstanding the multiple manifestations of psychoanalysis as it exists today, it can in almost all fundamental respects be traced directly back to Freud's original work. His main theory can briefly be summarized as the following:

1. Tripartite Personality Structure②**: The id, The ego, The superego**

In Freudian psychoanalytic theory, id, ego, and superego are the three aspects of the human personality.

The id, which embodies such drives as sex and aggression, represents the primitive, animal aspect of the self that Freud views as constituting the core of the psyche. It is the unconscious part of the mind and the basis of personality, containing all the inherited resources, especially instincts, which is the source of instinctual impulses that exist at birth. It is entirely non-rational and functions according to the pleasure-pain principle. Its working processes are completely unconscious in the adult, but it supplies the energy for conscious mental life, and it plays an especially important role in modes of expression that have a non-rational element, such as the making of art. The primary methods for unmasking its content, according to Sigmund Freud, are dream analysis and free association.

The ego is the conscious self. It is the part that remembers, evaluates, plans, and in other ways is responsive to and acts in the surrounding physical and social world. As a messenger of reality, the ego replaces the reign of the pleasure principle by that of the reality principle, imposing the constraints of the social environment. However, the ego is not coextensive with either the personality or the body; rather, it serves to integrate these and other aspects of the person, such as memory, imagination, and behavior. It mediates between the id and the superego by building up various defense mechanisms.

The superego is the ethical component of the personality, aiming for perfection. It comprises that organized part of the personality structure, mainly but not entirely unconscious. The superego and ego, responding to social demands, work in contradiction to the primitive impulses of the id. The Superego, which tells us what is right and

---

① 弗洛伊德把人的心理分为意识、前意识和无意识,后又分为意识和无意识(包括被压抑的无意识和潜伏的无意识)。认为存在于无意识中的性本能是人的心理的基本动力,是支配个人命运、决定社会发展的力量;并把人格区分为自我、本我和超我三个部分。

② 弗洛伊德后期关于人的个性(心理)结构模式,即将人分为"本我"、"自我"和"超我"三个构成部分。

wrong, strives to act in a socially appropriate manner, whereas the id just wants instant self-gratification.

Because our parents are our primary source of socialization, it might be said that the superego is the internalized voice of our parents. It is formed during the first five years of life in response to parental punishment and approval; children internalize their parents' moral standards as well as those of the surrounding society, and the developing superego serves to control aggressive or other socially unacceptable impulses. Violation of the superego's standards gives rise to feelings of guilt or anxiety.

In Freud's view, the superego is frequently in conflict with the id. The superego's drive to repress the id extends even into our dreams, so that socially unacceptable urges are expressed indirectly in dream symbols.

2. The Conscious and Unconscious Mind[①]

According to Freud the mind can be divided into two parts. The first part is the conscious mind, which includes everything that we are aware of. This is the aspect of our mental processing that we can think and talk about rationally. A part of this includes our memory, which is not always part of consciousness but can be retrieved easily at any time and brought into our awareness. Freud calls this ordinary memory the preconscious. The second part is the unconscious mind, which is a reservoir of feelings, thoughts, urges, and memories that outside of our conscious awareness. Most of the contents of the unconscious are unacceptable or unpleasant, such as feelings of pain, anxiety, or conflict. For Freud, the unconscious continues to influence our behavior and experience, even though we are unaware of these underlying influences.

3. Oedipus Complex

Freud coined the term "Oedipus Complex" from a Greek myth. Oedipus, the son of Laius, king of Thebes and Jocasta, killed his father without recognizing him after being away from his parents for long. Freud employs this term to denote the psychological, especially. sexual, drives developing usually from the ages 3 to 6, associated with the child's attachment to the parent of the opposite sex, and resentment of the parent of the same sex.

4. Psychosexual development

Freud believes that personality develops through a series of childhood stages — the oral, the anal, the phallic, the latency, and the genital, during which the pleasure-seeking energies of the id become focused on certain erogenous areas. This psychosexual energy, or libidinal drive, is described as the driving force behind behavior. Freud holds that if these psychosexual stages are completed successfully, the result is a healthy personality. If certain issues are not resolved at the appropriate stage, fixation can occur. A fixation is a persistent focus on an earlier psychosexual stage. Until this conflict is resolved, the

---

① 意识。弗洛伊德认为人的意识包括人的情感、思想和欲望,意识的作用在于接受来自外界与身体内部的情报,以其自由的可动的能量控制快乐的情绪。无意识,亦译"潜意识",指自己的意识所不能触及的心理过程和精神状态。它由人的以性欲为主导的原始的本能动机所组成,为社会道德、法律、宗教所不容。

individual will remain "stuck" in this stage, and anxiety would persist into adulthood as neurosis, a functional mental disorder. For example, a person who is fixated at the oral stage may be over-dependent on others and may seek oral stimulation through smoking, drinking, or eating.

Introductory remarks

The following selection is taken from Freud's work *Civilization and Its Discontent*, Part V. In this seminal book, he compares "civilized" and "savage" human lives in order to reflect upon the meaning of civilization in general. By enumerating the fundamental tensions between civilization and the individual, he attempts to prove that the primary friction stems from the individual's quest for instinctual freedom and civilization's contrary demand for conformity and instinctual repression. Many of humankind's primitive instincts (for example, the desire to kill and the insatiable craving for sexual gratification) are clearly harmful to the well-being of a human community. As a result, civilization creates laws that prohibit killing, rape, and adultery, and it implements severe punishments if such commandments are broken. This process, argues Freud, is an inherent quality of civilization that instills perpetual feelings of discontent in its citizens.

Civilization and Its Discontents[①](excerpt)

We have regarded the difficulties in the development of civilization as part of the general difficulty accompanying all evolution, for we have traced them to the inertia of libido[②], its disinclination to relinquish an old position in favor of a new one. It is much the same thing if we say that the conflict between civilization and sexuality is caused by the circumstance that sexual love is a relationship between two people, in which a third can only be superfluous or disturbing, whereas civilization is rounded on relations between larger groups of persons. When a love-relationship is at its height no room is left for any interest in the surrounding world; the pair of lovers are sufficient unto themselves, do not even need the child they have in common to make them happy. In no other case does Eros so plainly betray the core of his being, his aim of making one out of many; but when he has achieved it in the proverbial way through the love of two human beings, he is not willing to go further.[③]

---

① 《文明及其不满》,阐述文明抑制了本能的满足,但并不是说要抛弃文明。在论述文明及其合理性的同时,文章指出个体本能应在理性的指引下自愿作出牺牲。

② 力比多,指人追求性与满足的能量或势力。弗洛伊德把它看作是人的一切心理活动和行为的动力源泉,是性欲、性本能冲动。

③ In no other case does Eros... he is not willing to go further. 在其他任何情况下,爱洛斯都不会这样明显地暴露他的存在的核心,即他要使多结合为一的目的;但是当他以众所周知的通过两个人恋爱的方法达到这一目的时,他就不愿再往前走了。Eros:爱洛斯,(希腊)爱神。弗洛伊德赋予它以"人的爱的本能"之意。

From all this we might well imagine that a civilized community could consist of pairs of individuals such as this, libidinally satisfied in each other, and linked to all the others by work and common interests①. If this were so, culture would not need to levy energy from sexuality. But such a desirable state of things does not exist and never has existed; in actuality culture is not content with such limited ties as these; we see that it endeavors to bind the members of the community to one another by libidinal ties as well②, that it makes use of every means and favors every avenue by which powerful identifications can be created among them, and that it exacts a heavy toll of aim-inhibited libido in order to strengthen communities by bonds of friendship between the members③. Restrictions upon sexual life are unavoidable if this object is to be attained.

Men are not gentle, friendly creatures wishing for love, who simply defend themselves if they are attacked, but that a powerful measure of desire for aggression has to be reckoned as part of their instinctual endowment④. The result is that their neighbor is to them not only a possible helper or sexual object, but also a temptation to them to gratify their aggressiveness on him, to exploit his capacity for work without recompense, to use him sexually without his consent, to seize his possessions, to humiliate him, to cause him pain, to torture and to kill him. Homo homini lupus⑤; who has the courage to dispute it in the face of all the evidence in his own life and in history? This aggressive cruelty usually lies in wait for some provocation, or else it steps into the service of some other purpose, the aim of which might as well have been achieved by milder measures. In circumstances that favor it, when those forces in the mind which ordinarily inhibit it cease to operate, it also manifests itself spontaneously and reveals men as savage beasts to whom the thought of sparing their own kind is alien⑥. Anyone who calls to mind the atrocities of the early migrations, of the invasion by the Huns or by the so-called Mongols under Jenghiz Khan and Tamurlane, of the sack of Jerusalem by the pious Crusaders, even indeed the horrors of the last world-war, will have to bow his head humbly before the truth of this view of man⑦.

---

① From all this we might... by work and common interests: 从这些看来, 我们完全可以想象这样一个文化集体: 它的成员是具有双重性的个人, 其利比多在他们相互间获得满足, 也通过共同工作和共同利益的纽带联系在一起。

② in actuality culture is not content... by libidinal ties as well: 现实告诉我们, 文明并不满足于我们现在赋予集体的那些有限的关系。它的目标还在于通过利比多努力把集体成员联系在一起, 并利用各种手段达到此目的。

③ that it exacts a heavy toll... between the members: 它在最大程度上唤起了目标被抑制的利比多以便借助成员之间的友谊关系加强集体纽带。

④ Men are not gentle... as part of their instinctual endowment: 人类并不是那种只有受到攻击时才自卫的友善、需要爱的温顺动物, 相反, 人类这一动物被认为在其本能的天赋中具有强大的进攻性。

⑤ Homo homini lupus: (拉丁语) 英译为 "man is a wolf to [his fellow] man", 人对人是狼。(源自柏拉图)

⑥ In circumstances that favor it... sparing their own kind is alien: 在有利于这种进攻性的情况下, 当平时禁止它精神上的反对力量失去效用时, 它就会自动表现出人类是一种野兽, 对于这种野兽来说, 饶其同类的命不是其本性。

⑦ Anyone who calls to... this view of man: 只要想想种族迁徙或是匈奴人的入侵, 或是成吉思汗和帖木儿统治下的所谓蒙古人, 或是虔诚的十字军血洗耶鲁撒冷, 或是近期世界大战带来的恐怖, 人们都不得不承认这一人性的真理性。the Huns: 匈奴人; Jenghiz Khan: 成吉思汗(1162—1227), 即元太祖; Tamurlane: 帖木儿(1336—1405), 帖木儿帝国开国君主(1370—1405); Jerusalem: 耶路撒冷; Crusaders: 十字军。

The existence of this tendency to aggression which we can detect in ourselves and rightly presume to be present in others is the factor that disturbs our relations with our neighbors and makes it necessary for culture to institute its high demands①. Civilized society is perpetually menaced with disintegration through this primary hostility of men towards one another. Their interests in their common work would not hold them together; the passions of instinct are stronger than reasoned interests. Culture has to call up every possible reinforcement in order to erect barriers against the aggressive instincts of men and hold their manifestations in check by reaction-formations② in men's minds. The time comes when every one of us has to abandon the illusory anticipations with which in our youth we regarded our fellow-men, and when we realize how much hardship and suffering we have been caused in life through their ill-will. It would be unfair, however, to reproach culture with trying to eliminate all disputes and competition from human concerns. These things are undoubtedly indispensable; but opposition is not necessarily enmity, only it may be misused to make an opening for it③...

Men clearly do not find it easy to do without satisfaction of this tendency to aggression that is in them; when deprived of satisfaction of it they are ill at ease. There is an advantage, not to be undervalued, in the existence of smaller communities, through which the aggressive instinct can find an outlet in enmity towards those outside the group. It is always possible to unite considerable numbers of men in love towards one another, so long as there are still some remaining as objects for aggressive manifestations④. I once interested myself in the peculiar fact that peoples whose territories are adjacent, and are otherwise closely related, are always at feud with and ridiculing each other, as, for instance, the Spaniards and the Portuguese, the North and South Germans, the English and the Scotch, and so on. I gave it the name of narcissism⑤ in respect of minor differences, which does not do much to explain it. One can now see that it is a convenient and relatively harmless form of satisfaction for aggressive tendencies, through which cohesion amongst the members of a group is made easier. The Jewish people, scattered in all directions as they are, have in this way rendered services which deserve recognition to the development of culture in the countries where they settled; but unfortunately not all the massacres of Jews in the Middle Ages sufficed to procure peace and security for their Christian contemporaries. Once the apostle Paul⑥ had laid down universal love between all men as the foundation of his Christian community, the inevitable consequence in

---

① The existence of this tendency...for culture to institute its high demands: 这种好斗性存在于我们内心,可恰当地推测它也存在于其他人身上。正是这一点扰乱了我们和邻里间的关系,并迫使文明耗费了高昂的代价。
② reaction-formations: 反作用形成。
③ It would be unfair...misused to make an opening for it.: 指责文明试图从人类活动中消除冲突和竞争是不公平的。这些东西无疑是必不可少的。但是反对并不一定是敌对,它可能被误用,并给敌对创造了机会……
④ It is always possible to unite...objects for aggressive manifestations: 只要还存在着可以承受进攻性的人,就有可能通过互爱把相当数量的人联合在一起。
⑤ narcissism: "那咯索斯主义";"影恋";自恋。那咯索斯主义是希腊神话中爱恋自己在水中倒影的美少年,最后憔悴而死。
⑥ Paul: 圣徒保罗,《圣经》初期教会主要领袖。

Christianity was the utmost intolerance towards all who remained outside of it; the Romans, who had not rounded their state on love, were not given to lack of religious toleration, although religion was a concern of the state, and the state was permeated through and through with it. Neither was it an unaccountable chance that the dream of a German world-dominion evoked a complementary movement towards anti-semitism; and it is quite intelligible that the attempt to establish a new communistic type of culture in Russia should find psychological support in the persecution of the bourgeois. One only wonders, with some concern, however, how the Soviets will manage when they have exterminated their bourgeois entirely.

If civilization requires such sacrifices, not only of sexuality but also of the aggressive tendencies in mankind, we can better understand why it should be so hard for men to feel happy in it①. In actual fact primitive man was better off in this respect, for he knew nothing of any restrictions on his instincts. As a set-off against this, his prospects of enjoying his happiness for any length of time were very slight. Civilized man has exchanged some part of his chances of happiness for a measure of security. We will not forget, however, that in the primal family only the head of it enjoyed this instinctual freedom; the other members lived in slavish thraldom②. The antithesis between a minority enjoying cultural advantages and a majority who are robbed of them was therefore most extreme in that primeval period of culture. With regard to the primitive human types living at the present time, careful investigation has revealed that their instinctual life is by no means to be envied on account of its freedom③; it is subject to restrictions of a different kind but perhaps even more rigorous than is that of modern civilized man.

In rightly finding fault, as we thus do, with our present state of civilization for so inadequately providing us with what we require to make us happy in life, and for the amount of suffering of a probably avoidable nature it lays us open to — in doing our utmost to lay bare the roots of its deficiencies by our unsparing criticisms, we are undoubtedly exercising our just rights and not showing ourselves enemies of culture. We may expect that in the course of time changes will be carried out in our civilization so that it becomes more satisfying to our needs and no longer open to the reproaches we have made against it④. But perhaps we shall also accustom ourselves to the idea that there are certain difficulties inherent in the very nature of culture which will not yield to any efforts at reform. Over and above the obligations of putting restrictions upon our instincts, which we see to be inevitable, we are imminently threatened with the dangers

---

① If civilization requires such sacrifices... so hard for men to feel happy in it：如果文明把如此大的牺牲不仅强加于人类的性行为,而且还强加于人类的进攻行为的话,我们就能更好地理解为什么在这样一种文明里人们极难使自己感到幸福。
② slavish thraldom：奴隶般的压迫；奴隶的束缚。
③ With regard to the primitive human... on account of its freedom：至于今天仍存在的原始民族,经仔细调查已表明他们的本能生活绝不会因为其自由而受到嫉妒。
④ We may expect that... the reproaches we have made against it：我们可能期待在我们的文明中逐渐实现这样的变化,即它将更好地满足我们的要求,并且不再受到我们的指责。

of a state one may call 'la misere psychologique'① of groups. This danger is most menacing where the social forces of cohesion consist predominantly of identifications of the individuals in the group with one another, whilst leading personalities fail to acquire the significance that should fall to them in the process of group-formation. The state of civilization in America at the present day offers a good opportunity for studying this injurious effect of civilization which we have reason to dread. But I will resist the temptation to enter upon a criticism of American culture; I have no desire to give the impression that I would employ American methods myself...

Famous quotations

Where id is, there shall ego be②.

—— *An Outline of Lectures on Psychoanalysis*

Devout believers are safeguarded in a high degree against the risk of certain neurotic illnesses; their acceptance of the universal neurosis spares them the task of constructing a personal one③.

—— *The Future of an Illusion*

One feels inclined to say that the intention that man should be "happy" is not included in the plan of "Creation"④.

—— *Civilization and Its Discontents*

The poor ego has a still harder time of it; it has to serve three harsh masters, and it has to do its best to reconcile the claims and demands of all three... The three tyrants are the external world, the superego, and the id⑤.

—— *New Introductory Lectures on Psychoanalysis*

Thinking is an experimental dealing with small quantities of energy, just as a general moves miniature figures over a map before setting his troops in action.⑥

—— *New Introductory Lectures on Psychoanalysis*

The ego is not master in its own house.⑦

—— *A difficulty in the path of Psycho-Analysis*

Brainstorming

1. What is Freud's basic view about human nature?

---

① la misere psychologique：心理匮乏。
② 本我在哪里，自我就应在哪里。——《精神分析概要》
③ 虔诚的信徒在很大程度上避免了患上神经症的风险；对一种普遍性神经症的接受让他们免除了制造出一种个人化神经症的重任。——《幻象之未来》
④ 人总是倾向于说人应该"快乐"，这个意图并不包括在"创世"这个计划里。——《文明及其不满》
⑤ 可怜的自我处境艰难，它必须服务于三位严酷的主人，并且必须努力让每一位的提议和要求得到满足……这三个暴君是：外部世界，超我和本我。——《新心理分析导论》
⑥ 思考是一种使用少量能量的实验，如同一位将军在派遣军队实战前移动地图上的模型。——《新心理分析导论》
⑦ 自我不是它在自己家里的主人。——《心理分析之路中的一个困难》。

2. According to Sigmund Freud, wisdom comes from the achievement of maturity. Do you agree?

3. What is the link, for Freud, between sexual desire and military invasion?

4. What will possibly happen when individual desire is traded for social security and cohesion? What do you think will be Freud's solution to the problem?

5. Is nature and culture incompatible with each other? State your own position.

Supplementary reading

Freud rejects the ancient "dream book" mode of interpretation in terms of fixed symbols, and believes one had to recover the hidden meaning of a dream through the dreamer's (not the interpreter's) associations to particular elements. Such associations are a part of the process of free association, in which a patient is obliged to report to the analyst all thoughts without censorship of any kind. The results of his investigations have been used to speculate about the origins of morality, religion, and political authority. As an example, we take the following passage from Chapter II of his *The Interpretation of Dreams*[①].

The Method of Interpreting Dreams: An Analysis of a Specimen Dream (excerpt)

The title that I have chosen for my work makes plain which of the traditional approaches to the problem of dreams I am inclined to follow. The aim which I have set before myself is to show that dreams are capable of being interpreted; and any contributions I may be able to make towards the solution of the problems dealt with in the last chapter will only arise as by-products in the course of carrying out my proper task. My presumption that dreams can be interpreted at once puts me in opposition to the ruling theory of dreams and in fact to every theory of dreams with the single exception of Scherner's [pp. 109 ff.]; for 'interpreting' a dream implies assigning a 'meaning' to it—that is, replacing it by something which fits into the chain of our mental acts as a link having a validity and importance equal to the rest. As we have seen, the scientific theories of dreams leave no room for any problem of interpreting them, since in their view a dream is not a mental act at all, but a somatic process signalizing its occurrence by indications registered in the mental apparatus. Lay opinion has taken a different attitude throughout the ages. It has exercised its indefeasible right to behave inconsistently; and, though admitting that dreams are unintelligible and absurd, it cannot bring itself to declare that they have no significance at all. Led by some obscure feeling, it seems to assume that, in spite of everything, every dream has a meaning, though a hidden one, that dreams are designed to take the place of some other process of thought, and that we

---

① 《梦的解析》,用实例解释梦的材料、来源、本质和功用以及梦过程的心理机制和梦的解析方法。

have only to undo the substitution correctly in order to arrive at this hidden meaning.

Thus the lay world has from the earliest times concerned itself with 'interpreting' dreams and in its attempts to do so it has made use of two essentially different methods.

The first of these procedures considers the content of the dream as a whole and seeks to replace it by another content which is intelligible and in certain respects analogous to the original one. This is '*symbolic*' dream interpreting; and it inevitably breaks down when faced by dreams which are not merely unintelligible but also confused. An example of this procedure is to be seen in the explanation of Pharaoh's dream propounded by Joseph in the Bible. The seven fat kine followed by seven lean kine that ate up the fat kine—all this was a symbolic substitute for a prophecy of seven years of famine in the land of Egypt which should consume all that was brought forth in the seven years of plenty. Most of the artificial dreams constructed by imaginative writers are designed for a symbolic interpretation of this sort: they reproduce the writer's thoughts under a disguise which is regarded as harmonizing with the recognized characteristics of dreams. The idea of dreams being chiefly concerned with the future and being able to foretell it—a remnant of the old prophetic significance of dreams—provides a reason for transposing the meaning of the dream, when it has been arrived at by symbolic interpretation, into the future tense. It is of course impossible to give instructions upon the method of arriving at a symbolic interpretation. Success must be a question of hitting on a clever idea, of direct intuition, and for that reason it was possible for dream-interpretation by means of symbolism to be exalted into an artistic activity dependent on the possession of peculiar gifts.

The second of the two popular methods of interpreting dreams is far from making any such claims. It might be described as the '*decoding*' method, since it treats dreams as a kind of cryptography in which each sign can be translated into another sign having a known meaning, in accordance with a fixed key. Suppose, for instance, that I have dreamt of a letter and also of a funeral. If I consult a 'dream-book', I find that 'letter' must be translated by 'trouble' and 'funeral' by 'betrothal'. It then remains for me to link together the keywords which I have deciphered in this way and, once more, to transpose the result into the future tense. An interesting modification of the process of decoding, which to some extent corrects the purely mechanical character of its method of transposing, is to be found in the book written upon the interpretation of dreams [*Oneirocritica*] by Artemidorus of Daldis. This method takes into account not only the content of the dream but also the character and circumstances of the dreamer; so that the same dream-element will have a different meaning for a rich man, a married man or, let us say, an orator, from what it has for a poor man, a bachelor or a merchant. The essence of the decoding procedure, however, lies in the fact that the work of interpretation is not brought to bear on the dream as a whole but on each portion of the dream's content independently, as though the dream were a geological conglomerate in which each fragment of rock required a separate assessment. There can be no question that the invention of the decoding method of interpretation was suggested by disconnected and confused dreams.

It cannot be doubted for a moment that neither of the two popular procedures for interpreting dreams can be employed for a scientific treatment of the subject. The symbolic method is restricted in its application and incapable of being laid down on general lines. In the case of the decoding method everything depends on the trustworthiness of the "key"—the dream-book, and of this we have no guarantee. Thus one might feel tempted to agree with the philosophers and the psychiatrists and, like them, rule out the problem of dream-interpretation as a purely fanciful task.

But I have been taught better. I have been driven to realize that here once more we have one of those not infrequent cases in which an ancient and jealously held popular belief seems to be nearer the truth than the judgment of the prevalent science of today. I must affirm that dreams really have a meaning and that a scientific procedure for interpreting them is possible.

My knowledge of the procedure was reached in the following manner. I have been engaged for many years (with a therapeutic aim in view) in unravelling certain psychopathological structures—hysterical phobias, obsessional ideas, and so on. I have been doing so, in fact, ever since I learnt from an important communication by Josef Breuer that as regards these structures (which are looked on as pathological symptoms) unraveling them coincides with removing them. (Cf. Breuer and Freud, 1895.) If a pathological idea of this sort can be traced back to the elements in the patient's mental life from which it originated, it simultaneously crumbles away and the patient is freed from it. Considering the impotence of our other therapeutic efforts and the puzzling nature of these disorders, I felt tempted to follow the path marked out by Breuer, in spite of every difficulty, till a complete explanation was reached. I shall have on another occasion to report at length upon the form finally taken by this procedure and the results of my labors. It was in the course of these psycho-analytic studies that I came upon dream-interpretation. My patients were pledged to communicate to me every idea or thought that occurred to them in connection with some particular subject; amongst other things they told me their dreams and so taught me that a dream can be inserted into the psychical chain that has to be traced backwards in the memory from a pathological idea. It was then only a short step to treating the dream itself as a symptom and to applying to dreams the method of interpretation that had been worked out for symptoms.

To Freud, man is unable to tolerate too much reality, and that dreams are the contraband representations of the beast within man which are smuggled into awareness during sleep. The analysis of dreams is the key to unlocking the vital secrets of the unconscious mind.

Language Is a Game
—— Wittgenstein

Chapter 14

> *He was the kind of man who would never have noticed such small matters as bursting shells when he was thinking about logic.*
> —— *Bertrand Russell*

In this chapter
- Getting to know Wittgenstein
- Examining the basic conception of Wittgenstein's doctrines
- Getting clear on Wittgenstein's two distinct philosophies

Ludwig Wittgenstein

Born into a wealthy Viennese family in 1889, Wittgenstein (1889—1951) first studied engineering and then he traveled to England to continue his education in Manchester, where he developed an intense interest in logic. In 1911 he moved to Cambridge to study under Bertrand Russell, but his studies ended with the onset of the World War I. He enlisted in the Austrian army and was taken prisoner. During his time at the front and later in the prison camp he completed his first great philosophical work *Tractatus Logico-Philosophicus*. After his release from the camp he returned to Vienna. He gave up all the fortune inherited from his father to his sisters and embarked on an itinerant career as a village schoolteacher, a gardener and an architect, thinking that he had already solved all the philosophical problems. Because of his constant renewed philosophical activity, he later returned to Cambridge first as a research student and then worked there as a professor until his death in 1951.

In his early philosophy he strives to uproot the deeply entrenched traditions of thought. In his later philosophy he accepts, uses and transforms them. Considered by some to be the greatest philosopher of the 20th century, Ludwig Wittgenstein played a central role in 20th-century analytic philosophy. He continues to influence current philosophical thought in topics as diverse as logic and language, perception and intention, ethics and religion, aesthetics and culture.

Distinctive insights[①]

Wittgenstein was, unquestionably, a genius. He produced two distinct philosophies: the early Wittgenstein is epitomized in his *Tractatus Logico-Philosophicus*, while the later Wittgenstein, mostly recognized in the *Philosophical Investigations*, takes the more revolutionary step in critiquing all of traditional philosophy including its climax in his own early work. Both of the two doctrines have been and still are profoundly influential.

1. Language "Pictures" Reality

Throughout the *Tractatus* Wittgenstein aims to show that language must have a certain structure if it is to represent reality. Language "pictures" reality by mimicking its structure. Anything can be said can be expressed as a proposition with a sense, and propositions with sense concern only facts about things in the world. Like a picture, a sentence-picture shows how things stand in the world. Sentences that do not represent possible states of affairs cannot be said, but can at best be shown. These include such philosophical discourses as ethical statements, aesthetics, the meaning of life, the immortality of the soul, the nature of the language, the nature of logic, the nature of mathematics, the fundamental structure of the world and other religious theses. They are, though important to our lives, nonetheless nonsensical.

2. The Workings of Logic Manifest Themselves

Wittgenstein provides new insights into the relations between world, thought and language and thereby into the nature of philosophy by showing the application of modern logic to metaphysics, via language. According to him, logic is not a body of propositions, nor is it an axiomatic system. It represents the architecture or reality, and that the fact that propositions represent are possible facts. He describes such possibilities as "atomic facts". Atomic facts are what make propositions true or false. Logic is therefore concerned with all possible facts: a logical picture contains the possibility of the situation it represents and is then found true or false by being compared with reality. The truth of a compound proposition depends on the truth of its elementary components except in the case of tautologies such as "Either it is raining or it is not raining," which are true under all

---

① 早期主张逻辑原子主义,强调逻辑分析。提出语言图像论,把语言看成事态的逻辑图像。宣称哲学只是一种指出人们能明白地讲出什么和不能明白地讲出什么的"活动"。后期放弃语言图像论,认为哲学的任务在于澄清语言的意义。提出语言工具论,是日常语言哲学的奠基人。

possible conditions, or in the case of contradictions such as "It is raining but it is not raining," which are false under all conditions. In both of these sorts of cases we do not need to test the propositions against reality.

Logic in itself does not say anything, nor does it tell us anything about the world. Rather, it determines the form taken by things in the world. Propositions can represent facts, and thoughts can represent propositions, because they all share a common logic form. This concept of logic of Wittgenstein as consisting of form rather than content is that logic itself can not be explained, that is to say, logic should not stand in need of justification, nor should it need law to say what can and can not be the case because logic defines the boundaries of sense: any proposition that has sense has a logic form, and any proposition that is nonsense lacks logic form. Thus, we do not need laws, axioms, or anything else to tell us what is and is not allowed in logic. The workings of logic make themselves manifest in everything we say and experience.

3. Language as A Form of Life

In the *Investigation* Wittgenstein is as much concerned with language as he was in the *Tractatus*, but the nature of the concern is different. Whereas the *Tractatus* deals with the nature of propositions the *Investigations* concentrates largely on those propositions that describe mental life. In the *Tractatus* Wittgenstein bases everything on the idea that meaning and lack of meaning depend on the formal relationship in which a proposition stands to reality, while in the *Investigations* meaning is seen as a function of how we use words: human purposes and the forms of life in which human beings engage are what give language its meanings. There is no final analysis of propositions into logically proper names that are the names of the simple objects of the world. Philosophy "simply puts everything before us, and neither explains nor deduces anything"; its results "are the uncovering of one or another piece of plain nonsense"; philosophical problems are solved "not by giving new information, but by arranging what we have always known". Wittgenstein therefore comes to the conclusion that the philosopher's treatment of a question is like the treatment of an illness; that is, the philosophical treatment does not have the form of question-plus-answer but, as with an illness, when the problem is treated properly, it goes away.

Introductory remarks

Tractatus consists of seven numbered sections. Each is constructed around seven basic propositions, numbered by the natural numbers 1-7, with all other paragraphs in the text numbered by decimal expansions so that, e.g., paragraph 1.1 is (supposed to be) a further elaboration on proposition 1, 1.22 is an elaboration of 1.2, and so on, each section dealing with a certain issue. The sixth thesis, from which our selection is taken, is that many of our utterances that we take to be significant are in fact not so but are "unsayable" in that they are not analyzable as logical pictures of simple objects. Such utterances include remarks about what is good or bad and the propositions — now to be thought of as pseudo-propositions — of philosophy, including the claims of the *Tractatus* itself. The seventh section consists of only one remark: "What we cannot speak about we must pass over in silence".

Text

Tractatus Logico-Philosophicus①(excerpt)

6.4　All propositions are of equal value.

6.41　The sense of the world must lie outside the world. In the world everything is as it is, and everything happens as it does happen: in it no value exists ——and if it did exist, it would have no value. If there is any value that does have value, it must lie outside the whole sphere of what happens and is the case②. For all that happens and is the case is accidental. What makes it non-accidental cannot lie within the world, since if it did it would itself be accidental. It must lie outside the world.

6.42　So too it is impossible for there to be propositions of ethics. Propositions can express nothing that is higher.

6.421　It is clear that ethics cannot be put into words. Ethics is transcendental③. (Ethics and aesthetics are one and the same.)

6.422　When an ethical law of the form, 'Thou shalt...', is laid down, one's first thought is, 'And what if I do not do it?' It is clear, however, that ethics has nothing to do with punishment and reward in the usual sense of the terms. So our question about the consequences of an action must be unimportant. ——At least those consequences should not be events. For there must be something right about the question we posed. There must indeed be some kind of ethical reward and ethical punishment, but they must reside in the action itself④. (And it is also clear that the reward must be something pleasant and the punishment something unpleasant.)

6.423　It is impossible to speak about the will in so far as it is the subject of ethical attributes. And the will as a phenomenon is of interest only to psychology.

6.43　If the good or bad exercise of the will does alter the world, it can alter only the limits of the world, not the facts —— not what can be expressed by means of

---

① 《逻辑哲学论》(1921),提出逻辑图像论,用以建立一种能表达我们思想的符号体系的逻辑基础。维特根斯坦认为,我们语言中的命题都必须有一个明白而具体的意义,而这种意义就在于语言(命题)和实在(事实)之间有一种逻辑图像关系。

② in it no value exists... of what happens and is the case: 世界中不存在价值,如果真存在价值,它也会是无价值的。如果存在任何有价值的价值,那么它必定处在一切发生的和既存的事件之外。

③ transcendental: 超验主义的。超验主义的核心观点是主张人能超越感觉和理性而直接认识真理。

④ There must indeed be some kind... they must reside in the action itself: 确实应该有某种伦理的奖励和伦理的惩罚,但是它们必定包含于行动本身。

language. In short the effect must be that it becomes an altogether different world, It must, so to speak, wax and wane as a whole. The world of the happy man is a different one from that of the unhappy man.

6.431 So too at death the world does not alter, but comes to an end①.

6.4311 Death is not an event in life: we do not live to experience death. If we take eternity to mean not infinite temporal duration but timelessness, then eternal life belongs to those who live in the present②. Our life has no end in just the way in which our visual field has no limits.

6.4312 Not only is there no guarantee of the temporal immortality of the human soul, that is to say of its eternal survival after death; but, in any case, this assumption completely fails to accomplish the purpose fro which it has always been intended③. Or is some riddle solved by my surviving forever?

The solution of the riddle of life in space and time lies outside space and time. (It is certainly not the solution of any problems of natural science that is required.)

6.432 How things are in the world is a matter of complete indifference for what is higher. God does not reveal himself in the world.

6.4321 The facts all contribute only to setting the problem not to its solution.

6.44 It is not how things are in the world that is mystical, but that it exists.

6.45 To view the world sub specie aeterni④ is to view it as a whole —— a limited whole. Feeling the world as a limited whole —— it is this that is mystical.

6.5 When the answer cannot be put into words, neither can the question be put into words. The riddle does not exist. If a question can be framed at all, it is also possible to answer it.⑤

6.51 Skepticism is not irrefutable, but obviously nonsensical, when it tries to raise doubts where no questions can be asked⑥. For doubt can exist only where a question exists, a question not only where an answer exists, and an answer only something can be said.

6.52 We feel that even when all possible scientific questions have been answered, the problems of life remain completely untouched. Of course there are then no questions left, and this itself is the answer.

---

① So too at death the world does not alter, but comes to an end：同样，死不是世界的改变，而是世界的终止。

② If we take eternity to mean...belongs to those who live in the present：如果我们把永恒理解为无时间性，而并非无限时间的延续，那么活在当下的人，也就永恒地活着。

③ Not only is there no guarantee...which it has always been intended 不仅人的灵魂在时间上的不灭，或者说它在死后的永存，是没有保证的；而且在任何情形下，这个假定都达不到人们所不断追求的目的。

④ sub specie aeterni：(拉丁文)从永恒观点看。

⑤ When the answer cannot be...it is also possible to answer it：若答案不可说，其问题也就不可说。谜是不存在的。当一个问题可以形成，它也就可能得到解答。

⑥ Skepticism is not irrefutable...where no questions can be asked 怀疑论不是不可反驳的，而是因为它试图在不能提出问题的地方产生怀疑，所以显然是无意义的。irrefutable：不能反驳的，无可辩驳的；nonsensical：愚蠢的，荒谬可笑的。

6.521　The solution of the problem of life is seen in the vanishing of the problem①. (Is not this the reason why those who have found after a long period of doubt that the sense of life became clear to them have then been unable to say what constituted that sense?)

6.522　There are, indeed, things that cannot be put into words. They make themselves manifest. They are what is mystical.

6.53　The correct method in philosophy would really be the following: to say nothing except what can be said, i.e. propositions of natural science — i.e. something that had nothing to do with philosophy② and then, whenever someone else wanted to say something metaphysical, to demonstrate to him that he had failed to give a meaning to certain signs in his propositions. Although it would not be satisfying to the other person — he would not have the feeling that we were teaching him philosophy — this method would be the only strictly correct one.

6.54　My propositions serve as elucidations in the following way: anyone who understands me eventually recognizes them as nonsensical, when he has used them — as steps — to climb up beyond them. (He must, so to speak, throw away the ladder after he has climbed up it.) He must transcend these propositions, and then he will see the world aright③.

7. What we cannot speak about we must pass over in silence.④

Brainstorming

1. What is Wittgenstein's basic view about the origin of the world?
2. What should be done given the fact that our world is "a limited whole?"
3. Can you think of a certain existing world view which resembles Wittgenstein's proposition? State their similarities and differences.
4. Is there any relationship between Wittgenstein's ideas in *Tractatus* and that in *Philosophical Investigation*?
5. If mystical things can't be realized through language, how could it be possibly approached in Wittgenstein's sense? What does he mean by "pass over in silence"?
6. What advancement in philosophy would Wittgenstein probably expect if the ladders of his propositions are thrown away?

---

① The solution of the problem of life is seen in the vanishing of the problem：人生问题的解答在于这个问题的清除。

② The correct method in philosophy... had nothing to do with philosophy：哲学的正确方法是：除了可说的东西，即自然科学的命题，也就是与哲学无关的东西之外，就不再说什么。

③ He must transcend these propositions, and then he will see the world aright：他必须超越这些命题，才会正确地看世界。aright：=all right

④ 对于不能讲的事，必须保持沉默。(本条是《逻辑哲学论》的要旨。维特根斯坦力图给思想的表达划定界限，进而也在语言中划分这个界限，即"凡是能说的，都可以说清楚；对于不能说的，必须保持沉默。"

> **Supplementary reading**

The following selection is taken from Wittgenstein's "*Lectures on Philosophy*", in which he emphasizes that there are countless different uses of what we call "symbols," "words," and "sentences." He believes that the task of philosophy is to gain a perspicuous view of those multiple uses and thereby to dissolve philosophical and metaphysical puzzles. These puzzles were the result of insufficient attention to the working of language and could be resolved only by carefully retracing the linguistic steps by which they had been reached.

Lectures on Philosophy (excerpt)

We begin with the question whether the toothache someone else has is the same as the toothache I have. Is his toothache merely outward behavior? Or is it that he has the same as I am having now but that I don't know it since I can only say of another person that he is manifesting certain behavior? A series of questions arises about personal experience. Isn't it thinkable that I have a toothache in someone else's tooth? It might be argued that my having toothache requires my mouth. But the experience of my having toothache is the same wherever the tooth is that is aching, and whoever's mouth it is in. The locality of pain is not given by naming a possessor. Further, isn't it imaginable that I live all my life looking in a mirror, where I saw faces and did not know which was my face, nor how my mouth was distinguished from anyone else's? If this were in fact the case, would I say I had toothache in my mouth? In a mirror I could speak with someone else's mouth, in which case what would we call me? Isn't it thinkable that I change my body and that I would have a feeling correlated with someone else's raising his arm?

The grammar of "having toothache" is very different from that of "having a piece of chalk", as is also the grammar of "I have toothache" from "Moore has toothache". The sense of "Moore has toothache" is given by the criterion for its truth. For a statement gets its sense from its verification. The use of the word "toothache" when I have toothache and when someone else has it belongs to different games. (To find out with what meaning a word is used, make several investigations. For example, the words "before" and "after" mean something different according as one depends on memory or on documents to establish the time of an event.) Since the criteria for "He has toothache" and "I have toothache" are so different, that is, since their verifications are of different sorts, I might seem to be denying that he has toothache. But I am not saying he really hasn't got it. Of course he has it; it isn't that he behaves as if he had it but really doesn't. For we have criteria for his really having it as against his simulating it. Nevertheless, it is felt that I should say that I do not know he has it.

Suppose I say that when he has toothache he has what I have, except that I know it indirectly in his case and directly in mine. This is wrong. Judging that he has toothache is not like judging that he has money but I just can't see his billfold. Suppose it is held that

I must judge indirectly since I can't feel his ache. Now what sense is there to this? And what sense is there to "I can feel my ache"? It makes sense to say "His ache is worse than mine", but not to say "I feel my toothache" and "Two people can't have the same pain". Consider the statement that no two people can ever see the same sense datum. If being in the same position as another person were taken as the criterion for someone's seeing the same sense datum as he does, then one could imagine a person seeing the same datum, say, by seeing through someone's head. But if there is no criterion for seeing the same datum, then "I can't know that he sees what I see" does not make sense. We are likely to muddle statements of fact which are undisputed with grammatical statements. Statements of fact and grammatical statements are not to be confused.

The question whether someone else has what I have when I have toothache may be meaningless, though in an ordinary situation it might be a question of fact, and the answer, "He has not", a statement of fact. But the philosopher who says of someone else, "He has not got what I have", is not stating a fact. He is not saying that in fact someone else has not got toothache. It might be the case that someone else has it. And the statement that he has it has the meaning given it, that is, whatever sense is given by the criterion. The difficulty lies in the grammar of "having toothache". Nonsense is produced by trying to express in a proposition something which belongs to the grammar of our language. By "I can't feel his toothache" is meant that I can't try. It is the character of the logical cannot that one can't try. Of course this doesn't get you far, as you can ask whether you can try to try. In the arguments of idealists and realists somewhere there always occur the words "can", "cannot", "must". No attempt is made to prove their doctrines by experience. The words "possibility" and "necessity" express part of grammar, although patterned after their analogy to "physical possibility" and "physical necessity".

Another way in which the grammars of "I have toothache" and "He has toothache" differ is that it does not make sense to say "I seem to have toothache", whereas it is sensible to say "He seems to have toothache". The statements "I have toothache" and "He has toothache" have different verifications; but "verification" does not have the same meaning in the two cases. The verification of my having toothache is having it. It makes no sense for me to answer the question, "How do you know you have toothache?" by "I know it because I feel it". In fact there is something wrong with the question; and the answer is absurd. Likewise the answer, "I know it by inspection". The process of inspection is looking, not seeing. The statement, "I know it by looking", could be sensible, e.g., concentrating attention on one finger among several for a pain. But as we use the word "ache" it makes no sense to say that I look for it; I do not say I will find out whether I have toothache by tapping my teeth. Of "He has toothache" it is sensible to ask "How do you know?", and criteria can be given which cannot be given in one's own case. In one's own case it makes no sense to ask "How do I know?" It might be thought that since my saying "He seems to have toothache" is sensible but not my saying a similar thing of myself, I could then go on to say "This is so for him but not for me". Is there then a private language I am referring to, which he cannot understand, and thus that he cannot understand my statement that I have toothache? If this is so, it is not a matter of experience that he cannot. He is prevented from understanding, not because of a mental shortcoming but by a fact of grammar. If a thing is *a priori* impossible, it is excluded from language.

Famous quotations

The world is everything that is the case.①

—— *Tractatus Logico-Philosophicus*, 1

Logic must take care of itself.②

—— 5.473

The world of the happy is quite another than the world of the unhappy.③

—— 6.43

Resting on your laurels is as dangerous as resting when you are walking in the snow. You doze off and die in your sleep.④

—— *Culture and Value*

When I obey a rule, I do not choose. I obey the rule blindly.⑤

—— *Philosophical Investigation* §219

The world and life are one.⑥

—— *Tractatus Logico-Philosophicus*, 5.621

Philosophy is a battle against the bewitchment of our intelligence by means of our language.⑦

—— *Philosophical Investigation*

According to Wittgenstein, any proposition that does not picture facts is meaningless — for example "killing is bad." Our language is therefore limited to statements of facts about the world. He arrives at the conclusion that "The limits of my language are the limits of my world."

---

① 世界是由一切发生的事件所构成。——《逻辑哲学论》,第1节。(维特根斯坦认为世界是由事件而不是由事物构成。因为,世界是事件的总和,而不是事物的总和;那发生的情况,即事件,就是事态的存在。)
② 逻辑学必须关心它自身。——第5章第473节。
③ 幸福者的世界几乎是不幸者的世界的另一面。——第6章第43节。
④ 躺在你的胜利上休息如同当你在雪地里行走时小憩一样危险。你打着盹死去。——《文化与价值》
⑤ 当我遵守一个规则时,我不加选择,而是盲目遵从。——《哲学研究》,第219节。
⑥ 世界与生活是同一的。——《逻辑哲学论》,第5章,621节。
⑦ 哲学是一场战斗。在这场战斗中我们用语言对抗我们智力的盅惑。——《哲学研究》。

Living Authentically
—— Heidegger

Chapter 15

Heidegger never thinks "about" something.
He thinks something.

—— Arendt

In this chapter
- Getting to know Heidegger
- Confronting Heidegger's phenomenological ideas
- Appreciating his Being and Time

Martin Heidegger

Born in Messkirch, Germany, Heidegger (1889—1976) received his preparatory schooling in Freiburg University, where he came across the writings of his teacher Husserl, and became intensely interested in philosophy. He soon became well known as an inspirational lecturer. In 1928 he accepted his teacher Husserl's chair at Freiburg. In 1933, having been elected rector of the university he joined the Nazi Party. Although he stepped down as rector one year later, evidence shows his complicity with the Nazis until the end of the Second World War. Heidegger spent the last 30 years of his life traveling and writing until his death at the age of 86.

Heidegger sees himself as a philosopher with a mission to redeem a civilization that had sold out to technology, science and a calculating rationality; that had "fallen out of

Being" and that must be recalled and made once again 'at home' in Being. His writings are considerable and cover a wide range of topics: logic, philosophy of science, philosophy of history, ontology, metaphysics, language, technology, poetry, Greek philosophy and mathematics. In spite of the abstruseness of his ideas his influence spread very wide. Having contributed greatly to the field of phenomenology, existentialism, hermeneutics and post-structuralism, he is acknowledged to be one of the most important philosophers of the 20th century.

Distinctive insights[①]

Heidegger's lifelong project was to answer the "question of being" (Seinsfrage). This question asks, what is it to be an entity of things in general (rocks, tools, people, etc.)? He himself describes his philosophy as the Quest for Being.

1. *Dasein*[②] and Human Existence

What is it to be an entity of things? It is the question of ontology first posed by ancient Greek philosophers from Anaximander to Aristotle. Heidegger holds, however, that philosophers starting with Plato have gone astray in trying to answer this question because they have tended to think of being as a property or essence enduringly present in things. In other words, they have fallen into the "metaphysics of presence," which thinks of being as substance. For him, what is overlooked in traditional metaphysics is the background conditions that enable entities to show up as counting or mattering in some specific way in the first place. In his early works, Heidegger recasts the issue by asking: What is the meaning of being? Or, put differently, how do entities come to show up as intelligible to us in some determinate way? Heidegger thinks this question calls for an analysis of the entity that has some prior understanding of things: human existence or *Dasein* (the German word for "existence" or "being-amidst," used to refer to the structures of human that make possible an understanding of being). Heidegger's claim is that *Dasein*'s pretheoretical (or "preontological") understanding of being, embodied in its everyday practices, opens a "clearing" in which entities can show up as, say, tools, protons, numbers, mental events, and so on. This historically unfolding clearing is what the metaphysical tradition overlooked. He believes that rather than trying to find the abstract definition that looks at human life from the outside of the world, he attempts to provide a much more concrete analysis of "being" from what could be called an insider's position. To be human, he says, is to be a temporal event of self-manifestation that lets other sorts of entities first come to "emerge and abide" in the world. There is no pre-given human essence, instead, humans are self-interpreting beings, and what they make of themselves in the course of their active lives. Thus, as everyday agency, *Dasein* is not an

---

① 海德格尔毕生探求"存在"的意义，试图通过对人的生存状态的分析来揭示存在的意义，将烦、畏、死、良知等视作人生的基本结构，赋予它们本体论的意义。

② 此在，亦称"亲在"，在此存在着。海德格尔认为，时间是一切"存在领悟"的条件，于是此在即是时间。

object with properties, but is rather the "happening" of a life course "stretched out between birth and death."

2. Being and Time

When Heidegger asks about the meaning of being, he is not asking about abstract concepts, but about something very direct and immediate ones. He believes that the meaning of our being must be tied up with time; we are essentially temporal beings. When we are born, we find ourselves in the world as if we had been thrown here on a trajectory① we have not chosen. We simply find that we have come to exist, in an ongoing world that pre-existed us, so that at our birth we are presented with a particular historical, material, and spiritual environment. We attempt to make sense of this world by engaging in various pastimes — for example, we might go to university, or decide to make a living by writing, or attempt to find true love. Through these time-consuming projects we literally project ourselves toward different possible futures; we define our existence. However, sometimes we become aware that there is an outermost limit to all our projects, a point at which everything we plan will come to an end, whether finished or unfinished. This point is the point of our death. Death, Heidegger says, is the outermost horizon of our being; everything we can do or see or think takes place within this horizon. We cannot see beyond it.

3. Living Authentically

It is to Heidegger that we owe the philosophical distinction between authentic and inauthentic existence. According to Heidegger, to live authentically involves to clear-sightedly face up to one's responsibility for what one's life is adding up to as a whole, and to seize on the possibilities to fulfill oneself within his horizon. Heidegger says most of the time, wrapped up in various ongoing projects we exist in the thick of things — in the midst of life, that we forget about death. But in seeing our life purely in terms of the projects in which we are engaged, we miss a more fundamental dimension of our existence, and to that extent, he believes, we are existing inauthentically. When we become aware of death as the ultimate limit of our possibilities, we start to reach a deeper understanding of what it means to exist. For instance, when a good friend passes away, we may look at our own lives and realize that the various projects which absorb us from day to day feel meaningless, and that there is a deeper dimension to life that is missing. So we may find ourselves changing our priorities and projecting ourselves toward different futures. When, through anxiety and hearing the call of conscience, we face up to our being-toward-death, our lives can be transformed.

Introductory remarks

The following selection is from the first part of the introduction of Heidegger's

---

① trajectory: 轨道。

*Being and Time*① (1927). It consists of the lengthy two-part introduction, followed by Division One, the "Preparatory Fundamental Analysis of Dasein," and Division Two, "Dasein and Temporality." The book is an exploration of the meaning of being, and is an analysis of time as a horizon for the understanding of being. The basic idea of *Being and Time* is extremely simple: being is time.

In the passage, Heidegger explains the importance of the retrieve of the Question of Being. He proposes to understand being itself, as distinguished from any specific entities. And he argues that a true understanding of being can only proceed by referring to particular beings, and that the best method of pursuing being must inevitably involve a kind of hermeneutic circle, that is (as he explains in his critique of prior work in the field of hermeneutics), it must rely upon repetitive yet progressive acts of interpretation.

Text

The Necessity of an Explicit Retrieve of the Question of Being

This question has today been forgotten—although our time considers itself progressive in again affirming "metaphysics." All the same we believe that we are spared the exertion of rekindling a gigantomachia peri tes ousias②["a Battle of Giants concerning Being," Plato, Sophist 245e6-246e1]. But the question touched upon here is hardly an arbitrary one. It sustained the avid research of Plato and Aristotle but from then on ceased to be heard as a thematic question of actual investigation. What these two thinkers achieved has been preserved in various distorted and "camouflaged③" forms down to Hegel's Logic. And what then was wrested from phenomena by the highest exertion of thought, albeit in fragments and first beginnings, has long since been trivialized④.

Not only that. On the foundation of the Greek point of departure for the interpretation of being a dogma has taken shape which not only declares that the question of the meaning of being is superfluous but sanctions its neglect. It is said that "being" is the most universal and the emptiest concept. As such it resists every attempt at definition⑤. Nor does this most universal and thus indefinable concept need any definition. Everybody uses it constantly and also already understands what is meant by it. Thus what troubled ancient philosophizing and kept it so by virtue of its obscurity has become obvious, clear as day, such that who-ever persists in asking about it is accused of

---

① 《存在与时间》,试图通过对人的生存的基本结构的分析,探求存在的意义。
② rekindling a gigantomachia peri tes ousias: 重新开始巨人间关于存在的争论。gigantomachia=gigantomachy: 巨人间的战争,大国间的战争。
③ camouflaged: 伪装的。
④ trivialized: 无足轻重的,琐碎的,不重要的。
⑤ "being" is the most universal ... every attempt at definition: "存在"是最普遍最空洞的概念,所以它本身就反对任何下定义的企图。

an error of method.

At the beginning of this inquiry the prejudices that constantly instill and repeatedly promote the idea that a questioning of being is not needed cannot be discussed in detail. They are rooted in ancient ontology itself. That ontology can in turn only be interpreted adequately under the guidance of the question of being which has been clarified and answered beforehand. One must proceed with regard to the soil from which the fundamental ontological concepts grew and with reference to the suitable demonstration of the categories and their completeness.① We therefore wish to discuss these prejudices only to the extent that the necessity of a retrieve of the question of the meaning of being becomes evident. There are three such prejudices.

1. "Being" is the most "universal" concept: "*to on esti katholou mahsta panton.*" *Illud quod primo cadit sub apprehensione est ens, cuius intellectus includitur in omnibus, quaecumque quis apprehendit.* "An understanding of being is always already contained in everything we apprehend in beings."② But the "universality" of "being" is not that of genus. "Being" does not delimit③ the highest region of beings so far as they are conceptually articulated according to genus and species: *oute to on genos* ["Being is not a genus"]. The "universality" of being "surpasses" the universality of genus④. According to the designation⑤ of medieval ontology, "being" is a transcendence. Aristotle himself understood the unity of this transcendental "universal," as opposed to the manifold of the highest generic concepts with material content, as the unity of analogy. Despite his dependence upon Plato's ontological position, Aristotle placed the problem of being on a fundamentally new basis with this discovery. To be sure, he too did not clarify the obscurity of these categorical connections. Medieval ontology discussed this problem in many ways, above all in the Thomist and Scotist schools, without gaining fundamental clarity⑥. And when Hegel finally defines "being" as the "indeterminate immediate," and makes this definition the foundation of all the further categorical explications of his Logic, he remains within the perspective of ancient ontology—except that he does give up the problem, raised early on by Aristotle, of the unity of being in contrast to the manifold of "categories" with material content. If one says accordingly that "Being" is the most

---

① That ontology... and answered beforehand: 反过来,本体论只有借助于事先澄清和解答的存在问题为前题,本能得到充分的阐释。

② An understanding of being... everything we apprehend in beings: 无论一个人于存在者处把握到的是什么,这种把握总已经包含了对存在的某种领会。[源自托马斯·阿奎那(c.1225—1274)的《神学大全》; *to on esti katholou mahsta panton*: 引用自亚里士多德的《形而上学》。]

③ delimit: 定……的界限;作为……边界。

④ The "universality" of being "surpasses" the universality of genus: 存在的"普遍性"超乎一切族类上的普遍性。

⑤ designation: 名称;称呼。

⑥ Medieval ontology discussed... fundamental clarity: 中世纪本体论主要依据托马斯主义和司各脱主义的学说对这一问题进行了各种各样的讨论,但并没能从根本上弄清楚这个问题。(托马斯主义指托马斯·阿奎那的哲学和神学体系。司各脱主义指基督教神学家司各脱(1265—1308)的神学学说。)

universal concept, that cannot mean that it is the clearest and that it needs no further discussion①. The concept of "being" is rather the most obscure of all.

2. The concept of "being" is indefinable. This conclusion was drawn from its highest universality. And correctly so — *if definitio fit per genus proximum et differentiam specificam*②[if "definition is achieved through the proximate genus and the specific difference"]. Indeed, "being" cannot be understood as a being. *Enti non additur aliqua natura*: "Being" cannot be defined by attributing beings to it. Being cannot be derived from higher concepts by way of definition and cannot be represented by lower ones③. But does it follow from this that "being" can no longer constitute a problem? Not at all. We can conclude only that "being" is not something like a being. Thus the manner of definition of beings which has its justification within limits — the "definition" of traditional logic which is itself rooted on ancient ontology — cannot be applied to being④. The indefinability of being does not dispense with the question of its meaning but forces it upon us.

3. "Being" is the self-evident concept. "Being" is used in all knowing and predicating, in every relation to beings and in every relation to oneself, and the expression is understandable "without further ado." Everybody understands, "The sky is blue," "I am happy," and similar statements. But this average comprehensibility only demonstrates the incomprehensibility. It shows that an enigma⑤ lies *a priori* in every relation and being toward beings as beings. The fact that we live already in an understanding of being and that the meaning of being is at the same time shrouded in darkness proves the fundamental necessity of repeating the question of the meaning of "being".

If what is "self-evident" and this alone—"the covert judgments of common reason"⑥ (Kant)—is to become and remain the explicit theme of our analysis (as "the business of philosophers"), then the appeal to self-evidence in the realm of basic philosophical concepts, and indeed with regard to the concept "being," is a dubious procedure⑦.

But consideration of the prejudices has made it clear at the same time that not only is the answer to the question of being lacking but even the question itself is obscure and

---

① If one says accordingly…it needs no further discussion：因此人们要是说："存在"是最普遍的概念,那可并不就等于说：它是最清楚的概念,再也用不着进一步讨论了。

② if definitio fit per genus proximum et differentiam specificam：(拉丁文)如果定义来自最近的种属及其具体的差异。

③ Indeed, "being" can-not be understood…be represented by lower ones：的确"存在"不能被理解为存在者,令存在者归属于存在并不能成为"存在"的定义。存在既不能用定义方法从更高的概念导出,又不能由较低的概念来表现。

④ Thus the manner of definition of beings which has its justification within limits — the "definition" of traditional logic which is itself rooted on ancient ontology — cannot be applied to being：所以,虽然传统逻辑的"定义方法"可以在一定限度内规定存在者——传统逻辑本身就根植在古希腊存在论之中——但这种方法不适用于"存在"。

⑤ enigma：费解的事物；令人困惑的处境。

⑥ the covert judgments of common reason：通常理性的隐秘判断。〔源自康德〕

⑦ then the appeal to self-evidence…is a dubious procedure：在哲学的基础概念范围内,尤其涉及到"存在"这个概念时,求助于自明性实在是一种可疑的方法。

without direction①. Thus to retrieve the question of being means first of all to work out adequately the formulation of the question.

Brainstorming

1. What challenges does Heidegger pose against existing philosophical theories?
2. What does he consider it important to shatter these false myths about the notion of "being"?
3. Why does Heidegger say "this comprehensibility only demonstrate the incomprehensibility"?
4. What, do you think, Heidegger will primarily discuss in the following section of the present text?
5. Briefly outline how theories of "being" develop throughout western philosophy.
6. What do you think is Heidegger's own solution to the question of "being"?

Famous quotations

Why are there beings at all, and why not rather nothing? That is a question.②

—— *What is Metaphysics*

Language is the house of the truth of being.③

—— *Letter on Humanism*

In order to remain silent Dasein must have something to say.④

—— *Being and Time*

Man acts as though he were the shaper and master of language, while in fact language remains the master of man.⑤

—— *...poetically, Man Dwells...*

We should raise anew the meaning of being.⑥

—— *Being and Time*

We are the entities to be analyzed.⑦

—— *Being and Time*

Supplementary reading

The following passage is taken from *Being and Time*, the second section of Chapter I.

---

① not only is the answer to... is obscure and without direction：存在问题不仅尚无答案,甚至这个问题本身还是晦暗而茫无头绪的。
② 为什么有存在,而不是虚无,这是一个问题。——《什么是形而上学》。
③ 语言是存在的家园。——《有关人文主义的一封信》。
④ 为了保持沉默,此在必须说点什么。——《时间与存在》。
⑤ 人类表现得好像他是语言的创造者与主人,实际上语言仍旧主宰着人类。——《人,诗意的栖居》
⑥ 我们应当重新提起存在的意义这个问题。——《时间与存在》。
⑦ 我们是将要被分析的实体。——《时间与存在》。

Heidegger employs the term *Dasein* to describe the mode of existence of a human being and argues that human life is radically different from other forms of life because it is able to be aware of itself and to reflect on its Being. He regards the analysis as the pathway to an understanding of being itself.

The Formal Structure of the Question of Being (excerpt)

The question of the meaning of being must be formulated. If it is a—or even the—fundamental question, such questioning needs the suitable transparency. Thus we must briefly discuss what belongs to a question in general in order to be able to make clear that the question of being is an eminent one.

Every questioning is a seeking. Every seeking takes its direction beforehand from what is sought. Questioning is a knowing search for beings in their thatness and whatness. The knowing search can become an "investigation", as the revealing determination of what the question aims at. Besides what is asked, what is interrogated also belongs to questioning. What is questioned is to be defined and conceptualized in the investigating, that is, the specifically theoretical, question. As what is really intended, what is to be ascertained lies in what is questioned; here questioning arrives at its goal. As an attitude adopted by a being, the questioner, questioning has its own character of being. Questioning can come about as "just asking around" or as an explicitly formulated question. What is peculiar to the latter is the fact that questioning first becomes lucid in advance with regard to all the above-named constitutive characteristics of the question.

The question to be formulated is about the meaning of being. Thus we are confronted with the necessity of explicating the question of being with regard to the structural moments cited.

As a seeking, questioning needs prior guidance from what it seeks. The meaning of being must therefore already be available to us in a certain way. We intimated that we are always already involved in an understanding of being. From this grows the explicit question of the meaning of being and the tendency toward its concept. We do not know what "being" means. But already when we ask, "What is being?" we stand in an understanding of the "is" without being able to determine conceptually what the "is" means. We do not even know the horizon upon which we are supposed to grasp and pin down the meaning. This average and value understanding of being is a fact.

No matter how much this understanding of being wavers and fades and borders on mere verbal knowledge, this indefiniteness of the understanding of being that is always already available is itself a positive phenomenon which needs elucidation. However, an investigation of the meaning of being will not wish to provide this at the outset. The interpretation of the average understanding of being attains its necessary guideline only with the developed concept of being. From the clarity of that concept and the appropriate manner of its explicit understanding we shall be able to discern what the obscure or not yet elucidated understanding of being means, what kinds of obfuscation or hindrance of an explicit elucidation of the meaning of being are possible and necessary.

Furthermore, the average, vague understanding of being can be permeated by traditional theories and opinions about being in such a way that these theories, as the sources of the prevailing understanding, remain hidden. What is sought in the question of being is not completely unfamiliar, although it is at first totally ungraspable.

What is asked about in the question to be elaborated is being, that which determines beings as beings, that in terms of which beings have always been understood no matter how they are discussed. The being of beings "is" itself not a being. The first philosophical step in understanding the problem of being consists in avoiding the *mython tina diegeisthai*, in not "telling a story," that is, not determining beings as beings by tracing them back in their origins to another being—as if being had the character of a possible being. As what is asked about, being thus requires its own kind of demonstration which is essentially different from the discovery of beings. Hence what is to be ascertained, the meaning of being, will require its own conceptualization, which again is essentially distinct from the concepts in which beings receive their determination of meaning.

Insofar as being constitutes what is asked about, and insofar as being means the being of beings, beings themselves turn out to be what is interrogated in the question of being. Beings are, so to speak, interrogated with regard to their being. But if they are to exhibit the characteristics of their being without falsification they must for their part have become accessible in advance as they are in themselves. The question of being demands that the right access to beings be gained and secured in advance with regard to what it interrogates. But we call many things "existent" [seiend], and in different senses. Everything we talk about, mean, and are related to is in being in one way or another. What and how we ourselves are is also in being. Being is found in thatness and whatness, reality, the objective presence of things [Vorhandenheit], subsistence, validity, existence [Da-sein], and in the "there is" [es gibt]. In which being is the meaning of being to be found; from which being is the disclosure of being to get its start? Is the starting point arbitrary, or does a certain being have priority in the elaboration of the question of being? Which is this exemplary being and in what sense does it have priority?

If the question of being is to be explicitly formulated and brought to complete clarity concerning itself, then the elaboration of this question requires, in accord with what has been elucidated up to now, explication of the ways of regarding being and of understanding and conceptually grasping its meaning, preparation of the possibility of the right choice of the exemplary being, and elaboration of the genuine mode of access to this being. Regarding, understanding and grasping, choosing, and gaining access to, are constitutive attitudes of inquiry and are thus themselves modes of being of a particular being, of the being we inquirers ourselves in each case are. Thus to work out the question of being means to make a being—one who questions—transparent in its being. Asking this question, as a mode of being of a being, is itself essentially determined by what is asked about in its being. This being which we ourselves in each case are and which includes inquiry among the possibilities of its being we formulate terminologically as Da-sein. The explicit and lucid formulation of the question of the meaning of being requires a prior suitable explication of a being (Da-sein) with regard to its being.

But does not such an enterprise fall into an obvious circle? To have to determine beings in their being beforehand and then on this foundation first pose the question of being—what else is that but going around in circles? In working out the question do we not presuppose something that only the answer can provide? Formal objections such as the argument of "circular reasoning," an argument that is always easily raised in the area of investigation of principles, are always sterile when one is weighing concrete ways of investigating. They do not offer anything to the understanding of the issue and they hinder penetration into the field of investigation.

All being is "a being-towards-death", but only humans recognize this. Since we realize that our lives are temporal, we should face up to our responsibility and seize on the opportunities to fulfill ourselves. And only in this way can we live a meaningful and authentic life.

Man Makes Himself
—— Sartre

Chapter 16

Sartre's oeuvre is a unique phenomenon. No other major philosopher has also been a major playwright, novelist, political theorist, and literary critic. It is still too early to judge which facet of Sartre's extraordinary genius posterity will regard as the most important, but since his philosophy permeates his other works, its enduring interest is assured.

—— Thomas Baldwin

In this chapter
- Getting to know Sartre
- Surveying the philosophical view of "Existence precedes essence"
- Appreciating Sartre's "No Exit"

Jean-Paul Sartre

  Friedrich Nietzsche (1844—1990) once prophetically wrote: "Europe now philosophizes with hammer blows". One of those who hit hardest in the 20th century was Sartre.

  Born in Paris, Sartre was only 15 months old when his father died. He proved a gifted student when he studied in the prestigious école Normale Supérieure. It was here that he met his lifelong partner — feminist author and social theorist Simone de Beauvoir. After graduation, he worked first as a teacher and was appointed Professor of Philosophy at the University of Le Havre in 1931. Never married throughout his life, Sartre was noted for his relationship with Beauvoir. He was offered but declined Nobel Prize in Literature in 1964. Such was his influence and popularity that when he died his funeral procession should have been followed by a crowd of some 50,000 people.

Sartre is a playwright, novelist, screenwriter, political activist, biographer, and literary critic, but most of all, he is one of the leading figures in the 20th century French philosophy. In the last ten years in Sartre's life that the fewer and less accessible the books he published, the more famous he became and the more admiration he received especially from the young people. He had always been the figurehead for a political and philosophical attitude which transcended his actual published works. Being one of the key figures in the philosophy of existentialism, his work is known to students, intellectuals, revolutionaries, and even the general reading public the world over, and it continues to influence fields such as Marxist philosophy, sociology, critical theory and literary studies.

Distinctive insights[①]

Existentialism, as the "-ism" suggests, is a term used to cover a wide range of views which deals with the experience of existing as a human being. So its first concern should be giving an account of how an individual consciousness apprehends existence and from this concern flow its main preoccupations: considerations about freedom, choice, personal authenticity, relationships with the world and other people, and about the ways in which individual meanings and values are generated.

1. Existence Precedes Essence

To clarify what is meant by human being, Sartre gives the following illustration. He asks us to imagine a paper-knife — the kind of knife that might be used to open an envelope. This knife has been made by a craftsman who has had the idea of creating such a tool, and who had a clear understanding of what is required of a paper-knife. It needs to be sharp enough to cut through paper, but not so sharp as to be dangerous to human being. It needs to be easy to wield, made of an appropriate substance such as metal, bamboo, or wood, perhaps, but not butter, wax, or feathers, and should be fashioned to function efficiently. Sartre says that it is inconceivable for a paper-knife to exist without its maker knowing what it is going to be used for. Therefore, the essence of a paper-knife — or all of the things that make it a paper-knife and not a steak knife or a paper airplane — comes before the existence of any particular paper-knife.

Humans, of course, are not paper-knives. For Sartre, there is no preordained plan that makes us the kind of being that we are. We are not made for any particular purpose. We exist, but not because of our purpose or essence like a paper-knife does; our existence precedes our essence.

---

① 萨特把存在当作哲学的研究对象，认为个人存在是一切存在的出发点，人真正的存在可还原为先于主客体区分的个人的纯粹意识活动，由此可展现世界的存在；人的存在不同于物的存在，他是积极能动的超越存在，即不断谋划选择和创造，人的真正的存在就是人的自由，人就是在自由的创造活动中获得自己的规定性和本质，故，人的存在先于人的本质。

2. For-itself versus In-itself[①]

Sartre's primary question is what it is like to be a human being? For him, human reality consists of two modes of experience, being and nothingness. In both being and none-being, the human being exists both as an In-itself, an object of things, and as For-itself, a consciousness which is no-thing, but simply not that thing of which it is conscious. He describes the existence of the In-itself, of a phenomenon or thing, as "opaque to itself... because it is filled with itself". A thing has no inner and outer aspects, no consciousness of itself; it just exists physically. In contrast the For-itself, or consciousness, has no such fullness of existence.

3. Responsible Freedom

Since ancient times, the question of what it is to be human and what makes human so distinct from all other types of being has been one of the main preoccupations of philosophers. Their approach to the question assumes that there is such a thing as human nature, or an essence of what it is to be human. For Sartre, however, thinking about human nature in this way risks missing what is most important about human beings, and that is our freedom. By making choices, he believes, we are also creating a template for how we consider a human life ought to be. If I decide to become a doctor, then I am not just deciding for myself. I am implicitly saying that being a doctor is a worthwhile activity. This means that freedom is the greatest responsibility of all. We are not just responsible for the impact that our choices have upon ourselves, but also for the impact on the whole of mankind. And, with no external principles or rules to justify our actions, we have no excuses to hold for the choices that we make. This is Sartre's precious notion of freedom and its concomitant sense of personal responsibility.

4. Anguish

The notion of anguish, or dread, has become something of a trademark of Sartre's existentialism. Sartre maintains that we turn away from freedom because in recognizing it we experience anguish. Anguish is felt because where there is nothing to determine choice. It is possible that one might choose in the next moment, something appalling and terrible, from the thought of which one now turns away in horror.

Introductory remarks

The following passage is taken from Sartre's *Existentialisme est un humanisme* ("*Existentialism Is Humanism*"). By claiming that "existentialism is a humanism" Sartre does not want to say that existentialism is a kind of "Red Cross" (humanitarian) philosophy. He rather wishes to place his version of existentialism into the mainstream of the libertarian humanist tradition that could be traced back to the Renaissance and its stress

---

① 萨特将存在分为自在存在与自为存在,前者为意识之外的存在,后者为意识的存在,意识的存在为一切存在的意义和基础。人的存在特征是先于本质,即人先存在,后取得其本质,取得本质的过程即计划和意向的过程,人在这个过程中发挥他的自由。

on human creativity and freedom. Sartre described the human condition in summary form: freedom entails total responsibility, in the face of which we experience anguish, forlornness, and despair; genuine human dignity can be achieved only in our active acceptance of these emotions.

Existentialism Is Humanism① (excerpt)

My purpose here is to offer a defense of existentialism against several reproaches that have been laid against it.

First, it has been reproached as an invitation to people to dwell in quietism of despair②. For if every way to a solution is barred, one would have to regard any action in this world as entirely ineffective, and one would arrive finally at a contemplative philosophy. Moreover, since contemplation is a luxury, this would be only another bourgeois philosophy. This is, especially, the reproach made by the Communists.

From another quarter we are reproached for having underlined all that is ignominious in the human situation, for depicting what is mean, sordid or base to the neglect of certain things that possess charm and beauty and belong to the brighter side of human nature③: for example, according to the Catholic critic, Mlle. Mercier, we forget how an infant smiles. Both from this side and from the other we are also reproached for leaving out of account the solidarity of mankind and considering man in isolation. And this, say the Communists, is because we base our doctrine upon pure subjectivity — upon the Cartesian "I think"④: which is the moment in which solitary man attains to himself; a position from which it is impossible to regain solidarity with other men who exist outside of the self. The ego cannot reach them through the *cogito*⑤.

From the Christian side, we are reproached as people who deny the reality and seriousness of human affairs. For since we ignore the commandments of God and all values prescribed as eternal, nothing remains but what is strictly voluntary. Everyone can do what he likes, and will be incapable, from such a point of view, of condemning either the point of view or the action of anyone else.

It is to these various reproaches that I shall endeavor to reply today; that is why I have entitled this brief exposition "Existentialism is a Humanism." Many may be surprised at the mention of humanism in this connection, but we shall try to see in what sense we

---

① 《存在主义是一种人道主义》(1946),对存在主义基本原则作了详尽阐述,断言不存在设定人性范本的上帝,也不存在古典哲学倡导的普遍人性。人的生存状态展现出来的是,首先有人,人遭逢自己,在世界上涌现出来,然后才给自己下定义。

② it has been...despair:存在主义曾被指责为诱导人们安于一种绝望的无为主义。quietism:无为主义。

③ From another quarter...of human nature:在另一方面,我们被指责为偏重了人类处境中黯淡的一面,只看到下贱、卑鄙和低劣,却忽略了人性光明面中某些仁慈和美好的事物。from another quarter:另一方面;ignominious:耻辱的,可鄙的。sordid:肮脏的,卑鄙的;base:劣等的。

④ I think:"我思",笛卡儿的"我思故我在"命题。

⑤ The ego...through the cogito:自我不能透过思维而与他们相同。cogito:(拉丁文)我思。

understand it. In any case, we can begin by saying that existentialism, in our sense of the word, is a doctrine that does render human life possible; a doctrine, also, which affirms that every truth and every action imply both an environment and a human subjectivity①. The essential charge laid against us is, of course, that of over-emphasis upon the evil side of human life. I have lately been told of a lady who, whenever she lets slip a vulgar expression in a moment of nervousness②, excuses herself by exclaiming, "I believe I am becoming an existentialist." So it appears that ugliness is being identified with existentialism. That is why some people say we are "naturalistic," and if we are, it is strange to see how much we scandalize and horrify them, for no one seems to be much frightened or humiliated nowadays by what is properly called naturalism Those who can quite well keep down a novel by Zola such as La Terre③ are sickened as soon as they read an existentialist novel. Those who appeal to the wisdom of the people — which is a sad wisdom — find ours sadder still. And yet, what could be more disillusioned than such sayings as "Charity begins at home" or "Promote a rogue and he'll sue you for damage, knock him down and he'll do you homage④"? We all know how many common sayings can be quoted to this effect, and they all mean much the same — that you must not oppose the powers that be; that you must not fight against superior force; must not meddle in matters that are above your station. Or that any action not in accordance with some tradition is mere romanticism; or that any undertaking which has not the support of proven experience is foredoomed to frustration; and that since experience has shown men to be invariably inclined to evil, there must be firm rules to restrain them, otherwise we shall have anarchy⑤. It is, however, the people who are forever mouthing these dismal proverbs and, whenever they are told of some more or less repulsive action, say "How like human nature!" — it is these very people, always harping upon realism, who complain that existentialism is too gloomy a view of things. Indeed their excessive protests make me suspect that what is annoying them is not so much our pessimism, but, much more likely, our optimism⑥. For at bottom, what is alarming in the doctrine that I am about to try to explain to you is — is it not? — that it confronts man with a possibility of

---

① ...a doctrine that does...human subjectivity：是一种使人生成为可能的学说；这种学说宣称任何真理和行为都包含着环境和人的主观性。

② ...lets slip a vulgar expression in a moment of nervousness：神经过敏地说了一句粗俗的话。let slip：不经意中说出。

③ 《土地》，法国自然主义文学流派左拉(1840—1902)所著。

④ And yet...do you homage：然而，又有什么比"仁爱始于家庭"或者"升擢歹徒，他会反咬；将他击倒，他则崇拜"之类的话更让人感到嗒然若丧呢？("仁慈始于家庭"源于法国作曲家福莱(Gabriel Fauré, 1845—1924)的"仁慈始于家庭，但不应当止于家庭"。)

⑤ Or that any action...we shall have anarchy：或是，任何不依从一些传统的行为都只是浪漫主义；或是不根据过去经验的行为，都注定要失败的；既然经验显示出人总是倾向于罪恶，因此必须有严厉的规则来约束他们，否则我们就要陷于无政府状态。

⑥ it is these very people...much more likely, our optimism：就是这些重弹写实主义老调的人，在抱怨存在主义对事物的看法太过于阴郁。的确，他们那些过度的抗议倒使我怀疑触怒他们的不是我们的悲观，而是我们的乐观。harping upon：老生常谈。

choice. To verify this, let us review the whole question upon the strictly philosophic level. What, then, is this that we call existentialism?

Most of those who are making use of this word would be highly confused if required to explain its meaning. For since it has become fashionable, people cheerfully declare that this musician or that painter is "existentialist." A columnist in Clartes① signs himself "The Existentialist," and, indeed, the word is now so loosely applied to so many things that it no longer means anything at all. It would appear that, for the lack of any novel doctrine such as that of surrealism, all those who are eager to join in the latest scandal or movement now seize upon this philosophy in which, however, they can find nothing to their purpose. For in truth this is of all teachings the least scandalous and the most austere②: it is intended strictly for technicians and philosophers. All the same, it can easily be defined.

The question is only complicated because there are two kinds of existentialists. There are, on the one hand, the Christians, amongst whom I shall name Jaspers and Gabriel Marcel③, both professed Catholics; and on the other the existential atheists, amongst whom we must place Heidegger as well as the French existentialists and myself. What they have in common is simply the fact that they believe that existence comes before essence — or, if you will, that we must begin from the subjective④. What exactly do we mean by that?

If one considers an article of manufacture as, for example, a book or a paper-knife — one sees that it has been made by an artisan who had a conception of it; and he has paid attention, equally, to the conception of a paper-knife and to the pre-existent technique of production⑤ which is a part of that conception and is, at bottom, a formula. Thus the paper-knife is at the same time an article producible in a certain manner and one which, on the other hand, serves a definite purpose, for one cannot suppose that a man would produce a paper-knife without knowing what it was for. Let us say, then, of the paperknife that its essence — that is to say the sum of the formulae and the qualities which made its production and its definition possible — precedes its existence. The presence of such-and-such a paper-knife or book is thus determined before my eyes. Here, then, we are viewing the world from a technical standpoint, and we can say that production precedes existence.

When we think of God as the creator, we are thinking of him, most of the time, as a supernal artisan. Whatever doctrine we may be considering, whether it be a doctrine like that of Descartes, or of Leibnitz⑥ himself, we always imply that the will follows, more

---

① A columnist in Clartes:《光明报》专栏作家。
② For in truth...most austere:因为事实上这在所有的学说中是最少恶意中伤,也是最为严谨的。
③ 雅斯培(1883—1969),德国哲学家;加百利·马赛尔(1889—1973),法国哲学家。
④ or, if you will, that we must begin from the subjective:或者,如果你愿意,也可以说:主体必须作为一切的起点。
⑤ the pre-existent technique of production:先于存在的制作技巧。
⑥ Leibnitz:莱布尼茨(1646—1716),德国自然科学家,哲学家。

or less, from the understanding or at least accompanies it① so that when God creates he knows precisely what he is creating. Thus, the conception of man in the mind of God is comparable to that of the paper-knife in the mind of the artisan: God makes man according to a procedure and a conception, exactly as the artisan manufactures a paper-knife, following a definition and a formula. Thus each individual man is the realization of a certain conception which dwells in the divine understanding.② In the philosophic atheism of the eighteenth century, the notion of God is suppressed, but not, for all that, the idea that essence is prior to existence; something of that idea we still find everywhere, in Diderot in Voltaire③ and even in Kant. Man possesses a human nature; that "human nature," which is the conception of human being, is found in every man; which means that each man is a particular example of a universal conception, the conception of Man. In Kant, this universality goes so far that the wild man of the woods, man in the state of nature and the bourgeois are all contained in the same definition and have the same fundamental qualities. Here again, the essence of man precedes that historic existence which we confront in experience④.

Atheistic existentialism, of which I am a representative, declares with greater consistency that if God does not exist there is at least one being whose existence comes before its essence, a being which exists before it can be defined by any conception of it. That being is man or, as Heidegger has it, the human reality. What do we mean by saying that existence precedes essence? We mean that man first of all exists, encounters himself, surges up in the world — and defines himself afterwards. If man as the existentialist sees him is not definable, it is because to begin with he is nothing. He will not be anything until later, and then he will be what he makes of himself. Thus, there is no human nature, because there is no God to have a conception of it. Man simply is. Not that he is simply what he conceives himself to be, but he is what he wills, and as he conceives himself after already existing — as he wills to be after that leap towards existence. Man is nothing else but that which he makes of himself⑤. That is the first principle of existentialism. And this is what people call its "subjectivity," using the word as a reproach against us. But what do we mean to say by this, but that man is of a greater dignity than a stone or a table? For we mean to say that man primarily exists — that man is, before all else, something which propels itself towards a future and is aware that it is doing so. Man is, indeed, a project which possesses a subjective life, instead of being a kind of moss, or a fungus or a cauliflower. Before that projection of the self nothing exists; not even in the

---

① ...we always imply...accompanies it: 我们多少总认为理念先于创作,或者至少伴随而来。
② Thus, each individual...divine understanding: 所以,每个个体都是上帝睿智中某个概念的实现。
③ 狄德罗(1713—1784),法国唯物主义哲学家;伏尔泰(1694—1778),法国启蒙思想家。
④ the essence...in experience: 人的本质先于我们在经验中所遭逢到的历史存在。
⑤ Man is...makes of himself: 人除了自我塑造外,什么也不是。

heaven of intelligence: man will only attain existence when he is what he purposes to be①. Not, however, what he may wish to be. For what we usually understand by wishing or willing is a conscious decision taken — much more often than not — after we have made ourselves what we are. I may wish to join a party, to write a book or to marry — but in such a case what is usually called my will is probably a manifestation of a prior and more spontaneous decision. If, however, it is true that existence is prior to essence, man is responsible for what he is. Thus, the first effect of existentialism is that it puts every man in possession of himself as he is, and places the entire responsibility for his existence squarely upon his own shoulders②. And, when we say that man is responsible for himself, we do not mean that he is responsible only for his own individuality, but that he is responsible for all men. The word "subjectivism" is to be understood in two senses, and our adversaries play upon only one of them. Subjectivism means, on the one hand, the freedom of the individual subject and, on the other, that man cannot pass beyond human subjectivity. It is the latter which is the deeper meaning of existentialism. When we say that man chooses himself, we do mean that every one of us must choose himself; but by that we also mean that in choosing for himself he chooses for all men. For in effect, of all the actions a man may take in order to create himself as he wills to be, there is not one which is not creative, at the same time, of an image of man such as he believes he ought to be. To choose between this or that is at the same time to affirm the value of that which is chosen; for we are unable ever to choose the worse③. What we choose is always the better; and nothing can be better for us unless it is better for all. If, moreover, existence precedes essence and we will to exist at the same time as we fashion our image, that image is valid for all and for the entire epoch in which we find ourselves. Our responsibility is thus much greater than we had supposed, for it concerns mankind as a whole. If I am a worker, for instance, I may choose to join a Christian rather than a Communist trade union. And if, by that membership, I choose to signify that resignation is, after all, the attitude that best becomes a man④, that man's kingdom is not upon this earth, I do not commit myself alone to that view. Resignation is my will for everyone, and my action is, in consequence, a commitment on behalf of all mankind. Or if, to take a more personal case, I decide to marry and to have children, even though this decision proceeds simply from my situation, from my passion or my desire, I am thereby committing not only myself, but humanity as a whole, to the practice of monogamy⑤. I

---

① Before that projection of the self nothing exists; not even in the heaven of intelligence; man will only attain existence when he is what he purposes to be：在这个自我设计之先,无物存在。即使在睿智的上天也没有。人只有在他计划成为什么时才能获得存在。
② the first effect of existentialism... upon his own shoulders：存在主义的第一个作用是它使每一个人主宰他自己,把他存在的责任全然放在他自己的肩膀上。
③ To choose between... unable ever to choose the worse：我们在两者间选择时,同时也在肯定我们所选择对象的价值,因为我们不能选择没有价值。
④ that resignation... becomes a man：为人处事最好忍让为先。resignation：顺从,忍让。
⑤ monogamy：一夫一妻制。

am thus responsible for myself and for all men, and I am creating a certain image of man as I would have him to be. In fashioning myself I fashion man①.

This may enable us to understand what is meant by such terms — perhaps a little grandiloquent — as anguish, abandonment and despair②. As you will soon see, it is very simple. First, what do we mean by anguish? — The existentialist frankly states that man is in anguish. His meaning is as follows: When a man commits himself to anything, fully realizing that he is not only choosing what he will be, but is thereby at the same time a legislator deciding for the whole of mankind — in such a moment a man cannot escape from the sense of complete and profound responsibility③. There are many, indeed, who show no such anxiety. But we affirm that they are merely disguising their anguish or are in flight from it. Certainly, many people think that in what they are doing they commit no one but themselves to anything: and if you ask them, "What would happen if everyone did so?" they shrug their shoulders and reply, "Everyone does not do so." But in truth, one ought always to ask oneself what would happen if everyone did as one is doing; nor can one escape from that disturbing thought except by a kind of self-deception. The man who lies in self-excuse, by saying "Everyone will not do it" must be ill at ease in his conscience, for the act of lying implies the universal value which it denies. By its very disguise his anguish reveals itself. This is the anguish that Kierkegaard called "the anguish of Abraham."④ You know the story: An angel commanded Abraham to sacrifice his son; and obedience was obligatory, if it really was an angel who had appeared and said, "Thou, Abraham, shalt sacrifice thy son." But anyone in such a case would wonder, first, whether it was indeed an angel and secondly, whether I am really Abraham. Where are the proofs? A certain mad woman who suffered from hallucinations said that people were telephoning to her, and giving her orders. The doctor asked, "But who is it that speaks to you?" She replied: "He says it is God." And what, indeed, could prove to her that it was God? If an angel appears to me, what is the proof that it is an angel; or, if I hear voices, who can prove that they proceed from heaven and not from hell, or from my own subconsciousness or some pathological condition? Who can prove that they are really addressed to me?

Who, then, can prove that I am the proper person to impose, by my own choice, my conception of man upon mankind⑤? I shall never find any proof whatever; there will be no sign to convince me of it. If a voice speaks to me, it is still I myself who must decide whether the voice is or is not that of an angel. If I regard a certain course of action as

---

① In fashioning myself I fashion man：我塑造我自己，我也塑造了别人。
② perhaps a little...abandonment despair：或许有一点夸张——例如，焦虑，舍弃和绝望。grandiloquent：夸张的。
③ When a man commits himself...complete and profound responsibility：当一个人有所行动时,他充分地自觉他不只是选择他所意愿的,同时也是一个为全人类裁决的立法者——在这时刻,一个人就不能从一种整体与沉重的责任感中逃避开来。
④ This is the anguish that Kierkegaard...anguish of Abraham"：这种焦虑,就是克尔凯格尔所谓的"亚伯拉罕的焦虑"。亚伯拉罕为《圣经·旧约》中的人物；克尔凯格尔(1813—1855),丹麦哲学家、神学家。
⑤ Who, then...upon mankind：那么，谁能证明我是借我的决策把我对于人的概念来加诸全人类的适当人选呢？

good, it is only I who choose to say that it is good and not bad. There is nothing to show that I am Abraham: nevertheless I also am obliged at every instant to perform actions which are examples. Everything happens to every man as though the whole human race had its eyes fixed upon what he is doing and regulated its conduct accordingly. So every man ought to say, "Am I really a man who has the right to act in such a manner that humanity regulates itself by what I do." If a man does not say that, he is dissembling his anguish. Clearly, the anguish with which we are concerned here is not one that could lead to quietism or inaction. It is anguish pure and simple, of the kind well known to all those who have borne responsibilities. When, for instance, a military leader takes upon himself the responsibility for an attack and sends a number of men to their death, he chooses to do it and at bottom he alone chooses. No doubt under a higher command, but its orders, which are more general, require interpretation by him and upon that interpretation depends the life of ten, fourteen or twenty men. In making the decision, he cannot but feel a certain anguish. All leaders know that anguish. It does not prevent their acting, on the contrary it is the very condition of their action, for the action presupposes that there is a plurality of possibilities, and in choosing one of these, they realize that it has value only because it is chosen. Now it is anguish of that kind which existentialism describes, and moreover, as we shall see, makes explicit through direct responsibility towards other men who are concerned. Far from being a screen which could separate us from action, it is a condition of action itself.

And when we speak of "abandonment" — a favorite word of Heidegger — we only mean to say that God does not exist, and that it is necessary to draw the consequences of his absence right to the end. The existentialist is strongly opposed to a certain type of secular moralism which seeks to suppress God at the least possible expense. Towards 1880, when the French professors endeavored to formulate a secular morality, they said something like this: God is a useless and costly hypothesis, so we will do without it. However, if we are to have morality, a society and a law-abiding world, it is essential that certain values should be taken seriously; they must have an *a priori* existence ascribed to them. It must be considered obligatory *a priori* to be honest, not to lie, not to beat one's wife, to bring up children and so forth; so we are going to do a little work on this subject, which will enable us to show that these values exist all the same, inscribed in an intelligible heaven① although, of course, there is no God. In other words — and this is, I believe, the purport of all that we in France call radicalism — nothing will be changed if God does not exist; we shall rediscover the same norms of honesty, progress and humanity, and we shall have disposed of God as an out-of-date hypothesis which will die away quietly of itself. The existentialist, on the contrary, finds it extremely embarrassing that God does not exist, for there disappears with Him all possibility of finding values in an intelligible heaven. There can no longer be any good *a priori*, since there is no infinite

---

① inscribed in an intelligible heaven: 附属于一个睿智的天国。

and perfect consciousness to think it①. It is nowhere written that "the good" exists, that one must be honest or must not lie, since we are now upon the plane where there are only men. Dostoevsky② once wrote: "If God did not exist, everything would be permitted"; and that, for existentialism, is the starting point. Everything is indeed permitted if God does not exist, and man is in consequence forlorn, for he cannot find anything to depend upon either within or outside himself. He discovers forthwith, that he is without excuse. For if indeed existence precedes essence, one will never be able to explain one's action by reference to a given and specific human nature; in other words, there is no determinism — man is free, man is freedom. Nor, on the other hand, if God does not exist, are we provided with any values or commands that could legitimize our behavior. Thus we have neither behind us, nor before us in a luminous realm of values③, any means of justification or excuse. — We are left alone, without excuse. That is what I mean when I say that man is condemned to be free. Condemned, because he did not create himself, yet is nevertheless at liberty, and from the moment that he is thrown into this world he is responsible for everything he does. The existentialist does not believe in the power of passion. He will never regard a grand passion as a destructive torrent upon which a man is swept into certain actions as by fate, and which, therefore, is an excuse for them. He thinks that man is responsible for his passion. Neither will an existentialist think that a man can find help through some sign being vouchsafed upon earth for his orientation④: for he thinks that the man himself interprets the sign as he chooses. He thinks that every man, without any support or help whatever, is condemned at every instant to invent man. As Ponge⑤ has written in a very fine article, "Man is the future of man." That is exactly true. Only, if one took this to mean that the future is laid up in Heaven, that God knows what it is, it would be false, for then it would no longer even be a future. If, however, it means that, whatever man may now appear to be, there is a future to be fashioned, a virgin future that awaits him — then it is a true saying.

  You can see from these few reflections that nothing could be more unjust than the objections people raise against us. Existentialism is nothing else but an attempt to draw the full conclusions from a consistently atheistic position. Its intention is not in the least that of plunging men into despair. And if by despair one means — as the Christians do — any attitude of unbelief, the despair of the existentialists is something different. Existentialism is not atheist in the sense that it would exhaust itself in demonstrations of the non-existence of God. It declares, rather, that even if God existed that would make no difference from its point of view. Not that we believe God does exist, but we think that the real problem is not that of His existence; what man needs is to find himself again and

---

  ① There can no longer... to think it: 既然没有无限完美的意识加以思考,那么,先验的事物将不再有什么用处。
  ② 陀思妥耶夫斯基(1821—1881),俄国作家。
  ③ a luminous realm of values:光辉的价值领域。
  ④ Neither will... his orientation:存在主义否认一个人可以凭借某种天降标志来帮助他决定未来行动的方向。vouchsafed:赐予。
  ⑤ 蓬热(1899—1987),法国诗人。

to understand that nothing can save him from himself, not even a valid proof of the existence of God①. In this sense existentialism is optimistic. It is a doctrine of action, and it is only by self-deception, by confining their own despair with ours that Christians can describe us as without hope.

Brainstorming

1. How has existentialism been reproached? What is Sartre trying to achieve with this essay? What is his purpose?
2. What was the meaning of Sartre's paper-knife analogy?
3. What are some of the implications of the idea that "existence is prior to essence"? Does that mean that we do not have responsibilities to others?
4. What difference does it make if there is no God? What implication does this have on freedom?
5. If freedom is a good thing, why does Sartre say we are "condemned to be free"?
6. What are the implications of the existential emphasis on freedom for human behavior?
7. When I make what feels like a free choice, am I really acting freely?

Famous quotations

The world of explanations and reasons is not that of existence②.

—— *Nausea*

Consciousness is complete emptiness because the entire world is outside it.

—— *Being and Nothingness*③

My acts cause values to spring up like partridges④.

—— *Being and Nothingness*

Man is a useless passion⑤.

—— *Being and Nothingness*

Hell is other people⑥.

—— *No exit*

Never have I thought that I was happy possessor of a "talent"; my sole concern has been to save myself by work and faith⑦.

---

① what man needs... a valid proof of the existence of God：人所需要的是去重新发现他自己,去了解没有什么东西(即便有上帝存在的确切证据)能够从他的自身中拯救他。
② 解释和理性的世界不是存在的世界。——《恶心》
③ 意识是绝对的空无(因为整个世界在它之外)。——《存在与虚无》
④ 我的行为使得价值观如同鹧鸪一样跳跃。——《存在与虚无》
⑤ 人是一种无用的激情。——《存在与虚无》
⑥ 他人是地狱。——《禁闭》
⑦ 我从来未想到我是占有某种"才能"的幸福之人；我所唯一关注的事便是通过工作和信念拯救我自身。——《言语》

Chapter 16 Man Makes Himself — Sartre

—— *The Words*

Three o'clock is always too late or too early for anything you want to do①.

—— *Nausea*, *Friday*

Man is the future of man.②

—— *Existentialism Is Humanism*

Supplementary reading

Jean-Paul Sartre's *No Exit*③ (Huis Clos) is considered by many to be the author's best play and most accessible dramatization of his philosophy of existentialism. It is a one-act, four-character play, which represents a tight conflict of characters who need one another and, at the same time, desperately want to get away from one another, yet cannot leave. The three characters who are present in the excerpt are Joseph Garcin, a war defector and wife abuser; Inez Serrano, a working-class Spanish woman, who is slowly revealed to be a lesbian; and Estelle Rigault, a member of the French upper class. They are doomed to spend eternity together in a Second Empire drawing room; Sartre's metaphorical hell. This room is devoid of mirrors, windows and books. There is no means of extinguishing the lights and the characters have even lost their eyelids. They have nothing left but one another and the hell (or heaven) they choose to create. Sartre brilliantly gives the characters dual reasons for their eternal damnation: first, each committed abominable acts while alive, and second, and perhaps more importantly, each failed to live his or her life in an authentic manner. The following is an excerpt from the last section of the play.

ESTELLE: You won't gain anything. If that door opens, I'm going too.

INEZ: Where?

ESTELLE: I don't care where. As far from you as I can.

GARCIN: Open the door! Open, blast you! I'll endure anything, your red-hot tongs and molten lead, your racks and prongs and garrotes — all your fiendish gadgets, everything that burns and flays and tears — I'll put up with any torture you impose. Anything, anything would be better than this agony of mind, this creeping pain that gnaws and fumbles and caresses one and never hurts quite enough. Now will you open? (THE DOOR FLIES OPEN: a long silence.)

INEZ: Well, Garcin? You're free to go.

GARCIN: Now I wonder why that door opened.

INEZ: What are you waiting for? Hurry up and go.

GARCIN: I shall not go.

INEZ: And you, Estelle? So what? Which shall it be? Which of the three of us will leave? The barrier's down, why are we waiting? But what a situation! It's a scream!

---

① 三点钟,不管你要干什么,这总是一个太迟或者太早的时刻。——《恶心》
② 人是人的未来。——《存在主义是一种人道主义》
③ 《禁闭》,萨特的哲理剧代表作,重点探讨人与他人的关系问题,以戏剧形式重申了他的存在主义观点。

We're inseparables!

ESTELLE: Inseparables? Garcin, come and lend a hand. Quickly. We'll push her out and slam the door on her. That'll teach her a lesson.

INEZ: (Struggling) Estelle, I beg you, let me stay. I won't go, I won't go! Not into the passage.

GARCIN: Let go of her.

ESTELLE: You're crazy. She hates you.

GARCIN: It's because of her I'm staying here.

INEZ: Because of me? All right, shut the door. It's ten times hotter here since it opened. Because of me, you said?

GARCIN: Yes. YOU, anyhow, know what it means to be a coward.

INEZ: Yes, I know.

GARCIN: And you know what wickedness is, and shame, and fear. There were days when you peered into yourself, into the secret places of your heart, and what you saw there made you faint with horror. And then, next day, you didn't know what to make of it, you couldn't interpret the horror you had glimpsed the day before. Yes, you know what evil costs. And when you say I'm a coward, you know from experience what that means. Is that so?

INEZ: Yes.

GARCIN: So it's you whom I have to convince; you are of my kind. Did you suppose I meant to go? No, I couldn't leave you here, gloating over my defeat, with all those thoughts about me running in your head.

INEZ: Do you really wish to convince me?

GARCIN: That's the one and only thing I wish for now. I can't hear them any longer, you know. Probably that means they're through with me. For good and all. The curtain's down, nothing of me is left on earth — not even the name of coward. So, Inez, we're alone. Only you two remain to give a thought to me. She — she doesn't count. It's you who matter; you who hate me. If you'll have faith in me I'm saved.

INEZ: It won't be easy. Have a look at me. I'm a hard-headed woman.

GARCIN: I'll give you all the time that's needed.

INEZ: Yes, we've lots of time in hand. All time.

GARCIN: Listen! Each man has an aim in life, a leading motive; that's so, isn't it? Well, I didn't give a damn for wealth, or for love. I aimed at being a real man. A tough, as they say. I staked everything on the same horse... Can one possibly be a coward when one's deliberately courted danger at every turn? And can judge a life by a single action?

INEZ: Why not? For thirty years you dreamt you were a hero, and condoned a thousand petty lapses — because a hero, of course, can do no wrong. An easy method, obviously. Then a day came when you were up against it, the red light of real danger — and you took the train to Mexico.

GARCIN: I "dreamt," you say. It was no dream. When I chose the hardest path, I made my choice deliberately. A man is what he wills himself to be.

INEZ: Prove it. Prove it was no dream. It's what one does, and nothing else, that shows the stuff one's made of.

GARCIN: I died too soon. I wasn't allowed time to — to do my deeds.

INEZ: One always dies too soon — or too late. And yet one's whole life is complete at that moment, with a line drawn neatly under it, ready for the summing up. You are — your life, and nothing else.

GARCIN: What a poisonous woman you are! With an answer for everything.

INEZ: Now then! Don't lose heart. It shouldn't be so hard, convincing me. Pull yourself together, man, rake up some arguments. Ah, wasn't I right when I said you were vulnerable? Now you're going to pay the price, and what a price! You're a coward, Garcin, because I wish it! I wish it — do you hear? I wish it. And yet, just look at me, see how weak I am, a mere breath on the air, a gaze observing you, a formless thought that thinks you. Ah, they're open now, those big hands, those coarse, man's hands! But what do you hope to do? You can't throttle thoughts with hands. So you've no choice, you must convince me, and you're at my mercy.

ESTELLE: Garcin!

GARCIN: What?

ESTELLE: Revenge yourself.

GARCIN: How?

ESTELLE: Kiss me, darling——then you'll hear her squeal.

GARCIN: That's true, Inez. I'm at your mercy, but you're at mine as well.

INEZ: Oh, you coward, you weakling, running to women to console you!

ESTELLE: That's right, Inez. Squeal away.

INEZ: What a lovely pair you make! If you could see his big paw splayed out on your back, up your skin and creasing the silk. Be careful, though! He's perspiring, his hand will leave a blue stain on your dress

ESTELLE: Squeal away, Inez, squeal away!... Hug me tight, darling; tighter still—that'll finish her off, and a good thing too!

INEZ: Yes, Garcin, she's right. Carry on with it, press her to you till you feel your bodies melting into each other; a lump of warm, throbbing flesh... Loe's a grand solace, isn't it, my friend? Deep and dark as sleep. But I'll see you don't sleep.

ESTELLE: Don't listen to her. Press your lips to my mouth. Oh, I'm yours, yours, yours.

INEZ: Well, what are you waiting for? Do as you're told. What a lovely scene: coward Garcin holding baby-killer Estelle in his manly arms! Make your stakes, everyone. Will coward Garcin kiss the lady, or won't he dare? What's the betting? I'm watching you, everybody's watching, I'm a crowd all by myself. Do you hear the crowd? Do you hear them muttering, Garcin? "Coward! Coward!" —that's what they're saying... It's no use trying to escape, I'll never let you go. What do you hope to get from her silly lips? Forgetfulness? But I shan't forget you, not I! "It's I you must convince." So come to me. I'm waiting. Come along, now... Look how obedient he is, like a well-trained dog who comes when his mistress calls. You can't hold him, and you never will.

GARCIN: Will night never come?

INEZ: Never.

GARCIN: You will always see me?

INEZ: Always.

GARCIN: This bronze. Yes, now's the moment; I'm looking at this thing on the mantelpiece, and I understand that I'm in hell. I tell you, everything's been thoughtout beforehand. They knew I'd stand at the fireplace stroking this thing of bronze, with all those eyes intent on me. Devouring me. What? Only two of you? I thought there were more; many more. So this is hell. I'd never have believed it. You remember all we were told about the torture-chambers, the fire and brimstone, the "burning marl." Old wives' tales! There's no need for red-hot pokers. HELL IS — OTHER PEOPLE!

ESTELLE: My darling! Please—

GARCIN: No, let me be. She is between us. I cannot love you when she's watching.

ESTELLE: Right! In that case, I'll stop her watching. (She picks up the PAPER knife and stabs Inez several times.)

INEZ: But, you crazy creature, what do you think you're doing? You know quite well I'm dead.

ESTELLE: Dead?

INEZ: Dead! Dead! Dead! Knives, poison, ropes — useless. It has happened already, do you understand? Once and for all. So here we are, forever.

ESTELLE: Forever. My God, how funny! Forever.

GARCIN: For ever, and ever, and ever.

(A long silence.)

GARCIN: Well, well, let's get on with it...

The use or purpose of a tool, such as a paper-knife, dictates its form. Humans, according to Sartre, have no specific purpose, so we have to create our purpose for ourselves.

Sketch of the History of Western Philosophy

Ancient Philosophy
(700 BC—470)

Western philosophy is said to have begun in the sixth century B.C. at Miletus on the Ionian seaboard of Asian Minor; it was also the land of Homer. The first Milesian philosophers, Thales, Anaximander and Anaximenes, were open not only to oriental influences and the Homeric tradition but to mathematics of Egypt and Babylon and to the ideas and information that flowed along the trade routs passing through Ionia.

The main concern of these first western thinkers centered around Thales' basic question: "What is the world made of", which sparked a series of investigations. And the various different answers to these investigations form the foundations of scientific thought, and has forged a relationship between science and philosophy that still exists today.

As philosophy spread across the Greek world from Ionia, and in particular to Athens, philosophers began to focus their attention more on the role of the human being than on the explanation of the material world. They broadened the scope of philosophy to include new questions, such as "How do we know what we know?" and "How should we live our lives?" It was Socrates, who ushered in the short but huge influential period of Classical Greek Philosophy. Here we find the Greek creation of philosophy as "the love of wisdom," and the birth of metaphysics, epistemology, and ethics. Together with Plato and Aristotle, Socrates were the most influential of the ancient Greek philosophers. The work of these key philosophers was succeeded by the Stoics and Epicureans who were also concerned with practical aspects of philosophy and the attainment of happiness. Other notable successors are Pyrrho's school of skepticism and the Neoplatonists such as Plotinus who tried to unify Plato's thought with theology.

Raphael's School of Athens, depicting an array of ancient Greek philosophers engaged in discussion.

The Ancient Greek philosophical tradition broke away from a mythological approach to explaining the world, and it initiated an approach based on reason and evidence. Initially concerned with explaining the entire cosmos, the ancient Greek philosophers strived to identify its single underlying principle. Their theories were diverse and none achieved a consensus, yet their legacy was the initiation of the quest to identify underlying principles, and their ideas have been the starting points for subsequent philosophers.

The Medieval Age Philosophy
(470—1500)

Medieval philosophy is the philosophy of Europe in the era now known as medieval or the Middle Ages, the period roughly extending from the fall of the Western Roman Empire (476 A.D.) in the fifth century to the Renaissance in the sixteenth century.

Medieval philosophy is characteristically theological; the medieval thinkers did not consider themselves philosophers at all. The problems discussed throughout this period are the relation of faith to reason, the existence and simplicity of God, the purpose of theology and metaphysics, and the problems of knowledge, of universals, and of individuation.

Two Roman philosophers had a great influence on the development of medieval philosophy. One is St. Augustine, who is regarded as the greatest of the Church Fathers. He is primarily a theologian and a devotional writer, but much of his writing is philosophical. His themes are truth, God, the human soul, the meaning of history, the state, sin, and salvation. He stated that he would never allow his philosophical investigations to go beyond the authority of God. The other is St. Thomas Aquinas, who argued that philosophy is the handmaiden of theology. Aquinas placed more emphasis on reason and argumentation, and was one of the first to use the new translation of Aristotle's metaphysical and epistemological writing. His artful synthesis of Greek rationalism and Christian doctrine eventually came to define Catholic philosophy.

"Universal Man", illumination from Hildegard's *Liber divinorum operum*, 1165

Although numerous criticisms may be made of Medieval religious reflections on the truth, the universals, the existence of God, however, the kind of approach has merits because its often swift collapse into paradox and absurdity stimulates criticism and the pursuit of fresh lines of investigation. It certainly contributes to the at once passionate and innocent intensity of philosophers' research for truth and beatitude. Moreover, this tendency to provoke new questions and further enquiry meant that it had an enduring liveliness and interest so that it inspired an abundance of fresh thought, criticism, discussion and new developments in philosophy and theology for centuries to come. That inspiration is at work still.

Renaissance and the Age of Reason
(1500—1750)

Renaissance was the period of Europe that falls roughly between the Miedieval Ages and early 17th century, overlapping the Reformation and the early modern era. It was a cultural movement that profoundly affected European intellectual life, which is thought to begin in Italy with the Italian Renaissance and roll through Europe. It could be viewed as an attempt by intellectuals to study and improve secularly and worldly, both through the revival of ideas from antiquity, and through novel approaches to thought. Its influence affected literature, philosophy, art, politics, science, religion, and other aspects of intellectual inquiry.

"What a piece of work is a man, how noble in reason, how infinite in faculties, in form and moving how express and admirable, in action how like an angel, in apprehension how like a god!"
— from William Shakespeare's Hamlet

Renaissance philosophy is marked by a continued zeal for classical study, and by the developmental of a broad learning and the new view of the intellectual life which is now known as Humanism. Among the distinctive elements of Renaissance philosophy are the revival (renaissance means "rebirth") of classical civilization and learning; a partial return to the authority of Plato over Aristotle, who had come to dominate later medieval philosophy; and, influenced by the concept of humanism, which shaped the intellectual landscape throughout the early modern period, by emphasizing the worth of the individual. In the meantime, it was also marked by an intense interest in the visible world and in the knowledge derived from concrete sensory experience. In this way it not only revived the ideas of Greek and Roman thinkers, and applied them in critiques of contemporary government, but also gradually replaced the purely formal methods of thought that scholasticism had fostered with a new method for conducting scientific experiments, based on detailed observations and deductive reasoning, which indirectly inspired the passion for Scientific Revolution, which in turn, led to great contributions in the fields of astronomy, physics, biology, and anatomy.

The Modern Period
(1750—1900)

The major schools in Western philosophy during the 17th and 18th centuries are roughly divided into two groups: the "rationalism", mostly in France and Germany, which held that all knowledge must begin from certain "innate ideas" in the mind; and the "empiricism" in Britain, which by contrast, assumed that knowledge must begin with sensory experience.

In the late 18th century Immanuel Kant set forth a groundbreaking philosophical system which brought unity to rationalism and empiricism. By doing this he sparked a storm of philosophical work in Germany in the early 19th century, beginning with German idealism, which emphasized the central role that mind plays in organizing experiences, and that mind was also the source of our sense experience as well as the shaper of those experience. It culminated in the work of Hegel, who claimed that "The real is rational; the rational is real"; and Schopenhauer took idealism to the conclusion that the world is nothing but the futile endless interplay of images and desires.

However, there were other philosophical approaches, particularly the British utilitarianism, which rejected the role of rational intuition in our quest for knowledge, but rather, attempted to refine techniques for sorting and assessing sense experiences.

Søren Kierkegaard dismissed all systematic philosophy as an in adequate guide to life and meaning. For him life is meant to be lived, not a mystery to be solved.

While others saw in 19th-century Europe the symbols of power and security, Nietzsche grasped with prophetic insight the imminent collapse of the traditional supports of the values to which modern people committed themselves. By claiming "God is dead", he launched a sustained attack on all the established traditional Western values, rejecting all systematic philosophy and all striving for a fixed truth transcending the individual.

As a reaction against the dominating strands of neo-Hegelian thought, Western philosophy also witnessed a new direction of analytic philosophy, headed by figures such as Russell, which laid emphasis on clarity and argument (often achieved via modern formal logic and analysis of language) and a respect for natural sciences.

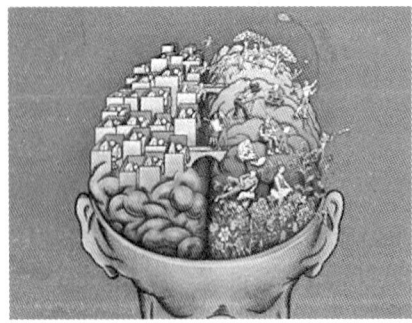

I take the limits of my own field of vision for the limits of the world.
— Arthur Schopenhauer

The Contemporary Time
(1900-Present)

Contemporary philosophy is the present period in the history of Western philosophy beginning at the end of the 19th century with the professionalization of the discipline and the rise of analytic and continental philosophy. Setting for a series of attempts to reform and preserve, and to alter or abolish the traditional knowledge systems, it mainly deals with the upheavals produced by a series of conflicts within philosophical discourse over the basis of knowledge, with classical certainties overthrown, and new social, economic, scientific and logical problems established. Difficult as it is to be classified into different schools, it appeared far more multicultural and colorful now than ever before.

Originally analytic and continental philosophy shared a common Western philosophical tradition up to Immanuel Kant. But later they started to differ on the importance and influence of subsequent philosophers on their respective traditions. The analytic program headed by Bertrand Russell and G. E. Moor in the early 20th century turned away from then dominant forms of Hegelianism, objecting its idealism and purported obscurity, and began to develop a new sort of conceptual analysis based on recent development in logic.

The continental approach, often labeled as making a broad range of philosophical views, tended to see their philosophical inquiries as closely related to personal, moral, or political transformation rather than treating philosophy in terms of discrete problems capable of being analyzed apart from their historical origins. The most representative schools are phenomenology (founded by Edmund Husserl), existentialism (led by Nietzsche and Jean-Paul Sartre), structuralism, post-structuralism, French feminism and Western Marxism.

Although contemporary philosophical schools have widely divergent interests, assumptions, and approaches, they often reject the established fundamental premises, characterized by precision and thoroughness about a narrow topic, and resistance to "imprecise or cavalier discussions about broad topics."

Directory

The Ancient Greek and Hellenistic Period

Thales of Miletus (c. 624—546 BC)
泰勒斯
Thales was regarded as the first known western thinker, and founder of the Milesian school, who seeks naturalistic, rational answers to fundamental questions, rather than to ascribe objects and events to the whims of capricious gods. He claims that water is the arche, and that earth floats on water like a raft.

Anaximander (c. 612—545 BC)
阿那克西曼德
Greek philosopher, reputedly known as the student and successor of Thales in the Milesian school. Like Thales, he thinks there is a single basic substance from which everything had evolved, but he describes the cosmos as originating from *apeiron* (the boundless).

Anaximenes
阿那克西美尼(c. 585—528 BC).
Following in the tradition of the Milesians, Anaximenes chooses air as something divine and something that causes life. He points out that just as air gives life to the human body, so a universal kind of air gives life to the cosmos.

Pythagoras of Samos
萨摩斯的毕达哥拉斯(c. 570—c. 495 BC)
Being the most famous pre-Socratic Greek philosopher, he was said the first to call himself a philosopher, or lover of wisdom. In contrast to the Milesians, Pythagoras and his followers believe that things consist of numbers. His originality also consists partly in his conviction that the study of mathematics is the best purifier of the soul. His ideas exercised a marked influence on Plato.

Heraclitus of Ephesus
赫拉克利特(c. 540—c. 480 BC)
Greek transitional figure between the Milesian philosophers and the later pluralists, Heraclitus is famous for his insistence on ever-present change in the universe, as stated in his famous saying, "No man ever steps in the same river twice." He also stresses unity of opposites in the world of change by a single source or *arche* of natural substances, namely, fire.

Parmenides of Elea
巴门尼德(c. 510—c. 550 BC)
Being the founder of the Eleatic school of philosophy, Parmenides was the first Greek thinker who can properly be called an ontologist of metaphysician. He holds that

"all is one" by arguing that "the real" or "what-is" or "being" must be ungenerable and imperishable, indivisible, and unchanging. According to him, "the real" is a unique entity which may be referred to as Being, or the All, or the One. These ideas strongly influenced the whole of Western philosophy, perhaps most notably through its effect on Plato.

Empedocles
恩培多克勒斯(c. 495—435 BC)
A Greek philosopher, Empedocles created a physical theory in response to Parmenides while reasserting the motion of Heraclitus that we live in an ever-changing world. He explains this phenomenal change by positing that four elements (his "roots", *rizomata*), earth, water, air and fire continually combine, move apart, and recombine in a finite number of ways. This idea remained part of Western thinking up till the Renaissance period.

Anaxagoras
阿拉克萨克拉(c.500—428 BC)
Following Parmenides, this Greek philosopher elaborates a theory of matter according to which nothing comes into being or perishes. In his cosmogony, an initial chaos of complete mixture gives way to an ordered world when *noûs* (mind) begins a vortex motion that separate cosmic masses of ether (the bright upper air), air, water, and earth. Anaxagoras' theory of mind provides the first hint of a mind-matter dualism.

Democritus of Abdera
德谟克利特(c.460—c.370 BC)
Following in the tradition of his mentor Leucippus, this Greek philosopher became the founder of atomism. He posited the existence of a plurality of tiny invisible beings — the atoms — and not-being — the void; or empty space, and that atoms do not come into being or perish, but they do move in the void, making possible the existence of the world. Democritus is considered by many to be the "father of modern science".

Protagoras
普罗泰格拉(c.490—c.420 BC)
Greek philosopher, he was the most famous and perhaps the first Sophist. He insists there is no objective truth; the world is for each person as it appears to that person. His statement that man is the measure of all things is believed to have created a major controversy, which was very revolutionary for the time and contrasting to other previous philosophical doctrines that claimed the universe was based on something objective, outside the human influence.

Gorgias
高尔吉亚(c. 483—376 BC)
He was a Greek philosopher from Sicily. Like other Sophists, he doesn't believe in objective truth. He holds that different people have different virtues: for example, women's virtue differs from men's. Since there is no truth (and if there were we couldn't know it), we must rely on opinion, and so speakers who can change people's opinions have greater power — greater than the power produced by any other skill.

Thrasymachus (c. 459—400 BC)
特拉西马库斯

Greek Sophist from Bithynia, he asserts that justice is only what benefits the stronger, i.e., the ruler. From the point of view of those who are ruled, then, justice always serves the interest of someone else, and rulers who seek their own advantage are unjust.

Epicurus (341—271 BC)
伊壁鸠鲁

Hellenistic philosopher and founder of Epicureanism, he is famous for his hedonistic ethics, which holds that pleasure is our innate natural goal, to which all other values, including virtue, are subordinated. Philosophers' task is to show how pleasure can be maximized, and pain minimized. This is acquired for the body through simple way of life that satisfies only our natural and necessary desires, and for the soul through the study of physics, which achieves the ultimate pleasure—"freedom from disturbance" (cataraxia), by eliminating the two main sources of human anguish, the fears of the gods and of death.

Socrates (469—399 BC)

Greek philosopher and often referred to as one of the founders of Western philosophy, Socrates is best known for his dictum that only an examined life is worth living. Socrates lived with a disregard for pleasure and pain — e.g., walking barefoot in snow; he believes that in every circumstance a virtuous person is better off than a non-virtuous one, because the virtuous person uses properly whatever is present. He also stresses that the soul is more important than the body, and neglects the body for the soul. Socrates' thoughts and way of life had a profound impact upon many of his contemporaries, and through Plato's portrayal of him, he has become a major source of inspiration and ideas for later generations of philosophers.

Antisthenes (c. 445—c. 365 BC)
安提斯泰尼

Founder of Cynics, Antisthenes stresses the soul as more important than the body with disregard for pleasure and pain.

Diogenes of Sinope (c. 400—c. 325 BC)
西诺普的第欧根尼

Greek philosopher, he pursues the line of thought of Antisthenes by emphasizing the self-sufficiency and the soul, but he takes the disregard for pleasure to asceticism. By refusing to live by the current standards of customs, he apparently wants to replace them with the genuine standards of nature — but nature in the sense of what was minimally required for human life, which an individual human could achieve, with society. Because of this, he was called a Cynic, from the Greek word *kuon* (dog), because he was as shameless as a dog.

Zeno of Citium (334—262 BC)
季蒂昂的芝诺

Founder of Stoicism, Zeno declares that man has been given a rational soul with which to exercise free will. No one is forced to pursue a "good" life. It is up to the individual to choose whether to put aside the things over which he has little or no control, and be indifferent to pain and pleasure, poverty and riches. Zeno is convinced that he will achieve a life that is in harmony with nature in all its aspects, good or bad, and live in accordance with the rulings of the supreme lawgiver. Major representatives of Stoicism are Cicero (西塞罗, 106—43 BC), Seneca (塞内加, c. 1—65), Epictetus (艾比克泰德, c. 55—c. 135), and the Emperor Marcus Aurelius (马尔库斯·奥列里乌斯大帝, 21—80)

Pyrrho of Elis (361—270 BC)
爱里斯的皮浪
Pyrrho was the first noted Greek philosopher to place doubt at the center of his thinking and is regarded as the founder of skepticism, who treats the suspension of judgment about beliefs as the only reasonable reaction to the fallibility of the senses, and to the fact that both sides of any judgment can seem to be equally valid. This idea was taken over by the skeptical Academy, and two centuries later, a revival of skepticism adopted his name, called Pyrrhonism. Major representatives of skeptics are Arcesilaus (阿塞西劳斯, c. 316—241 BC) and Sextus Empiricus (塞克斯都·恩皮里克, c. 200)

Lucretius (99 or 94—55 BC)
卢克莱修
Roman philosopher, Lucretius is known as an orthodox Epicurean for his emphasis on the role of even the most technical aspects of physics and philosophy in helping to attain emotional peace and dismiss the terrors of popular religion.

Plotinus (c. 204—270)
普罗提诺
A Greco-Roman Neo-Platonist from Egypt, Plotinus pursues the line of thought Plato had set forth in his vivid myths and allegories, by combining a speculative description of reality with a religious theory of salvation. More than Plato, he not only describes the world, but also gives an account of its source, of our place in it, and how we overcome our moral and spiritual difficulties in it. In this case, Plotinus' theory became a major strand in most of medieval philosophy.

Porphyry (c. 232—c. 304)
波菲利
Not known for original thought, this Greek Neo-Platonist philosopher has dedicated himself to explicating Aristotle's logic and defending Plotinus's version of Neo-Platonism.

The Medieval Age

Hypatia of Alexandria (c. 370—415)
亚历山大的海巴夏
Greek Neo-Platonist philosopher, she appears to have been a very popular female philosophy teacher at that time. She presumably professed a standard Neo-Platonist curriculum, using mathematics as a ladder to the intelligible world.

Boethius (c. 480—525)

波爱修

As a Roman philosopher, Boethius shares the common Neo-Platonist view that the Platonist and Aristotelian systems could be harmonized by following Aristotle in logic and natural philosophy, and Plato in metaphysics and theology. His commitment to an ontology that includes not just Aristotelian natural forms but also Platonist Forms existing apart from matter implies a strong realist view of universals.

John Scotus Erigena (c.810—877)

爱留根纳

An Irish-born scholar and theologian, he holds that there is only one predestination, to good, since evil is strictly nothing. Thus no one is compelled to evil by God's foreknowledge, since, strictly speaking, God has no foreknowledge of what is not. He also treats the universe as a procession from God, everything real in nature being a trace of God, and then a return to God through the presence of nature in human reason and man's union with God.

St. Anselm of Canterbury (1033—1109)

坎特伯雷的安瑟尔谟

Italian-born English philosophical theologian, Anselm follows Augustine's doctrine of divine illumination, which gave him direct access to certain truth. He argues that the most accessible proofs of the existence of God are through value theory, and he insists that humans were made for beatific intimacy with God and therefore are obliged to strive into God with all of their powers, he emphatically includes reason or intellect along with emotion and will.

St. Thomas Aquinas (1225—1274)

托马斯·阿奎那

An Italian philosophical theologian and the father of Thomism, Aquinas produces a powerful philosophical synthesis that combined Aristotelian and Neo-Platonic elements within a Christian context in an original and ingenious way. His influence on Western thought is considerable, and much of modern philosophy is conceived as a reaction against, or as an agreement with, his ideas, particularly in the areas of ethics, natural law, metaphysics, and political theory.

The Renaissance Time

Pico della Mirandola (1463—1494)

皮科·德拉·米兰多拉

Pico is known as the most vivid representative of Italian Renaissance humanism. His philosophy is mainly regarded as a celebration of man's freedom and dignity. Great weight has been placed on his most famous work, On the Dignity of Man (1486), in which he saw man set apart from the rest of creation, and is completely free to form his own nature, that is, he is free to choose between good and evil.

Niccolo Machiavelli (1469—1527)
尼可罗·马基雅维利

An Italian political theorist, Machiavelli is commonly considered the father of political science in the West, whose philosophy came to be identified later with Machiavellianism, the doctrine that envisioned a double standard of behavior, one for rulers and the other for the people. The masses, he holds, need to follow Christian ethics as a necessary means of securing peace within society, while the rulers, in contrast to the morality of the masses, must have the freedom to adjust their acts to the requirements of each occasion without feeling bound to any objective moral rules.

Desiderius Erasmus (1466—1536)
德西德里乌斯·伊拉斯谟

Erasmus is a Dutch philosopher, known as an important figure in Renaissance humanism. He stresses within philosophy and theology the function of philosophical precision, grammatical correctness, and rhetorical elegance. He has been call the first modern intellectual because he tries to influence and reform the mentality of society by working within the shadow of ecclesiastical and political leaders.

Thomas Hobbes (1588—1679)
托马斯·霍布斯

As a political philosopher, the English Hobbes is often regarded as the father of modern totalitarianism, whose most famous *Leviathan* (1651) strongly influenced all subsequent English moral and political philosophy. Hobbes strongly favors the establishment of a government with the power to make and enforce laws. This government, which gets both its right to govern and its power to do so from the consent of the governed, has as its primary duty the people's safety. As long as the government provides this safety the citizens are obliged to obey the laws of the state in all things. Thus, the rationality of seeking lasting preservation requires seeking peace; this in turn requires setting up a state with sufficient power to keep the peace. Anything that threatens the state stability of the state is to be avoided.

Early Modern Period

Baruch Spinoza (1632—1677)
巴鲁赫·斯宾诺莎

The Dutch philosopher is generally regarded as one of the most important figures of the 17th century rationalism. His philosophical system has the notion that good and evil are relative concepts, claiming that nothing is intrinsically good or bad except relative to a particular individual. Things that had classically been seen as good or evil, Spinoza argues, are simply good or bad for humans. Spinoza believes in a deterministic universe in which "All things in nature proceed from certain necessity and with the utmost perfection." Nothing happens by chance in Spinoza's world, and nothing is contingent. Besides, Spinoza's position is also known as "substance monism", which claims that all things are ultimately aspects of a single thing, as opposed to "substance dualism", which asserts that there are ultimately two kinds of things in the universe, most commonly defined as "mind" and "matter".

Gottfried Leibniz (1646—1716)

戈特弗里德·莱布尼兹

The German rationalist Leibniz's distinction between truths of reasoning and truths of fact marks an interesting twist in the debate between rationalism and empiricism. Leibniz's best known contribution to metaphysics is his theory of monads, as exposited in *Monadologie*. Monads, he claims, are to the metaphysical realm what atoms are to the physical/phenomenal. They can also be compared to the corpuscles of the Mechanical Philosophy of René Descartes and others. They are the ultimate elements of the universe.

John Locke (1632—1704)

约翰·洛克

As an English proponent of empiricism, Locke argues that knowledge, thus understood, is "short and scanty" — much too short and scanty for the living of life. Life requires the formation of beliefs on matters where knowledge is not available. Thus, he set out to demonstrate that the best explanation of the world as we experience it is corpuscular theory, namely the theory that everything in the world is made up of submicroscopic particles, or corpuscles, which we can have no direct knowledge of, but which, by their very existence, make sense of phenomena that would otherwise be difficult or impossible to explain.

Adam Smith (1723—1790)

亚当·斯密

The Scottish philosopher Adam Smith is commonly regarded as the founder of modern political economy and a major contributor to ethics and the psychology of morals. His philosophy ranges from the motivation of wealth to the psychological causes of religious and political fanaticism. At the same time, while trying to show how virtue and liberty can complement each other, he also expresses his full awareness of the potentially dehumanizing force of what was later called "capitalism", and sought remedies in schemes for liberal education and properly organized religion.

Jeremy Bentham (1748—1832)

杰里米·边沁

As a British philosopher of ethics and political-legal theory, Bentham's orientation is grounded in British empiricism. Convinced that all human activity is driven by only two motivating forces — the avoidance of pain and the pursuit of pleasure, he argues forcefully that all social and political decisions should be made with the aim of achieving the greatest happiness for the greatest number of people. He believes that the moral worth of such decisions relates directly to their utility, or efficiency, in generating happiness or pleasure.

Johann Gottlieb Fichte (1762—1814)

约翰·戈特利布·费希特

Fichte is a German philosopher and a proponent of an uncompromising system of transcendental idealism. His philosophy earned him a reputation as a brilliant exponent of Kantianism by adopting Kant's method — stripped of the concept of the unknowable thing-in-itself, and transform Kant's critical idealism into a metaphysical idealism. He thus concludes that every object and indeed the entire universe is a product of mind.

G. W. F. Hegel (1770—1831)
黑格尔
Hegel is one of the most influential and systematic German idealists, also well known for his philosophy of history and of religion. His central idea is that all phenomena, from consciousness to political institutions, are aspects of a single Spirit (by which he means "mind" or "idea") that over the course of time is reintegrating these aspects into itself. This process of reintegration is what he calls "dialectic", and it is one that we (who are all aspects of Spirit) understand as "history".

Arthur Schopenhauer (1788—1860)
阿瑟·叔本华
Schopenhauer is a German philosopher known for his pessimism and philosophical clarity. His central idea is that the fundamental reality is will, which he equates with the Kantian thing-in-itself. Unlike Kant, Schopenhauer insists that one can immediately know the thing-in-itself through experience of an inner, volitional reality within one's own body. He uses the word "will" to express this pure energy that has no driving direction, and yet is responsible for everything that manifests itself in the phenomenal world.

Ludwig Feuerbach (1804—1872)
路德维希·费尔巴哈
As a materialist, the German philosopher Feuerbach incorporates much of the philosophical thinking into his theory, but while Hegel regards an Absolute Spirit as the guiding force in nature, he sees no reason to look beyond our experience to explain existence. According to him, humans are not an externalized form of an Absolute Spirit, but the opposite: we have created the idea of a great spirit, a god, from our own imaginations and longings. Therefore, we should focus more on human justice rather than on heavenly righteousness.

Late Modern Period

Auguste Comte (1798—1857)
奥古斯特·孔德
Comte is a French philosopher known as the founder of positivism. In conformity with empiricism, Comte holds that knowledge of the world arises from observation. He went beyond many empiricists, however, in denying the possibility of knowledge of unobservable physical objects. He conceives of positivism as a method of study based on observation and restricted to the observable.

Ralph Waldo Emerson (1803—1882)
拉尔夫·沃尔多·爱默生
The American philosopher believes in the unity of nature, with every single particle

of matter and each individual mind being a microcosm of the entire universe. A strong proponent of personal integrity and self-reliance as the only moral imperatives, he stresses that every human being has the power to shape his own destiny.

Soren Kierkegaard (1813—1855)
索伦·克尔凯郭尔

The Dutch philosopher attempts to examine what "it means to be a human being", not as a part of some great philosophical system, but as a self-determining individual. He claims that our lives are determined by our actions, which are themselves determined by our choices. So how we make those choices is critical to our lives.

Karl Marx (1819—1883)
卡尔·马克思

Marx is a German socialist philosopher, and known as one of the greatest thinkers of the 19th century. Marx claims in his *The Communist Manifesto* that all historical change comes about as the result of an ongoing conflict between dominant (upper) and subordinate (lower) social classes, and that the roots of these conflicts lie in economics. The only solution, according to him, is for all the instruments of economic production (such as land, raw materials, tools, and factories) to become common property, so that every member of society could work according to their capacities, and consume according to their needs. This was the only way to prevent the rich from living at the expense of the poor.

Friedrich Engels (1820—1895)
弗里德里希·恩格斯

Engels, a German socialist philosopher, is referred to as the founder of what is later called Marxism. As a central figure in the socialist movement, he sought to make it not only true, but also a finely tuned instrument of working-class emancipation which would lead to a world without classes.

Charles S. Peirce (1839—1914)
查尔斯·皮尔士

Peirce is an American philosopher, and the founder of the philosophical movement called pragmatism. Peirce believes that many debates in science, philosophy and theology are meaningless. He claims that they are often debates about words, rather than reality, because they are debates in which no effect on the senses can be specified. His idea that we do not acquire knowledge simply by observing, but by doing and that we rely on that knowledge only so long as it is useful, has become the founding pragmatic maxim.

William James (1842—1910)
威廉·詹姆士

James is American pragmatic philosopher. His central idea is that the truth of an idea depends on how useful it is; namely, whether or not it does what is required of it. He claims that the truth of an idea is not a stagnant property inherent it. Truth happens to an idea. It becomes true, is made truth by events. Its verity is in fact an event, a process. Any idea, if acted upon, is found to be true by the action we take; putting the idea into practice is the process by which it becomes true.

Ferdinand De Saussure (1857—1913)

费尔迪兰·德·索绪尔

This Swiss philosopher is commonly known as the founder of the school of structural linguistics. Turning his back on a long tradition that says language is about the relationships between words and things, Saussure sees language as made up of systems of "signs", with the signs acting as the basic units of the language. A sign, he claims, is made up of a "signifier" — a sound-image, and the "signified", or concept, which means that it is a system of relations between sound-images and concepts. However, the relationship between the signified and the signifier is arbitrary. Saussure's theory on language formed the basis of modern linguistics, and influenced many philosophers and literary theorists.

John Dewey (1859—1952)

约翰·杜威

Being a pragmatic philosopher, Dewey's attention is not focused on abstract problems divorced from people's lives. For him, philosophy starts from our everyday human hopes and aspirations, and from the problems that arise in the course of our lives. He believes that it should be a way of finding practical responses to these problems. He insists that philosophizing is not about being a "spectator" who looks at the world from afar, but about actively engaging in the problems of life.

Henri Bergson (1859—1941)

亨利·柏格森

Bergson is a French philosopher of vitalism, or theory of life. He stresses the full importance of our faculty of intuition, which, he claims, allows us to grasp an object's uniqueness through direct connection. He believes that our intuition is linked to *élan vital*, a life-force (vitalism) that interprets the flux of experience in terms of time rather than space.

Alfred North Whitehead (1861—1947)

艾尔弗雷特·诺斯·怀特海

Whitehead is an English philosopher. His process philosophy was based on his conviction that traditional philosophical categories are inadequate in dealing with the interactions between matter, space, and time, and that "the living organ or experience is the living body as a whole" and not just the brain.

The Contemporary Period

Rudolph Carnap (1891—1970)

鲁道夫·卡尔纳普

Carnap, the German-born American philosopher, is one of the leaders of the Vienna Circle. He is best known for his statement that many philosophical questions are meaningless, since the way they were posed amounted to an abuse of language. Therefore, an operational implication of this opinion was taken to be the elimination of metaphysics from responsible human discourse.

Hans-Georg Gadamer (1900—2002)

汉斯-格奥尔格·伽达默尔

Though being a leading proponent of hermeneutics, the German philosopher Gadamer sought to shift the focus of hermeneutics from the problems of obscurity and misunderstanding to the community of understanding that participants in a dialogue share through language. He goes on to point out that our understanding is always from the point of a particular point in history. For him, our prejudices and beliefs, the kinds of questions that we think are worth asking, and the kinds of answers with which we are satisfied are all the product of our history. We can not stand outside of history and culture, so we can never reach an absolutely objective perspective.

Karl Jaspers (1883—1969)

卡尔·雅斯贝尔斯

As a German existentialist, Jaspers' philosophical aim is to seek the reality that underlies human life — a reality that he calls *Existence*. For him, to deal with existence, philosophers must consider their immediate inner and personal experience. They had to achieve a thorough understanding of philosophical, political, and religious history as well as an adequate assessment of the present situation. Existential thinking, he says, is "the philosophic practice of life."

Karl Popper (1902—1994)

卡尔·波普尔

Popper is an Austrian-born British philosopher, best known for his contributions to philosophy of science and to social and political philosophy. He is interested in the method by which science find out about the world. Science depends on experiment and experience. In other word, it is empirical, or based on experience. However, theories that are untestable are not part of the natural sciences. This does not mean they are not the kinds of theories that the sciences deal with. This idea of falsifiability does not mean we are justified in having a belief in theories that cannot be falsified. Beliefs that stand up to repeated testing, and that resist our attempts at falsification, can be taken to be reliable. But even the best theories are always open to the possibility that a new result will show them to be false.

Maurice Merleau-Ponty (1908—1961)

莫里斯·梅洛·庞蒂

Merleau-Ponty is a French philosopher of phenomenology, responsible for introducing the phenomenology of Husserl into France. Because he seeks to emphasize not only the existential nature of the human subject, but above all, its bodily nature, his philosophy could be characterized as a philosophy of the lived body or the body subject. It was he who first made the body central theme of a detailed philosophical analysis. This provided an original perspective from which to rethink such perennial philosophical issues as the nature of knowledge, freedom, time (temporality), language and intersubjectivity.

Simone De Beauvior (1908—1986)

西蒙·德·波伏娃

Like her life-long partner Sartre, the French existentialist and feminist Beauvior attempts to produce an existentialist ethics based upon the recognition of radical human freedom as "projected" toward an open future. She rejects inauthenticity and condemns the "spirit of seriousness whereby individuals identify themselves wholly with certain fixed qualities, values, tenets, or prejudices.

Claude Lévi-Strauss (1908—2009)
克劳德·列维-斯特劳斯
Strauss is a French anthropologist and ethnologist, generally referred to as "father of modern anthropology". He argues that the "savage" mind had the same structures as the "civilized" mind and that human characteristics are the same everywhere. These observations culminated in his famous book *Tristes Tropiques*, which positioned him as one of the central figures in the structuralist school of thought, which has been defined as "the search for the underlying patterns of thought in all forms of human activity". His ideas reached into fields including humanities, sociology and philosophy.

Willard Van Orman Quine (1908—2000)
威拉德·冯·奥曼·奎因
Quine is American philosopher, who believes that language is not, as many philosophers assert, about the relationship between objects and verbal signifiers, but about knowing what to say and when to say it. He claims that language is a social art, and, the sense of someone uttering a word, and of this utterance being meaningful comes not from some mysterious link between words and things, but from the patterns of our behavior, and the fact that we learned to participate in language as a social art.

John Austin (1911—1960)
约翰·奥斯丁
Austin is an English philosopher, and a leading exponent of postwar "linguistic" philosopher. Unlike some other philosophers, Austin does not believe that philosophical problems all arise out of observations from "ordinary language", nor does he necessarily find solutions there; he dwelt, rather, on the authority of the vernacular as a source of nice and pregnant distinctions, and he holds that rigorous analysis of how language operates in ordinary everyday usage can lead to the discovery of the subtle linguistic distinctions needed to solve profound philosophical problems.

Roland Barthes (1915—1980)
罗兰·巴特
Barthes is a French post structuralist, whose principal message is that words are merely one kind of sign whose meaning lies in relations of difference between them, including reading subject and the structuring effect that the subject has on the literary work.

John Rawls (1921—2002)
约翰·罗尔斯
Being an American philosopher, Rawls is widely recognized as one of the leading political philosophers of the 20th century. His approach falls into the tradition known as social contract that individuals enter into because it yields benefits that exceed what they can attain individually. He believes that a just society maximizes the worth to the least

advantaged of the basic liberties shared by all. It is governed by a liberal-democratic constitution that protects the basic liberties and provides citizens with equally effective rights to participate in electoral processes and influence legislation. Furthermore, it incorporates a modified market system that extensively distributes income and wealth — either a "property-owning democracy" with widespread ownership of means of production, or liberal socialism.

Nel Nodding (1929—)

奈尔·诺丁

As a American feminist, Nodding is noted for her feminist view that much of our intellectual heritage was not only formed by men but reflects a male way of looking at the world. She insists that the male-oriented ethical theories should be replaced with ones that are female-oriented, because for her, "To construct an ethics free of gendered views may be impossible in a thoroughly gendered society." To counterbalance male theories, therefore, female-oriented theories need to be proposed, and perhaps at some future time, we can transcend them both with gender-neutral approaches.

Michel Foucault (1926—1984)

米歇尔·福科

The idea that man is an invention of recent date was first proposed by French philosopher Foucault. He is interested in how our discourse — the way in which we talk and think about things — is formed by a set of largely unconscious rules that arise out of the historical conditions in which we find ourselves. What we take to be the "common sense" background to how we think and talk about the world is in fact shaped by these rules and these conditions. However, the rules and conditions change over time, and consequently so do our discourses. For this reason, an "archaeology" is needed to unearth both the limits and the conditions of how people thought and talked about the world in previous ages. We cannot take concepts that we use in our present context and assume that they are somehow eternal, and that all we need is a "history of ideas" to trace their genealogy. For Foucault, it is simply wrong to assume that our current ideas can be usefully applied to any previous point in history. Besides, Foucault suggests that not only is this idea of "man" an invention of recent date, it is also an invention that may be close to coming to its end — one that may soon be erased "like a face drawn in the sand at the edge of the sea."

Noam Chomsky (1928—)

诺姆·乔姆斯基

Chomsky is a distinguished American linguist and philosopher, whose best-known scientific achievement is the establishment of a rigorous and philosophically compelling foundation for the scientific study of the grammar of natural language. With the use of tools from the study of formal languages, he gives a far more precise and explanatory account of natural language grammar than had previously be given. The most central of his theory is that there is an innate set of linguistic principles shared by all humans, and the purpose of linguistic inquiry is to describe the initial state of the language learner, and account for linguistic variation via the most general possible mechanisms.

Jacques Derrida (1930—2004)
雅克·德里达

Derrida is the French author of deconstructionism, and a leading figure in the postmodern movement. He seeks to demonstrate that the origin of geometry, conceived by Husserl as the guiding paradigm for Western thought, was a supratemporal idea of perfect knowing that serves as the goal of human knowledge. Thus the origin of geometry is inseparable from its end or *telos*, a thought that Derrida later generalized in his deconstruction of the notion of origin as such. He argues that this ideal cannot be realized in time, hence cannot be grounded in lived experience, hence cannot meet the "principle of principles" Husserl designated as the prime criterion for phenomenology, the principle that all knowing must ground itself in consciousness of an object that is coincidentally conscious of itself. This revelation of the aporia at the core of phenomenology in particular and Western thought in general was not yet labeled as a deconstruction, but it established the formal structure that guided Derrida's later deconstructive revelations of the metaphysics of presence underlying the modernism in which Western thought culminates.

Richard Rorty (1931—)
理查德·罗蒂

Rorty is an American philosopher, notable for the breadth of his philosophical and cultural interests. His position is neither analytic nor continental, but rather pragmatic, which involves a rejection of the representationalism that has dominated modern philosophy from Descartes through logical positivism. He attempts to argue against the idea that knowledge is a matter of correctly representing the world, like some kind of mental mirror. He insists that this view of knowledge cannot be upheld. He suggests that knowledge is not so much a way of mirroring nature as "a matter of conversation and social practice." When we decide what counts as knowledge, our judgment rests not on how strongly a "fact" correlates to the world, so much as whether it is something "that society lets us say." What we can and cannot count as knowledge is therefore limited by the social contexts that we live in, by our histories, and by what those around us will allow us to claim. "Truth," said Rorty, "is what your contemporaries let you get away with saying."

Slavoj Žižek (1949—)
斯拉沃热·齐泽克

The Slovenian philosopher Žižek remains tremendously popular in both academic and popular demographics, synthesizing Lacanian, Hegelian, and Althusserian Marxist thought in discussions of popular culture and politics. He is also involved with the contemporary thrust to step beyond postmodernism and the linguistic turn of the 20th century.

Glossary

Absolute
The Absolute is the concept of an unconditional reality which transcends conditional, everyday existence.

Agnosticism
It is the view that the truth value of certain claims—especially claims about the existence or non-existence of any deity, but also other religious and metaphysical claims—is unknown or unknowable.

Allegory of the cave
It is often said by scholars to represent Plato's own epistemology and metaphysics. It is intimately connected to his political ideology, that only people who have climbed out of the cave and cast their eyes on a vision of goodness are fit to rule.

Anthropology
Anthropology is the study of humanity. It has origins in the humanities, the natural sciences, and the social sciences.

Analytic
Analytic is a term Aristotle used for hip syllogism and for the discussion of the conditions of demonstrative knowledge presented in his *Prior Analytics* and *Posterior Analytics*.

Analytic philosophy
Analytic philosophy is a generic term for a style of philosophy that emphasizes the use of scientific methods to develop and solve philosophical problems.

Antinomy
This term refers to a pair of opposed propositions, called a thesis and antithesis, each of which seems to be supported by formally valid argument, but which are inconsistent with one another.

Anthropomorphism
It is a form of personification (applying human or animal qualities to inanimate objects) and similar to prosopopoeia (adopting the persona of another person).

A priori
It is a term used in the theory of knowledge to distinguish what comes before experience (the opposite is a posteriori).

A posteriori
This term literally means after experience; a posterior knowledge is that derived from experience. This is in contrast with a priori knowledge.

Being
Being is a general term in metaphysics referring to ultimate reality or existence. True being, for Plato, is the realm of the external forms.

Dasein
Dasein is a crucial term for Heidegger, but it is generally left untranslated. It is used for the modes of human being. Human being must have a place there in the world and must be considered as Being-in-the-world.

Determinism

It is the philosophical proposition that every event, including human cognition, decision and action, is causally determined by an unbroken chain of prior occurrences.

Dionysian

It is a concept in Nietzsche's philosophy referring to the forces of life.

Dogma

Historically, a dogma is a religious doctrine proclaimed by scripture or the Church, which requires popular acceptance without rational justification.

Dualism

Dualism is a set of beliefs which begins with the claim that the mental and the physical have a fundamentally different nature.

Ego

The ego is the real "I" or genuine self. It has a conscious part and an unconscious part. It represents characteristic human values of prudence and rationality.

Eidos

It is the distinctive expression of the cognitive or intellectual character of a culture or a social group.

Eidetic reduction

It is a technique in the study of essences in phenomenology whose goal is to identify the basic components of phenomena.

Electra complex

In Neo-Freudian psychology, the Electra complex, as proposed by Carl Gustav Jung, is a girl's psychosexual competition with mother for possession of father.

Empiricism

It is the doctrine that all knowledge ultimately comes from experience, denying the notion of innate ideas or a priori knowledge about the world.

Epicureanism

It was founded by Epicurus. It in fact refers to a middle-path philosophy defining happiness as success in avoiding pain, in order to produce a state of tranquility.

Epistemology

It is the theory of knowledge, which inquires into what can be known, with what degree of certainty and under what conditions.

Eros

Eros is the Greek god of erotic love. It came to be symbolic of various aspects of love.

Existentialism

It is a philosophy that emphasizes the uniqueness and isolation of the individual experience in a hostile or indifferent universe. Existentialism regards human existence as unexplainable, and stresses freedom of choice and responsibility for the consequences of one's acts.

Foundationalism

This term may be used in the rationalist sense, referring especially to Descartes's project of constructing a system of knowledge on a foundation of clear and distinct ideas of reason.

Four Causes

Four Causes refers to a principle in Aristotelian science that is used to understand change. These causes are called, respectively, the formal cause, the material cause, the efficient cause, and the final cause.

Genealogy

Genealogy is an inquiry into origin and descent. It begins with the present and goes backward in time until a difference is located.

Greatest happiness principle

It is a principle providing the central idea of classical utilitarianism. According to this principle, an action is moral if it produces the greatest happiness for the greatest numbers of people involved.

Golden Mean

In philosophy, especially that of Aristotle, the golden mean is the desirable middle between two extremes, one of excess and the other of deficiency.

Hedonism

Hedonism is the ethical view that pleasure is the greatest good, and that pleasure should be the standard in deciding which course of action to pursue.

Hermeneutics

Hermeneutics is the study of the theory and practice of interpretation.

Hume's Fork

It is a term used in two different senses. In one sense, it is Hume's distinction between ought and is; in another sense, Hume's fork is his claim that there are only two valid kinds of reasoning: demonstrative reasoning and empirical reasoning.

Id

Id contains bodily appetites and unconscious instincts.

Idealism

It is the view that mind is the ultimate reality in the world.

Idols of the cave

This term is coined by Sir Francis Bacon. It is one of the earliest treatises arguing the case for the logic and method of modern science. The idols of the cave are the idols of the individual man.

Immaterialism

This theory contends that individuals can only directly know sensations and ideas of objects, not abstractions such as "matter."

Instrumentalism

Instrumentalism is the view that a scientific theory is a useful instrument in understanding the world.

James-Lange view

It is the view that emotions are feelings generated by characteristic bodily changes in response to external stimuli. Hence emotion follows bodily changes rather than causes them.

Last man

The last man is a term used by the philosopher Friedrich Nietzsche. It refers to a weak-willed individual, one who is tired of life, takes no risks, and seeks only comfort and security.

Libido

It is Freud's term for the psychophysical energy or motive force produced by sexual instinct. It is the energy of the id, and can be directed either toward the self or an object.

Logical positivism

Logical positivism confines knowledge to science. It divides all meaningful propositions into two categories: analytic propositions and synthetic propositions.

Metaphysics

Metaphysics is the branch of philosophy concerned with the question of the ultimate nature of reality. It goes beyond particular things to inquire about more general questions.

Metatheory

A metatheory is a theory whose subject matter is some other theory. In other words it is a theory about a theory.

Monism

It is the metaphysical and theological view that there is only one principle, essence, substance, or energy.

Narcissism

Narcissism is self-love or an erotic interest in oneself. Freud believed that narcissism exists when the libido is directed toward the self.

Necessary truth

Logically necessary truths are based on the principle of contradiction, having negations that are logically impossible.

Neo-Platonism

It is the modern term for a school of religious and mystical philosophy, based on the teachings of Plato and earlier Platonists.

Nihilism

It is a philosophical view that the world, and especially human existence, is without meaning, purpose, comprehensible truth, or essential value.

Nominalism

Nominalism is primarily a position on the problem of universals, which dates back at least to Plato, and is opposed to realism—the view that universals do exist over and above particulars.

Oedipus complex

In Greek myth, Oedipus, acting according to his destiny, killed his father and married his mother. According to Freud, in the mental life of a male child there is desire for his mother as a sexual object and hatred for his father as a rival.

Ontology

Ontology is the philosophical study of the nature of being, existence or reality as such, as well as the basic categories of being and their relations.

Peripatetics

The Peripatetics were members of a school of philosophy in ancient Greece. The school dates from around 335 BC when Aristotle began teaching in the Lyceum.

Phenomenalism

Phenomenalism is the view that physical objects do not exist as things in themselves but only as perceptual phenomena or sensory stimuli (e.g. redness, hardness, softness, sweetness, etc.) situated in time and in space.

Phenomenological reduction

Phenomenological reduction is a means of detecting the intentional or essential structure of experience. By turning away from the sense-contents of one's own stream of experiences, one can concentrate on what is essential, basic, and irreducible in experience.

Philosopher-king

Philosopher kings are the rulers, or Guardians, of Plato's *Utopian Kallipolis*. Plato used the term philosopher here in its original sense of a lover of knowledge and not for a professional role.

Platonism

It is the school of philosophy founded by Plato. It is often used to refer to Platonic idealism, the belief that the entities of the phenomenal world are imperfect reflections of an ideal truth.

Pluralism

It is the view that there are more than one or two separate substances making up the world. This stands in contrast with both monism and dualism.

Positivism

It is an approach to the philosophy of science, deriving from Enlightenment thinkers like Pierre-Simon Laplace and many others.

Pragmatism

Pragmatism is a movement consisting of varying but associated theories, originally developed by Charles S. Peirce and William James and distinguished by the doctrine that the meaning of an idea or a proposition lies in its observable practical consequences.

Pre-Socratics

It is a term invented by historians of philosophy to group together the Greek thinkers living between approximately the first half of the sixth century b.c. and Socrates' lifetime.

Quietism

Quietism in philosophy is an approach to the subject that sees the role of philosophy as broadly therapeutic or remedial.

Rationalism

It is a theory or method based on the thesis that human reason can in principle be the source of all knowledge. It is opposed with empiricism.

Realism

It is a view of a reality ontologically independent of conception, perception, etc.

Representation

In general, it is an item in the mind, picture, model, copy, or other thing which stands for something else because of a likeness or on some other grounds.

Scholasticism

It is a school of philosophy taught by the academics of medieval universities circa 1100—1500. Scholasticism attempted to reconcile the philosophy of the ancient classical philosophers with medieval Christian theology.

Skepticism

Skepticism is a school or method of doubt regarding what is held as knowledge. It is a critical philosophical attitude, questioning by systematic arguments the reliability of knowledge claims and our ability to establish objective truth.

Structuralism

It is an approach or theory that studies underlying structural relationships between concepts. Structuralism is a methodology that emphasizes structure rather than substance and relations rather than things.

Subjective idealism

This theory contends that individuals can only directly know sensations and ideas of objects, not abstractions such as "matter."

Superego

The superego is a human's moral faculty and is the agent of conscience. It represents an individual's social personality, and acts as a deputy for the culture outside oneself.

Syllogism

A syllogism is a formally valid inference to a conclusion from two premises (a major premise and a minor premise). The premise containing the predicate of the conclusion is the major premise, and the premise containing the subject of the conclusion is the minor premise.

Synthetic proposition

Synthetic proposition is a proposition whose predicate concept is not contained in its subject concept; it is defined in Kant's terms as a sentence, or judgment in which the predicate adds new information to the subject.

Tautology

A tautology is a logical formula which is true whatever the truth-possibilities of its constituent propositional variables. It is not concerned with any subject-matter, but exhibits the logical properties of genuine propositions or restates the same idea in different words.

Teleology

Teleology is any philosophical account which holds that final causes exist in nature.

Transcendentalism

It is a group of new ideas that advocates that there is an ideal spiritual state that "transcends" the physical and empirical and is only realized through a knowledgeable intuitive awareness that is conditional upon the individual.

Transcendental idealism

It is a view according to which our experience is not about the things as they are in themselves, but about the things as they appear to us.

Utilitarianism

It is an ethical doctrine that judges actions in terms of the amount of happiness it generates. The best action results in the most happiness and the least pain for the greatest number of people.

Ubermensch

Ubermensch is a worldly antithesis of God, a union of the strongest mind and strongest body. For Nietzsche, it is the realization of the profoundest human potentialities and gifts, the overcoming or negation of the mediocrities of the merely human.

Unmoved Mover

Unmoved Mover is the substance that initiates movement without itself being moved, also called the prime mover.

Voluntarism

It refers to any philosophical position that holds the concept of will as the central explanatory principle.

References

Atkinson, Sam. *The Philosophy Book*. USA: Dorling Kindersley Limited, 2011

Audi, Robert. *The Cambridge Dictionary of Philosophy (Second Edition)*. New York: Cambridge University Press, 2009

Cahn, Steven M. *Classics of Western Philosophy (Seventh Edition)*. USA: Hackett Publishing Company, Inc., 2006

Collinson, Diané. *Fifty Major Philosophers: A Reference Guide*. Great Britain: Biddles Ltd, Guidford and King's Lynn, 1987

Durant, Will. *The Story of Philosophy*. USA: Washington Square Press, 1961

Gottlieb, Anthony. *The Dream of Reason: A History of Western Philosophy*. UK: Penguin, 2001

Hobson, John M. *The Eastern Origins of Western Civilization*. New York: Cambridge University Press, 1965

Honderich, Ted. *The Oxford Companion to Philosophy*. New York: Oxford University Press, 1995

Horner, Chris & Westacott, Emrys. *Thinking through Philosophy: An Introduction*. UK: Cambridge University Press, 2008

Hospers, John. *An Introduction to Philosophical Analysis (Fourth Edition)*. Great Britain: T. J International Ltd, 1997

Morris, Tom. *Philosophy for Dummies*. USA: Wiley Publishing, Inc., 1999

Solomon, Robert C. & Higgins, Kathleen M. *The Big Questions: A Short Introduction to Philosophy*. USA: Wadsworth Publishing Co Inc, 2009

Stumpf, S. E.& Fieser, J. *A History of Philosophy: Socrates to Sartre and Beyond*(西方哲学史——从苏格拉底到萨特及其后),北京:北京大学出版社,2006

尼古拉斯·布宁,余纪元编著,《西方哲学英汉对照辞典》,北京:人民出版社,2001

孙有中,编著,《西方思想经典导读》,北京:外语教学与研究出版社,2008

严忠志,编译,《读点哲学》,上海:上海科技教育出版社,2001

中国社会科学院哲学研究所《哲学译丛》编辑部编,《英汉哲学术语词典》,北京:中共中央党校出版社出版发行,1991

张志伟,《西方哲学十五讲》,北京:北京大学出版社,2004

张致祥,主编,《西方引语宝典》,北京:商务印书馆,2004